Pithári

Soúvles

Ghthín

Amourghí

Pinakotí

Kolokítha

Téntsero

Tsoukáli

Kazáni

Kappamás

Ghthin Xílino

Tipári

Tentserí

Stámnos

Kanní

Mílos Kaffé

Bríki

Mangáli

Flintzáni

Vitinári

Greek Islands Cooking

Greek Islands Cooking

THEONIE MARK

Illustrated
by Maris Platais

B. T. Batsford Ltd, London

To my husband, Robert,
and my three sons,
Morgan, Ted and Burton

0 7134 1283 6
PRINTED IN GREAT BRITAIN BY
WEATHERBY WOOLNOUGH, NORTHANTS
FOR THE PUBLISHERS
B. T. BATSFORD LTD, 4 FITZHARDINGE STREET,
LONDON W1H 0AH

Acknowledgments

I wish to thank my mother, Maria Diakidis, for her recipes and constant guidance, her people for all the wonderful things I learned from them, and my husband Robert, who helped me appreciate those things, encouraged me to write them in this book, and came to my rescue daily with English grammar; my mother-in-law, Dorothy Mark, for her long, helpful visits, and my wonderful sons for sampling my tested recipes. I wish to thank my agent and friend, Ellen Neuwald, for her moral support; David Otte, for his reassurance; Mary Rackliffe and Mary Purcell, for their much-appreciated editorial assistance; and my typist, Ruth Bastide, for putting up with all those Greek words. I would also like to thank my American friends at WGBH-TV, Boston: Michael Rice, Sylvia Davis, Peggy MacLeod, Pauline Mercer, and — in South Devon, England — Ann Irving, all of whose enthusiasm about Greek islands cooking helped me bring this book to realization.

Contents

Introduction

I remember my visits to my mother's family in the village, particularly in the autumn, when the days were still warm and the wind blew lightly. I used to walk the uphill road framed with whispering eucalyptus trees that led from their house to the narrow streets of the village, passing young men returning from the fields either on donkeys or on foot and followed by their goats or a cow, and young women with their heads wrapped in beaded white scarves, carrying on their shoulders their empty water jugs to fill them with the spring water that ran from the village fountain. And the old people sitting on low stools at their doorsteps, as is customary in the afternoons, smiling and greeting people passing by. The children gathering at dusk in the village storyteller's house — an old Homeric custom — where she continued the adventure story she had started days before and which kept the children still and glued to her every word. Washday by the river, where clothes were beaten with wooden paddles in the bubbling water by cheerful women; and looking at the birds, of so many kinds, that scattered away as one approached the wiry shrubs on the riverbanks. I remember the harvest of olives in autumn, and of wheat and grapes in summer; the humour and laughter of these people whose way of life is shared by other villagers on other islands that lie in the blue seas of Greece. Some of these islands are large and green with vegetation, others are smaller with earth-coloured mountains, each a world of its own with its own history marked by the multifarious invaders of the past.

But what I remember most of all is my grandmother's and aunts' cooking: one-pot meals they skilfully prepared with ingredients they had raised, fresh and natural with that good, healthy quality that islanders learned to appreciate in food long ago. Using traditional methods of preparation, holding the vegetables gently, they sliced or minced them and combined them with olive oil and scarlet-skinned tomatoes and fresh herbs and set them to cook in clay or copper pots over the open fire of their primitive kitchens. And my aunts, while preparing their favourite dishes, always sang songs of the sea or lullabies to their babies, a tradition passed down through the centuries and still observed today.

It is nostalgia for these places, for the foods and customs associated with them, for the simple life in the villages and the cosmopolitan cities that inspired me to compile the recipes in this book. Also, the repeated requests I have had from my American friends when I have found it impossible to explain to them by word of mouth how each dish was prepared — saying only 'You use a little of this and a dash of that', which is the way of cooking in the islands, since there are no written recipes in the families. Instead, cooking methods are passed down by example and in conversation from mothers to daughters, who, by watching over and over again, memorize the preparation of the many generations of dishes. I felt great pleasure writing these recipes because each one brought a story from the past, a personal feeling and an image of the seasons and the activities that go with them in the Greek islands, so familiar to many Greeks like myself who left their village or city behind them to travel through the world, carrying with them memories of their youth and of a world so different from the one we are living in now. My own cooking — which has been greatly influenced by my mother and her people and our Sephardic Jewish friends and neighbours in the city we lived in — began when I married my American husband and came to America more than a dozen years ago and started introducing him and his friends to my native island dishes — dishes that range from earthy peasant ones to the more sophisticated cooking of the city.

In compiling this collection I have kept in mind the busy lives of many women today who are involved in earning a living and don't have as much time to spend in the kitchen as our mothers and grandmothers did in the past. Many of the dishes in this collection can be prepared ahead of time, using fresh ingredients, and then frozen without detriment to their flavour or appearance. I believe in using fresh produce, and the results are more economical and healthier if one takes advantage of the seasonal vegetables of the region. Root vegetables, greens and cabbages are at their peak in winter, and fresh beans, tomatoes, aubergines (eggplants) and other vegetables in summer. Even though out-of-season vegetables are available all year round in many places, they are grown somewhere else and transported and are therefore more expensive and not as good as those grown locally. This is one of the reasons why I have divided the book into the four seasons, giving in each section a selection of recipes — all traditional, most at their best in that particular season — with appetizers, soups, salads, meat and fish, vegetable dishes and the much-loved Greek pastries. There is an additional section that includes breads, pastas, rice and egg dishes, and sauces, all of which are used throughout the year.

Besides the dishes and procedures inherited by Greeks virtually unchanged from their forefathers (such as the well-known *kakkaviá*, a thick fish soup; and brown lentil soup; the skewering of lambs and birds; the roasting of pigs; many breads and rolls and the honeyed cheese cakes, all of which date back hundreds of years, some mentioned in Homer's *Iliad* and *Odyssey*, others by Plato, and many more quoted in *The Deipnosophistae* by the Greek grammarian Athenaeus, AD 200) the islanders also adopted food patterns left behind by invaders, developing versions of their own, and thus adding many variations to their rather simple cooking by using new herbs — dill weed, flat-leafed parsley, savory, bay leaf, thyme and mint — fresh in summer and dried in winter, including a few which are reserved for winter dishes only — cumin, coriander and allspice. Flavourings of wine, vinegar and lemon are present in both types of island cooking: *kavourthistá*, which always starts with the frying of meat and vegetables before they are put on to stew, making the dish richer in colour but also heavier; and *yahnistá*, which starts with the gentle sautéing of onion and then the addition of the remaining ingredients which are stewed — a favourite method of summer cooking. The sweet spices of cinnamon, nutmeg, clove and mastic are used in cakes, cookies and pastries, with honey and sugar syrups for topping.

Village cooking differs slightly from city cooking in that

less elaborate, on-top-of-the-stove dishes — some baked at weekends when the oven is lit for bread-making — are more usual. In the city, many everyday dishes are baked in community ovens for a small fee, with instructions given to the baker for them to be ready at a specified time. Charcoal fires or small kerosene stoves were the means of cooking in city homes in the past, but they have now been replaced with modern electric or gas appliances. Cooking utensils are the most beautiful feature of island kitchens, coming in graduated sizes and varied shapes: tin-lined copper ones with brass handles, glazed clay pots and water jugs, wooden spoons and paddles. They are the same utensils used in past centuries and are all handed down from mother to daughter as part of the dowry (which emphasizes the importance of learning how to cook so as to avoid the tense situation of a newly-wed husband having to return to his mother for better meals — a well-known and much-exercised custom!).

I remember when I was a girl how many times my grandmother emphasized to me the two most important things a women should learn — to cook and to light a fire. Of course the life of women, particularly in the cities, has changed considerably since my grandmother's time and so have the kitchens, but one thing that remains the same is that cooking is still one of the many ways in which women express themselves and give pleasure to their friends and families. In Greece and throughout the world many important occasions are still celebrated with cooking and feasting and there is the centuries-old tradition of welcoming friends and guests in the home. Everyday cooking in Greece is done by the woman, whether she works outside or at home, and there are three daily meals. The smallest and simplest meal is breakfast, consisting only of a cup of coffee, tea or hot milk, with buttered toast and honey. The largest and most elaborate meal is served at midday — when the cities shut down for a four-hour break — with soup, salad, meat or fish, side dishes of vegetables and freshly baked bread (but not butter), and fresh fruits of the season for dessert. A long nap follows the meal, with the men and women returning to their work in late afternoon. The evening meal, served four to five hours after the midday one, is smaller and is usually a thick soup or a one-pot meal with crusty bread, with fruits for dessert. Sweet pastries and puddings are usually eaten between meals, accompanied by a cup of coffee or a glass of water.

Table settings and eating customs in the islands are much like those of the rest of Europe and America, with the exception that men are served first and according to age, starting with the oldest. Village eating customs differ considerably from the city, with the largest meal served in the evening, after the men return from the fields and have washed and relaxed. This dinner is served on low, round, wooden tables placed on the raised floor of the kitchen area and set with forks, spoons and knives and surrounded with pillows for everyone to sit on while dining. Two or three dishes are served in beautifully designed earthenware bowls for everybody to choose and eat from, accompanied by thick slices of round wheat bread, olives and pickles, cold water from the clay jug for the children and wine from the home supply for the husband and wife.

It is for those who have not yet travelled to the Greek islands and are not yet familiar with the land, the people and the food, that I describe in this book the spectrum of colour of the natural landscape, the sea and cloudless skies, and the customs associated with the food today; and for those who already know Greece I just remind you of the warmth of the sun and the taste of the foods: with all of you I share my recipes, together with the happiness that I have had writing this book for you.

The precise measurements and quantities I have given in these recipes are the standard American ones (see Table of Measures and Equivalents pp. 277—79). I suggest that when you have tried out a recipe you use your own judgment and feel free to alter it to your own preference by adding more or less of the herbs and seasoning to suit your taste, a practice frequently used by family cooks in the islands.

The Greek ingredients in these recipes are readily available in Greek or Middle Eastern shops. Pots and pans may be of enamel, cast iron, heavy aluminium, stainless steel or, of course, tin-lined copper, old or modern, which is a good heat conductor and very decorative in the kitchen. Ordinary aluminium pans can be used for the baking of sweet pastry. In many of the recipes electric gadgets are suggested as alternative methods, but the minimum of simple utensils and the use of your hands are the main implements needed in the preparation of this home cooking of the Greek islands.

SPRING

Spring

In springtime in the islands when the young wheat comes up, the fields are green, and all around the hills are like velvet; then the people celebrate the many beautiful customs of the season.

March the first is when spring officially starts on most of the islands — where the weather is warmer than in other parts of Greece — and in the villages it used to be announced by a man called the *skopós*, the field guard, whose duty was to protect the wheat fields and keep stray animals from invading them. On the day before the first of March, the *skopós* would go up into the mountains and blow his *moungrístra* (conch shell) to announce the coming of spring; then the next morning the children would go for walks in the fields with their teachers, singing songs and bringing back the first flowers, beautiful anemones. I think the loveliest month of all in the Greek islands is May, which abounds with flowers everywhere you look. There the young girls celebrate the first day of May by arising very early in the morning and going to the fields to catch the magic, a custom filled with beauty and ancient mysticism. I remember when I was young my friends and I would begin preparations the night before by cooking picnic foods, and the next morning we would get up early in silence — not speaking to anybody so we would not lose the magic — pack our picnic basket, and go out. When we arrived in the fields we picked flowers — yellow marguerites, bluebells and poppies — and made the traditional wreaths, and only after that did we speak and begin our picnic. Then we sang songs of May and played games, and when we returned home we hung the wreaths on our front doors — and that was the magic brought home.

In spring Greek people go on outings and picnics more often than in any other season. The sun is comfortably warm then, the air smells fresh, and the sea is so calm that you can see your face reflected in its waters and so clean that you can see the smallest details on the bottom. I remember the family picnics when I was growing up, riding to beautiful places in a car left from another era that seemed very long to me then, with a convertible top and extra folding seats in the middle — which I loved to sit on; stopping by the seashore or a grassy field, we would spread the various "finger foods" on the striped *sendòna* (a thick hand-woven spread my grandmother had made) and sitting around it we would feast. The finger foods were *tirotrígona*, cheese triangles made of fresh cheese and herbs wrapped in thin dough; or meatballs made from spring lamb and mint; lots of olives and cheese; and of course stuffed vine leaves (*dolmáthes*). All these my mother would prepare the evening before, after my father's announcement that we would go on an outing the next day, bringing such excitement to all of us children that we would spend hours that night thinking what we would like to do most on our day of fun. My older brother loved to take pictures, and the rest of us hiked to the mountains. Whenever we visited a Turkish friend of my parents in the country we all played with his beautiful goldfish in the pond, and when we were at the seashore we spent hours collecting colored pebbles from the beach. Then when I was in my teens, my brothers, their friends and I organized bicycle excursions, taking the winding road that led us to beautiful Kalithea, a place where mountains and sea come close together with pine groves stopping short at the edge of the clear water. On the way we would stop and picnic with the food we carried in our bicycle baskets — chicken pie and *spanakópitta* (spinach pie), each cooked in a pie crust — and with them we would have refreshing fruit drinks that we chilled in the running water from the spring.

Spring is also the season when Greeks fast in preparation for Easter, the most important holy day in Greece, and a great feast. There are the baking of many bracelet-shaped cookies and of sweet spiced breads which tempt you to break your long fast; the roasting of lambs on Easter Sunday, with the aroma filling the whole village; and the cracking of the red-dyed eggs called *tsóungrisma* by children dressed in their newest clothes competing to see whose egg is the strongest. New spring vegetables from the farms are then available, tender and green, and are cooked with spring lamb to make the most delicate of dishes. Plump young chickens are cooked with delicious stuffings, and the fish markets in the cities are full once again of fresh seafood. Butter and milk are also available at this time of the year and are used to make white sauces for the creamed dishes, so unlike the usual tomato sauces of the other seasons.

Appetizers

Orektiká are appetizers and many of them are finger foods, an interesting feature of Greek island cooking, which are very convenient for serving and come in many varieties. There are neat little pastry envelopes stuffed with meat, cheese, or greens that vary with the seasons and leaves of the grapevine stuffed with meat, rice and fresh dill weed. These finger foods are served by housewives and also in *tavérnas* and restaurants in the spring, along with other spring appetizers such as large, cooked legumes and fresh seafood.

In the seashore *tavérnas*, shrimps are at their best cooked in wine and herbs and served in their shells, which are removed just before eating. In the countryside, where there are small cafés now, in the same places where my parents used to take us on

Sunday picnics, stuffed grape leaves and giant white lima beans are served. There are still flowers, wild daisies and red poppies that cover the fields where I used to pick them and spend hours making garlands for my hair.

STUFFED GRAPE LEAVES

Dolmáthes

The leaves of the grapevines are very tender in the spring, and stuffed with the ground meat of spring lamb, they become the delicacy so well-known throughout Greece as *dolmáthes*. Eaten usually hot but sometimes cold, they are just the right shape and size to pass around to your guests before dinner. You may use fresh vine leaves or those preserved in brine and sold in jars in the markets. If you are planning to use fresh leaves and you haven't cultivated a grapevine in your garden, use the wild grapevines that grow over stone walls and fences in most parts of this country. But you must make sure that they have not been sprayed with pesticides.

In the New England area, where I live, we have wild Concord grapevines, which are very good to use. The best time to pick leaves is May and June, and you start by holding up the very tip of one of the many branches (choosing only the tender new ones). You count down the leaves — one, two, three — and pick the third and sometimes the fourth leaf; they are the right size to use, and leaves below the fourth will be too tough. In no time you will collect a lot of leaves. When you get home, snip the stem from each leaf with your fingers, pile the leaves in stacks of ten, drop each stack in boiling water, press the leaves down with a wooden spoon for a few seconds to scald them until they are pliable, and then remove them to a plate and let them cool. If you are in no hurry to use the leaves, put them in a plastic bag, sprinkle them with water, and store them in the refrigerator, where they will keep for several days.

When you are using leaves preserved in brine, just rinse them under cold water before you stuff them and use less salt in the stuffing. The leaves can be stuffed ahead of time and kept refrigerated in the pan without water added until you are ready to cook them. Any pot with a lid can be used to cook them. (*Makes 30 to 40 dolmáthes.*)

⅓ cup olive oil
1 finely chopped onion
1 pound lean ground lamb
½ cup uncooked rice
⅓ cup pine nuts
2 tablespoons tomato paste

½ cup chopped fresh or
   1 tablespoon dry dill weed
¾ cup water
40 to 50 grape leaves,
   prepared as above
Salt and pepper to taste

Heat the olive oil in a skillet, add the onion, and cook it until it becomes translucent. Add the meat and cook it until it crumbles, then add the rice, pine nuts, tomato paste, dill weed and water.

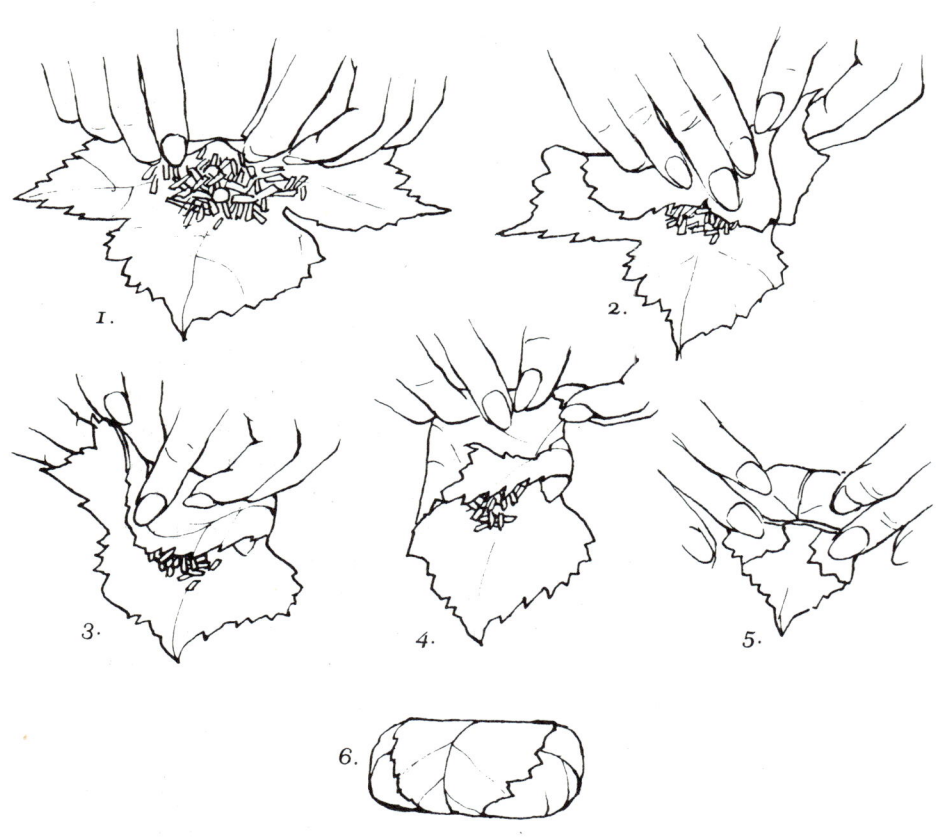

Season, mix, and cook over moderate heat for 10 minutes or until the water is absorbed, and then let it cool.

Cover the bottom of a pot that has a lid with some of the scalded leaves so that the stuffed leaves will not be burned. To stuff each leaf, place it upside down (veins up) on the palm of your hand; the tip of the leaf should line up with your middle finger and the base of the leaf should rest on the heel of your hand. Now put a tablespoon of stuffing in the center of the leaf and then fold the leaf like an envelope — first the two halves of the base of the leaf, then the two sides of the leaf, as shown — and roll it up, tucking in the edges as you go, toward the tip of the leaf, which you tuck underneath so that the leaf will not unroll. You will see that the shiny side of the leaf is on the outside. Place the stuffed leaves side by side in the pan to cover the bottom, then put a second layer on top of the first one, and so on until you have put in all the stuffed leaves. If you have some unstuffed leaves left, place them on top of the last layer. Add water to 1 inch below the top of the stuffed leaves, place a saucer upside down on top of the leaves, and press it down gently. Cover the pot with the lid and cook the leaves over moderate heat for about half an hour or until the rice is done (to test whether the rice is cooked open one of the stuffed leaves). Let the *dolmáthes* cool slightly before serving.

SHRIMPS IN THEIR SHELLS

Garíthes

On all the islands and along the coastline of the Greek mainland, small shrimps are cooked in their shells with wine and herbs to give them a delightful flavor. They are chilled and served in a large bowl, and each person shells and eats his own. If fresh shrimps are not available, use frozen, unshelled ones, but first defrost them overnight in the refrigerator or in clam juice (page 274). (*Serves 4 to 6.*)

2 *pounds shrimps in their shells*	6 *sprigs flat-leaf parsley, stems and all*
2 *mashed garlic cloves*	1 *cup dry white wine*

½ cup olive oil

1 teaspoon salt

Pepper to taste

Rinse the shrimps briefly under running cold water and set them aside to drain. Combine all the ingredients but the shrimps in a large saucepan, bring to a boil over moderate heat, and boil for 1 minute. Remove the saucepan from the heat, add the shrimps, and gently stir with a wooden spoon to baste them with the wine and herbs. Return the saucepan to the heat, bring the liquid to a boil again, reduce the heat, and simmer the shrimps uncovered for 5 minutes until they turn pink, stirring occasionally so they will cook evenly. Remove the pan from the fire and let the shrimps cool in their juice, then chill them. Remove the shrimps with a slotted spoon to a large bowl and serve them.

CHEESE TRIANGLES

Tirotrígona

Little tidbits of stuffed pastry are made with eggs and herbs and the marvelous combination of Greek *fétta* cheese and *mizíthra* (known as ricotta in this country and found in all local markets). The triangles can be made ahead of time and frozen, ready to be baked for a snack or party appetizer. The dough is a thin pastry called *phíllo;* see page 273 for how to work with it and how to make the triangles. (*Makes 2 to 3 dozen triangles.*)

1 cup crumbled *fétta cheese*

½ *cup drained* mizíthra *or ricotta cheese*

2 *medium-size eggs, lightly beaten with a fork*

¼ *cup chopped fresh flat-leaf parsley*

White pepper to taste

½ *pound* phíllo *pastry in standard-size sheets (about 10″ x 15″ or 12″ x 18″)*

¼ *cup olive oil*

Preheat the oven to 350°. Combine the cheeses in a small bowl, then add the eggs, parsley and pepper and stir until well mixed. Spread the *phíllo* on a board or a table and cut it into 3″ x 10″ or 3″ x 12″ strips. Using two layers of *phíllo* for each strip, put about 1 tablespoon of filling at one end of a strip and fold it as you

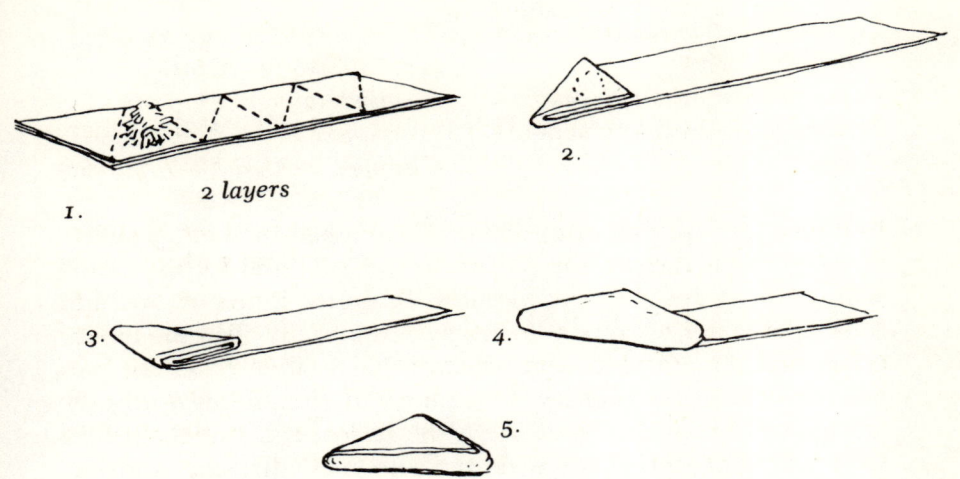

1. 2 layers
2.
3.
4.
5.

would a flag, in triangle form, to the end. When you have folded all the strips into triangles, place them on an oiled baking sheet and brush the tops with olive oil. Bake about 20 minutes until the triangles are puffed and golden. Serve them piping hot.

FREEZING DIRECTIONS: Cheese triangles may be kept uncooked in the freezer for a month; simply freeze them on the baking sheet covered with plastic wrap. After they harden they may be kept in sealed plastic or tied bags. When you are ready to cook them, place them still frozen on an oiled baking sheet, brush the top with olive oil, and bake in the upper third of a preheated 250° oven for about 25 minutes until they are puffed and golden.

GIANT WHITE LIMA BEANS WITH DRESSING

Ghíghes Plakí

In the early spring these large legumes are cooked and chilled and served with other appetizers along with *retsína*, the lightly flavored, chilled resin wine Greeks like so much. The Greek variety of giant lima beans, unlike the American variety, doesn't split in the process of cooking. If Greek beans are unavailable, use the packaged ones found in American markets. (*Serves 6.*)

1 pound giant white lima
  beans
1 chopped medium-size onion
2 chopped stalks celery with
  tops

2 tablespoons tomato paste
Salt and pepper to taste
½ cup lemon-oil dressing
  (page 254)
Chopped fresh flat-leaf parsley

In a medium-size pan bring the beans to a boil in about 3 quarts of water, then remove the pan from the heat and let the beans soak, covered, for about 30 minutes. Drain the liquid off and add fresh cold water to come 1 inch above the beans. Add the onion, celery and tomato paste and season to taste, then cover the pan and cook the beans over low heat for 30 to 40 minutes until they are tender. Drain the liquid from the beans, transfer them to a large bowl, drench them with the lemon-oil dressing and stir them gently. Sprinkle them with parsley and chill.

Soups

When the last of the spring rains leaves a chill in the air, a kettle of soup cooking on the stove is a welcome sight to families in the village and city alike. Some of the island soups are easy to make, combining the first greens of spring and the dried legumes you have left after the winter; other, more elaborate ones, like island Easter soup, demand long preparation. Unlike the Easter soup made in most other parts of Greece, this one uses the knuckles as well as the innards of milk-fed lambs. It is a nutritious dish on Easter Sunday morning after the midnight mass, the first meat meal after the long fast.

A favorite soup of all Greeks is chicken-egg-lemon, which is served on Sundays and when there are unexpected guests — that is, if you like them. My aunt always served this soup when my brothers and parents and I were visiting her and the other relatives of my mother's in the village, and often I watched her make it from scratch. Usually we arrived unannounced to visit our relatives — an accepted village custom — just a short car ride from the city where we lived; and we always stayed with my Aunt Katerina, whose large, beautiful, old whitewashed stone house looks down on the village and the patchwork of fields that stretch all the way to the sea. In back of the house there are magnificent graduated mountains against the blue sky, with rows and rows of olive trees ascending the rolling hills. After the greetings everybody would think of food, and one of the men in the family would go out and catch one or two of the chickens roaming about the yard, wring their necks, and give them to the women of the house to pluck and prepare for the soup. The whole preparation was done quickly while the women gossiped and exchanged news. The fresh chickens were put to cook whole to make the rich broth, and then when the rice was added and the soup was made, the eggs were beaten in a small bowl with forks (which made a lovely sound, one that always let me know what I was having to eat) to make the egg-lemon sauce. Then the whole-cooked chickens were fried in olive oil to a gentle golden brown and served as the main part of the second course after the soup.

CHICKEN-EGG-LEMON SOUP

Soúppa Avgolémono

The special flavor of this soup is achieved by the tanginess of the fresh lemon juice which, combined with the beaten eggs, gives the soup its delicate golden color. This soup is served as a first course to a Greek meal. (*Serves 6.*)

8 cups chicken stock (page 255)
½ cup uncooked rice
Salt and pepper to taste

3 medium-size eggs, separated
1 teaspoon water
Juice of 1 or 2 lemons

In a large saucepan bring the chicken stock to a boil, add the rice, and bring it again to a boil, stirring occasionally; then reduce the heat to moderate, cover the pan, and cook until the rice is soft, 15 to 20 minutes. Season with salt and pepper and remove the saucepan from the fire. Put the egg whites in a shallow bowl with 1 teaspoon of water and beat them with a fork or an electric mixer until they peak. Add the yolks and beat for 5 minutes longer until the eggs are fluffy and light yellow. Slowly and continuously beating with a fork, add the juice of 1 lemon to the eggs and then, while still beating, add ½ cup of the stock a little at a time; this must be done to keep the eggs from curdling. Pour the egg mixture into the soup and stir gently;

taste it, and if more tanginess is desired, add more lemon juice. Serve immediately.

SPINACH AND LENTIL SOUP

Spanáki me Fakkí

Leaves from the first spinach plants of spring are added to cooked lentils to make a thick soup much loved by all villagers after a chilly spring day's work in the fields. (*Serves 4.*)

1 pound fresh spinach leaves	5 thinly sliced scallions
1 cup dry brown or green	1 mashed garlic clove
lentils	½ teaspoon ground cumin
¼ cup olive oil	Salt and pepper to taste

Cut the spinach leaves in half, wash them, and set them aside to drain. In a large saucepan, cook the lentils in approximately 4 cups of water over moderate heat, covered, for 30 minutes until they are soft and mealy. Heat the olive oil in a small skillet and sauté the scallions until they are tender, then add them with the oil to the lentils. Also add the garlic, cumin and spinach leaves. Cover the pan and cook the mixture over moderate heat for 15 minutes, and when the spinach settles add salt and pepper to taste and mix thoroughly. The soup can be made to the desired thickness by adding more or less water. Serve it very hot as part of the main meal.

ISLAND EASTER SOUP

Soúppa Pashaliní

To make this soup, the knuckles and the tender, thin casing of a milk-fed lamb are scrubbed, and the casings are turned inside out and washed in a dozen changes of water and drained. Then coarse sea salt, onion wedges and lemon slices are rubbed vigorously against the casings to clean them, again they are rinsed in cold water, then the sparkling-clean casings are wrapped around the knuckles like thread on a spool and securely tied. The tripe is scalded, scraped and washed (see page 274 for directions), and

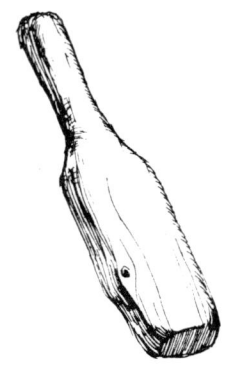

cut in small pieces; then it is put in a large pan with the casing-wrapped knuckles, covered with water and spices, and simmered over a low fire for several hours. This is a very rich soup and can be used as the main dish with your favorite bread, with a Greek salad before or after it. It is served to a Greek family at the beginning of the Easter feast. The knuckles and casings are available in this country in areas with a substantial Greek population, but only at Easter time, and have to be ordered in advance. (*Serves 4 to 6.*)

The small casings, knuckles	*Salt and pepper to taste*
and tripe of a milk-fed	
lamb	EGG-LEMON SAUCE
1 large sliced onion	*3 eggs, separated*
1 bay leaf	*Juice of 1 large lemon*

Divide the casings in 4 equal amounts, turn them inside out with a small, smooth stick about the thickness of a pencil, then proceed with the cleaning as described above. Wrap an equal amount of casing around each knuckle and tie it in a knot or with a thread so that it will not unwind during cooking. Cut the cleaned tripe in 1-inch-square pieces and place it in a large soup pot with the casings, knuckles, onion and bay leaf in enough water to cover them. Bring the water to a boil over moderate heat and with a spoon remove the froth from the top. Reduce the heat, cover, and simmer for 2 hours or until the meat is tender. Add salt and pepper to taste and more water if needed to keep the meat covered throughout cooking. Remove the pot from the heat.

Prepare egg-lemon sauce I as on page 251, using the ingredients listed here and one cup of the soup. Stir the sauce into the soup and serve immediately.

Salads

Young leaves of lettuce and other tender vegetables and greens make the unpretentious salads of spring. As a general rule, spring salads are made of cut-up raw greens and lettuce, with scallions, radishes, cheese, and olives sometimes added, and dressed with olive oil and lemon or vinegar. But Greek people love to boil vegetables that have not yet matured and use them for salads; these vegetables range from wild to domesticated and from the bean family to the thistle family. On one of my many visits to the village I remember having a delicious dish made from the stalks of wild thistle plants that had been stripped of their spiny leaves and defuzzed, then boiled and dressed with garlic sauce. Daisy plants can be prepared the same way while they are still tender and before they flower, and the dish is called *amarángous*. Another very old, favorite recipe my mother prepared every spring is a dish of artichokes and fresh fava beans (*anghináres ke koukía*). I remember a song I sang as a child about these two ingredients, which went like this:

> *One, two, three,*
> *Artichokes and fava beans*
> *And the best tomatoes found,*
> *Only a penny a pound.*

LETTUCE OR DANDELION SALAD

Maroulosaláta e Rathíkia

Crisp romaine lettuce grows on the island from spring until the middle of summer and is made into salads by itself and with the flavoring of bits of fried bacon. Fresh dandelion leaves can also be prepared this way when picked young from a pesticide-free area or bought at the market. (*Serves 4.*)

1 large head romaine lettuce or ½ pound dandelion greens	*½ cup lemon-oil dressing (page 254)*
Freshly ground pepper and salt to taste	*½ cup cooked bacon, cut in bits*

Remove each leaf from the base of the lettuce and discard the tough, outside ones; then wash the tender leaves under running cold water and put them in a basket to drain or pat them with a paper towel to remove the excess water. Bunch the leaves together in groups of 3 to 4 and cut them crosswise in ¼-inch-wide strips into a salad bowl. If dandelion greens are used, clean them the same way as the lettuce leaves; if they are small do not cut them at all, and if they are large cut them in half. Just before serving, season the greens with salt and pepper, add the dressing, and toss the salad by turning the greens over and over to coat them evenly. Sprinkle the bacon bits over the salad and toss it again.

LETTUCE, RADISH AND CHEESE SALAD

Maroúli me Rapanákia ke Tirí Saláta

When they are in season, fresh red radishes and scallions are served by themselves as vegetables with meals and very often they are added to salads along with white *fétta* cheese to give the green salad color and texture contrast. (*Serves 4.*)

1 head romaine lettuce   *5 scallions*

10 *little red radishes*	*⅓ cup olive oil*
¼ cup fétta *cheese, crumbled*	*¼ cup chopped fresh flat-leaf*
Juice of 1 lemon	*parsley*
Freshly ground pepper to taste	*Salt to taste*

Wash and drain the lettuce and cut it into a salad bowl as in the preceding recipe. Peel the outside skin off the scallion bulbs, cut off their whiskers, and trim off all but 2 inches of the green tails. Bunch them together and cut the white parts crosswise in thin circles and slice the greens, and add them to the lettuce. Wash the radishes and cut the tips off both ends; without peeling them, cut them in thin circles and add them to the salad bowl. Sprinkle the cheese, lemon juice and pepper over the salad, then add the olive oil and parsley and toss the greens gently to coat them evenly. *Fétta* is salty, so do not add salt until just before serving, and then only as needed.

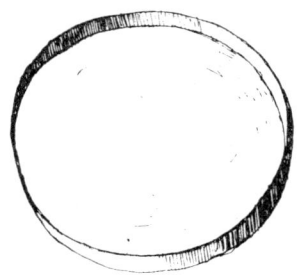

ARTICHOKE AND FRESH FAVA BEAN SALAD

Anghináres ke Koukiá

Fresh fava beans or broad beans are used whole when small and not mature and cut in half when large. When the beans inside the thick pods are full-grown, sometimes they are shelled and combined with some immature beans, and sometimes used just by themselves, cooked and made into a salad dressed with lemon oil. Fresh fava beans can be found in season in Greek and Middle Eastern stores and in some supermarkets. Small fresh artichokes trimmed down to the tenderest part or frozen artichoke hearts are used combined with the beans to make this dish. (*Serves 4.*)

1 pound fresh fava beans
4 to 6 small artichokes or
   1 package frozen artichoke
   hearts
Juice of 1½ lemons

1½ teaspoons salt
Lemon-oil dressing (page
   254)
Pepper and additional salt to
   taste

Prepare the lemon-oil dressing and set it aside. Snip the ends off the fava pods and place them in cold water with the juice of ½ lemon added to prevent them from turning brown. Trim the bottoms off the artichokes and remove most of the leaves down to the tender part, then cut off their tips and split them in half, or in quarters if they are medium-size or large. With a knife remove the fuzz and spiny little leaves from the center of the artichokes and immediately rub them with the juice of another ½ lemon to keep them from turning brown. Bring to a boil 3 quarts of water with the juice of the third ½ lemon and 1½ tablespoons salt added to it; drain the cold water from the beans and add them with the artichokes to the boiling water. Cook the beans and artichokes uncovered over moderate heat until they are tender but still firm, approximately 25 to 35 minutes, then drain them. While they are still hot, add the dressing and season them with pepper and salt. Serve warm or cold.

Fish and Shellfish

The fair weather of spring takes the fishing boats to sea again, and when they return, they bring back enough fish of many kinds and sizes to fill the marble basins of the city fish market of Rhodes. The fish market, an octagonal stone building with a raised open platform and four wide stairways ascending to it, surmounted by arches which support a dome, stands in the center of the circular marketplace, the *agorá*. On top of the dome is a large fish weathervane that peaks higher than the other buildings around it. The fishermen stand at the head of the stairs and shout to the passersby, praising the freshness of their fish and describing them by kind and color and the seas they were caught in. Some of the fish are from island waters, while others, like the European shad (*kóklanos*) are caught as far away as Turkey, where they go upriver early in the spring to spawn. Shad is available only once a year, and when it is in the market it causes great excitement among the housewives, who rush to get it before it is all sold out and prepare it in the traditional island way, poached with herbs and served with homemade mayonnaise. Shad roe, a delicacy throughout Europe, always makes a luxurious lunch when it is sautéed and served surrounded with lemon wedges.

Highly prized among sea shellfish is *pínna*, a very large bivalve with a wedge-shaped shell harvested from the sandy bottoms of deep waters throughout the Mediterranean. In the past fishermen used to cook *pínna* in the shells over the coals of their wood fire on the beach, in a manner similar to the New England clambake, to make their day's supper. Now a new version of the dish is prepared with a combination of seafood cooked in shells in the oven, which makes a delicious first course or lunch depending on the size of the shells used.

POACHED FISH WITH HERB MAYONNAISE

Psári Vrastó me Mayonéza

A poached shad, pike, or striped bass is enhanced by the fragrance of the herb mayonnaise so many island women prepare when these fish are in season. The trick of poaching a fish is to have it come out in one piece and as attractive as it was before it was cooked. There must be enough liquid in the poaching pan to cover the fish. A poaching rack is often used to lower the fish into the stock to cook, but if you don't have one, then cook the fish wrapped and tied in clean cheesecloth, and then lift it out very carefully to prevent it from breaking. (*Serves 4 to 6.*)

1 fish, 3½ to 4 pounds, shad, pike or bass
1 cup herb mayonnaise (page 253)

STOCK
1 cup dry white wine

1 crushed garlic clove
1 bay leaf
4 sprigs flat-leaf parsley
Peel of ½ lemon
2½ cups water

Combine the stock ingredients in a saucepan and boil them covered for 5 minutes, then set the stock aside to cool. Have the fishman scale, gut, and degill the fish, leaving the head and tail intact (see page 270 for instructions for doing it yourself). Rinse the fish under cold water and either put it on the poaching rack or wrap it, tied, in clean cheesecloth, then place it in a poacher or a shallow pan large enough to hold both the fish and the stock. Pour the cool stock in with the fish and bring it slowly to a boil, then quickly reduce the heat to low and gently simmer the fish until it is cooked and its flesh flakes easily when tested with a fork (approximately 10 minutes per pound). Lift the fish from the stock to drain and transfer it from the rack or cheesecloth to a warm platter. Decorate around the fish with leaves of rocket or watercress. Serve it hot or cold accompanied by a bowl of herb mayonnaise.

SHAD ROE SAUTÉED

Avghotáraho

The distinctive taste of shad roe is retained when the roe is gently sautéed in sweet butter, sprinkled with fresh parsley and lemon juice, then served with boiled new potatoes and a green salad. (*Serves 4.*)

4 shad roes	*pepper to taste*
Flour for rolling	*¼ cup minced fresh flat-leaf*
1 cup unsalted butter (2	*parsley*
sticks)	*Juice of ½ lemon*
Salt and freshly ground	*Lemon wedges for garnish*

Wash the roes, being careful not to puncture their thin outer membranes, and place them in a saucepan with enough cold water to cover them. Slowly bring the water to a boil, then remove the pan from the heat immediately. Let the roes cool in the liquid, drain them and pat them dry, and dip them in flour, gently shaking off any excess. Melt the butter in a heavy skillet until it foams, place the roes in it, and sauté them on all sides for 10 minutes, then season them with salt and pepper. Lower the heat and cook them slowly, covered, for 10 to 15 minutes longer, occasionally turning them over and checking to see that the heat is low enough not to burn the butter. Remove the roes to a warm platter, then mix the parsley in with the butter in the skillet and pour it over the roes. Sprinkle them with lemon juice and serve with lemon wedges on the side.

SEAFOOD IN THE SHELL

Thalasiná se Ostrakón

Here is a dish served beautifully in large scallop or clam shells, which can be purchased from stores that sell cooking utensils. The filling can be prepared in advance, stored in the refrigerator, then put in the shells to bake just a little while before serving. The shells are served individually and make either a first course or a main course. Traditionally, the filling was made from the sweet flesh of the *pínna* and other shellfish available in the islands. In one of her visits to me in the States my mother made this dish with succulent scallops, fillets of haddock, and hard-boiled Easter eggs. This recipe is her own version of the dish. (*Makes enough filling for eight 4-inch scallop shells.*)

1 cup white sauce (page 250)
½ pound haddock fillets
¼ pound bay or cape scallops
2 tablespoons salt butter
2 minced scallions, green tops included
Salt and white pepper to taste

2 tablespoons chopped fresh flat-leaf parsley
2 coarsely chopped hard-boiled eggs
¼ cup fine bread crumbs
⅛ cup grated kephalotíri or Parmesan cheese

Make the white sauce and set it aside, covered.

Preheat the oven to 375°. Cut the haddock fillets in ½-inch cubes; rinse the scallops in cold water, then drain them and pat them dry in a towel. If the scallops are larger than the fish cubes, cut them in half; otherwise leave them whole.

Melt the butter in a large skillet over moderate heat and cook the scallions for 1 minute until soft, then add the haddock and scallops and sauté them until the fish flakes when tested with a fork and the scallops are no longer translucent. Season them with salt and lots of white pepper, then add the parsley, stir gently, and remove them from the heat. Now mix in the chopped eggs and the white sauce. At this point the mixture will be a little loose. Distribute the seafood mixture in the shells, sprinkle the tops with bread crumbs and cheese, and place the shells on a cookie sheet or aluminum foil to catch the drippings. Bake the shells 15 to 20 minutes until the mixture bubbles and the top browns. Serve hot.

Poultry

At the end of spring, when the grapes were still sour and green, their tart juice was used to flavor chicken dishes my grandmother used to make. She loved to take walks in the fields, always holding a long, thick stick in one hand to support herself when she got tired and to protect herself from any poisonous snake that came her way, and in the other hand a willow basket that she would fill with the fresh fruits, vegetables or wild greens of the season. Sometimes in the later part of spring she would bring back in her basket some of those green, not-yet-ripe grapes, which she would squeeze and strain, and with their juice she would make an old version of a chicken dish called *órnitha aguritháti* that we all loved. Today, because I have so few cultivated grapevines around me here, I can't bear to cut my grapes unripe; and since lemons are so plentiful all year round, I use them instead of grapes and call the dish *órnitha lemonáti*.

Another way to cook a young spring chicken is to rub it all over with lemon, then stuff it and pot-braise it on top of the stove in a tomato-base sauce flavored with any of a variety of herbs. The next day, if you have some chicken left over, you can concoct a delicious combination of chicken and mushrooms to make a filling for *ornithópitta*, a chicken pie frequently used during the *Apókria* season (like Mardi Gras week) in the islands. The chicken used for all these dishes should be young broilers or roasters so that the meat will be tender.

LEMONY CHICKEN

Órnitha Lemonáti

The delicate flavor of this dish is created by the lemon rind and fresh spring herbs — as well as by using butter instead of olive oil. (*Serves 6.*)

1 3- to 4-pound chicken
1 lemon
Salt and white pepper
4 tablespoons salt butter
5 chopped scallions

½ cup chopped fresh flat-leaf
parsley
1 mashed garlic clove
1 teaspoon grated lemon rind

Cut the chicken in serving pieces, then wash it and pat it dry with a towel to remove all moisture. Rub the chicken pieces inside and out with half the lemon, squeezing it to cover the pieces with juice, and then set the chicken aside for the juice to be absorbed. Season the chicken with salt and pepper, rubbing them in with your hand. Melt the butter in a heavy enamel casserole, add the chicken pieces, and sauté them for 15 minutes over moderate heat, turning them so that they will brown on all sides. Mix in the scallions, parsley and garlic and the juice of the remaining ½ lemon and sprinkle the grated lemon rind on top. Place 1 cup of water in the casserole, then cover it and simmer over low heat

for about 1 hour until the chicken is tender. If you wish to thicken the chicken sauce, dilute 1 tablespoon of flour in ¼ cup water, add it to the sauce, and cook a few minutes longer.

RED POT-ROASTED CHICKEN

Órnitha Kokkinistí

This dish every housewife fusses over and prepares with precision, stuffing the chicken with pine nuts and rice to make a perfect meal. (*Serves 4 to 6.*)

1 4- to 5-pound roasting
   chicken
½ lemon
½ cup olive oil

STUFFING
¼ cup olive oil
6 scallions
Chopped chicken giblets
½ pound chopped beef or
   lamb
½ cup uncooked rice
1 tablespoon tomato paste

2 tablespoons chopped fresh
   flat-leaf parsley
½ cup pine nuts
1 teaspoon powdered thyme
Salt and pepper to taste

SAUCE
½ cup chicken stock
2 tablespoons tomato paste
   diluted with ½ cup water
1 garlic clove, slit in half
Salt and pepper to taste

Wash the chicken inside and out and pat it dry with a towel. Rub the ½ lemon all over the outside of the chicken and set the chicken aside to absorb the lemon juice.

TO MAKE THE STUFFING, heat the ¼ cup of olive oil in a skillet and sauté the scallions over moderate heat until they are soft, then add the giblets and sauté them until their red color disappears; add the ground meat and stir it until it crumbles. Mix the rice in with the meat and add the tomato paste, parsley, pine nuts, thyme, salt and pepper and ¾ to 1 cup water and simmer uncovered, stirring frequently, for about 12 to 15 minutes or until the water is absorbed and the rice is half cooked. Remove the stuffing from the heat. When it is cool, loosely. stuff the cavity of the chicken, then turn the chicken breast-side up and sew the opening with a needle and thick thread. Turn the tips of the wings under the chicken to make a platform while it cooks. If there is any stuffing left over, cook it until the rice is soft and serve it with the meat.

Heat the ½ cup olive oil over moderate heat in a heavy casserole and place the stuffed chicken in it to brown all over, turning it gently with wooden spoons and being careful not to break or burn the skin. Pour out the excess oil, leaving 2 tablespoons in the casserole with the chicken.

TO MAKE THE SAUCE, add the sauce ingredients to the chicken, cover, and simmer over low heat, occasionally basting the bird with the sauce, for about 45 to 60 minutes. Remove the chicken to a warm platter and strain the sauce into a gravy boat, to be poured over the chicken when it is served.

CHICKEN PIE

Ornithópitta

To the islanders, outdoor eating is irresistible, whether it is by the sea, in the mountains, or in their own yards, under the shade of the grapevine trellis. This double-crusted pie is an ideal dish to serve outdoors and can be made in advance and eaten hot or cold. (*Serves 4 to 6.*)

PASTRY DOUGH
2½ cups sifted flour
½ teaspoon salt
⅔ cup unsalted butter, diced
Approximately ⅓ cup ice-cold
   water

FILLING
1 cup white sauce (page 250)
3 tablespoons salt butter
5 scallions, including some of
   the green tails
1 cup sliced mushrooms,

preferably brown
2 cups diced cooked chicken
2 tablespoons fresh chopped
   or 1 teaspoon dry powdered
   thyme
¼ cup chopped fresh flat-leaf
   parsley
1 mashed garlic clove
¾ cup chicken stock (page
   255)
2 lightly beaten eggs
Salt and pepper to taste

TO MAKE THE DOUGH, mix the flour and salt in a bowl, add the butter and rub in the flour with your fingers until pieces of dough the size of white beans form. Add half the ice water and mix with your hands, pushing the flour inward from the sides of the bowl and up from the bottom. Add more water a little at a time, still mixing, then press the dough together and, picking up the loose particles from the bowl, form it into a ball. Divide the dough in half, wrap each half in wax paper, and refrigerate for half an hour.

Make the white sauce and set it aside. Cook the scallions in the butter until they are soft but not brown, then add the mushrooms and sauté them over moderate heat for 1 minute. Stir in the chicken, thyme, parsley, garlic and stock and cook for 2 minutes longer. Remove the pan from the heat, let it cool slightly, mix in the white sauce and the eggs, add the salt and pepper, and set the filling aside.

Preheat the oven to 400°. On a lightly floured board or table, roll out the dough into 2 round crusts ¼ inch thick and 1 inch larger all around than a 9-inch pie plate. Line a 9-inch pie plate with one of the shells, then carefully pour in the filling and cover it with the other shell. Flute the edges of the pie by pressing them together all around with your fingertips and with a knife cut the excess dough off the edges; brush the top of the crust with some milk if you want it to brown, then puncture the top crust in several places with a fork so that the steam can escape when the pie is cooking. Bake it for 15 minutes at 400°, then reduce the heat to 325° and bake the pie 25 minutes longer until it is golden. Let the pie cool slightly before cutting it. Serve hot or cold.

Lamb

Young lambs, born on the mountains from January to March, are fed on the new leaves of the spring savory and thyme, which give a gentle aroma to their flesh. Spring is the best season for lamb in the islands, and by Easter time, when most of the new lambs are ready for market, thousands of them, with their heads decorated in festive blues and pinks, are brought down to the cities from the *mándras,* the camping grounds of the shepherds, to be sold to each city family that has not raised one of its own. Traditionally, each village family raises a milk-fed lamb or kid to be slaughtered, prepared, stuffed and baked in the outdoor bee-hive oven the day before Easter for the feast. After the oven is heated from a fire of pine and sweet-smelling *askinós* wood and the lamb or kid is inside, the door and cracks of the oven are sealed with clay to keep out drafts and keep the temperature even so that the lamb can cook overnight without burning.

There are other traditional meals made with lamb; the delicious meatballs (*keftéthes*) and roasted leg of lamb (*arní toú foúrnou*), both of which people in the cities especially like to have on Sundays because preparation is simple. A leg of lamb can be prepared early in the morning or even the night before, then one or two hours before serving time it is taken to the neighborhood ovenhouse and left with the attendant, who cooks it in time for it to be picked up for dinner. *Keftéthes* are made of ground lamb mixed with herbs and fried; they are served with a salad for a quick meal. The villagers' favorite lamb dish is a stew, *arnáki yahnistó*. Made with fresh vegetables or pasta and cooked over an open fire in a clay pot, it is a foundation for endless variations of dishes.

LEG OF LAMB

Arní tou Foúrnou

Lamb cooks very quickly if it is young and tender. A leg of spring lamb weighs approximately 3 to 4 pounds and should cook in about 1 hour. If potatoes are going to be used with it, they should be cooked with the meat so that its juices give them a good flavor. (*Serves 5.*)

1 3- to 4-pound leg of lamb
2 slivered garlic cloves
2 teaspoons dry rosemary
   crushed with your fingers
½ cup olive oil

Salt and pepper to taste
6 medium-size nonbaking
   potatoes
2 tablespoons tomato paste
   diluted in ½ cup water

Preheat the oven to 375°. Place the leg of lamb in a pan and with a small knife remove any fat. Cut 2 deep 2-inch-long gashes on opposite sides of the leg all the way to the bone. Tuck the slivered garlic and a little of the rosemary into the gashes and pour some

olive oil onto the leg and rub it all over with your hands. Sprinkle the remaining rosemary over the leg, rub it gently, and then season it with salt and pepper.

Peel and quarter the potatoes and if they are large cut them in wedges. Rinse them under cold water and drain them. Toss them in a bowl with some salt and pepper and arrange them around the leg in the roasting pan. Spoon the diluted tomato paste over the potatoes, then drizzle the remaining olive oil on them; this will make them crisp and rosy as they bake. Finally, pour ½ cup of water into the bottom of the pan and roast the leg for 15 minutes at 375°, then reduce the heat to 350° and bake it for 45 minutes longer, checking from time to time to see that there is always a little water in the bottom of the pan.

MEATBALLS WITH MINT

Keftéthes

Ground lamb made into meatballs is popular throughout Greece, with each section of the country offering its own particular variation. In the islands we make *keftéthes* with fresh mint, which gives them a refreshing taste. (*Serves 6.*)

1 finely chopped large onion
1½ pounds ground lamb
2 large peeled and diced
    tomatoes or 1 16-ounce can
    strained tomatoes
½ cup chopped fresh mint
3 tablespoons grated
kephalotíri *or Parmesan*
    cheese
¼ cup fine bread crumbs
3 tablespoons flour
Salt and pepper to taste
Olive oil for frying
Flour for rolling

Cook the onion in ¼ cup water in a small saucepan over moderate heat until it gets soft and most of the water is evaporated; then set it aside to cool. Combine the onion, meat and all the other ingredients except the oil and flour in a large bowl, and blend with your hands or a wooden spoon until the mixture is well mixed and smooth. Spoon it out with a tablespoon — or a teaspoon if smaller balls are preferred — and roll the pieces over the flour to cover them entirely; then pick them up 1 at a time and jiggle them from hand to hand to shake off the excess flour. Roll them in between your palms to round them up. Heat ¼ inch olive oil in a skillet and add the meatballs a few at a time to fry over moderate heat until they are cooked inside, turning them around until they are evenly brown and firm. Test the inside by cutting one in half; if it is still soft, it should be cooked longer, but the meatballs should not be too dry.

LAMB WITH PASTA

Youvétsi

This everyday family dish is made with pieces of lamb and a pasta called *kritharáki* that used to take my mother hours to prepare by hand. *Kritharáki* looks like little grains of barley (but don't confuse it with barley) and can be bought in boxes in American supermarkets under the Italian name "orzo." A green leafy salad is always served with this dish. (*Serves 4 to 6.*)

2 pounds lean lamb	teaspoons dried savory
½ cup olive oil	1 mashed garlic clove
1 chopped medium-size onion	Salt and pepper to taste
6 large fresh tomatoes	2 cups uncooked kritharáki or
¼ cup chopped fresh or 1½	orzo

Cut the meat into pieces about 2 inches square and 1 inch thick and pat them dry with a towel to remove any excess moisture so that the oil will not spatter during the frying. Heat the olive oil in an ovenproof casserole over moderate heat and add the meat a few pieces at a time to brown on all sides. When all the meat is browned, return it to the casserole and stir in the onion and cook for 1 minute, then add the tomatoes, savory, garlic, salt and pepper and simmer covered over low heat for about 25 to 30 minutes or until the meat is almost cooked. Preheat the oven to 350°. Parboil the *kritharáki* or orzo according to the directions on the package, then drain it and add it to the lamb and mix well. Place the casserole in the preheated oven for 20 minutes or until the liquid is absorbed. If the orzo absorbs all the moisture of the meat sauce before it is fully cooked, then add more hot water, stir, and cook longer.

LAMB STEW

Arnáki Yahnistó

The flavor of this basic Greek stew varies depending on the vegetables cooked with it. It can be prepared ahead of time and refrigerated while slightly undercooked, or it can be kept on hand
frozen for a quick beginning for many delicious dishes. Any vegetables to be cooked in the stew should be added about ½ hour
before the meat is done. (*Serves 4 to 6.*)

2 pounds lean lamb
⅓ cup olive oil
1 chopped onion
2 tablespoons tomato paste
*   diluted in ¾ cup water*

1 mashed garlic clove
½ cup chopped fresh flat-leaf
*   parsley*
Salt and pepper to taste

Cut the lamb in pieces about 2 inches square and 1 inch thick
and pat them dry with a towel to remove the excess moisture.
Heat the olive oil in a heavy casserole over moderate heat and
brown the meat on all sides, a few pieces at a time. When all
the pieces have been browned, return them to the casserole. Add
the onion and cook for 1 minute or until it becomes soft. Add
the diluted tomato paste, garlic, parsley, salt and pepper, and
cover and simmer gently until the meat is almost tender. The
sauce should be thick, so add about 1 tablespoon flour diluted
in ¼ cup water to thicken it. If it comes out too thick, thin it
with a little more water.

Vegetables

Próima zarzavatiká are the vegetables that come up in the early part of spring and brighten up the marketplace with their different shapes and shades of green. They are all prepared with the minimum of cooking to preserve their flavor and freshness. Peas, plump in their shiny pods, are one of the first to arrive in the market. They are shelled and cooked quickly in a light sauce and they retain their emerald-green color and sweet taste. Another early arrival is spinach; its dark green crinkled leaves are seasoned with herbs and mixed with cheese and baked between pie

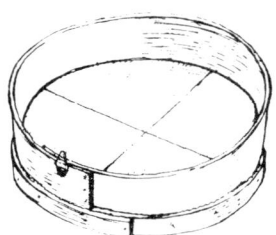

crusts to make the Greek *spanakópitta*. There is also the perennial artichoke, which bears its global fruits in spring; they can be picked small then or larger later on, to be combined with fresh tomatoes to make a delightful accompaniment to spring lamb dishes. If potatoes are underestimated by many people, they are not by the villagers, who unearth them small, almost the size of marbles, boil them in their skins, and serve them drenched with butter and sprinkled with fresh mint leaves.

Some of these gifts of nature, when cooked in the simplest way, will win a place on your table and give you new experiences in eating.

SPINACH PIE

Spanakópitta

Spanakópitta translates very badly into English, but I have not met a Greek who did not like it, and most of my American friends love it, too. It is made with beautiful green crinkly-textured spinach, scallions, dill weed and the Greek *fétta* cheese, which are combined and baked in a breadlike dough in a pie dish. (*Serves 4 to 6.*)

FILLING
1/3 *cup olive oil*
1 *large diced onion*
6 *to 8 peeled and coarsely diced scallions*
1 1/2 *pounds washed and coarsely chopped fresh spinach with large stems removed*
3/4 *cup coarsely chopped fresh or about 1/3 cup dry dill weed*
1 1/2 *cups crumbled* fétta

cheese
Pepper to taste

CRUST
1/2 *cake yeast or 1/2 envelope powdered yeast*
1/2 *cup lukewarm water*
1 1/2 *cups white flour*
1/2 *cup sifted whole-wheat flour*
1 *teaspoon salt*
5 *tablespoons olive oil*

TO MAKE THE FILLING, heat the olive oil in a large cast-iron or enamel saucepan (don't use aluminum, which gives spinach a metallic taste). Add the onion and scallions and cook them over moderate heat until they are soft but not brown. Place the spinach on top of the onions, and cover and cook for 5 minutes or until the spinach has settled, then stir the mixture with a wooden spoon and remove the pan from the heat. Mix the dill weed, *fétta* cheese and pepper into the spinach and set it aside to cool. Do not add salt; the saltiness of the *fétta* cheese is quite sufficient for the whole dish.

TO MAKE THE CRUST, prepare the yeast by dissolving it in ½ cup of lukewarm water and set it aside. In a large bowl mix the white and whole-wheat flours and salt and then make a little well in the center of the bowl. Place 3 tablespoons of the olive oil and the dissolved yeast in the well, and with your hands mix them into the dough by pushing the flour from the sides of the bowl inward toward the middle, then up from the bottom. Knead the dough until it is smooth and pliable. If any loose particles are left in the bottom of the bowl, add a few drops of water and knead some more. Cover the dough and allow it to rise in the bowl to twice its size, then punch it down and knead it again.

Preheat the oven to 375°. Now divide the dough in 2 and roll each half out on a floured board into a crust ¼ inch thick and 1 inch larger all around than a 9-inch pie plate. Oil the bottom and sides of the pie plate lightly and gently fit in one of the crusts. Pour the excess liquid off the spinach filling and put the filling evenly into the pie crust, then lay the top crust over it. Flute the edges of the crusts by pressing them together with your fingertips. Cut any excess dough from the edge of the pie with a knife, then pour the remaining 2 tablespoons olive oil on top of the crust and spread it all over with your hands. Prick designs in the top crust with a fork so the steam can escape during cooking. Bake 45 minutes or until the crust is golden.

SPINACH RICE

Spanakórizo

This spinach is loved even by children when it is made with fragrant oregano and served piping hot. (*Serves 4.*)

1 pound fresh spinach	*½ cup uncooked short-grain*
¼ cup olive oil	*rice*
5 chopped scallions, including	*2 tablespoons chopped fresh*
the green tops	*or 1 teaspoon dry oregano*

Salt and pepper to taste　　　　*Parmesan cheese*
Grated kephalotíri *or*

Remove and discard the stems from the spinach leaves, then wash the leaves, drain them, cut them in half, and set them aside. Sauté the scallions in the olive oil in an enamel saucepan over moderate heat until they are soft, then stir in the rice, and when it turns milky pour into it approximately 2¾ cups of cold water. Bring the rice to a boil, reduce the heat to low, cover, and simmer over low heat until the rice is almost cooked, 25 to 30 minutes. Season the rice with oregano, salt, and pepper, then put the spinach on top of it and cover the pot until the spinach settles. Stir the rice and spinach well together, adding a little more water if needed; cover it and cook 5 minutes longer. Serve at once with a sprinkle of cheese on top.

FRESH PEAS IN LIGHT SAUCE

Pizélia Aspra

This is a dish my mother always prepared in the spring. The peas were shelled and sometimes some tender pods were included, and all were simmered in a sauce made from fresh butter brought specially from the village, This can be served as a side dish with any meat or fish dish. (*Serves 4.*)

2½ pounds fresh peas in their
　shells
4 tablespoons salt butter or
　olive oil
5 chopped scallions
2 tablespoons flour

1¼ cups hot chicken stock
　(page 255) or hot water
1 tablespoon lemon juice
2 tablespoons fresh dill weed
White pepper and salt to taste

Shell the peas and set them aside. Heat the butter or olive oil in a saucepan and add the scallions and cook them over low heat until they are soft. Add the flour and stir for a few seconds, being careful not to let it brown; remove the pan from the heat and pour in the chicken stock or water, stirring constantly. Then return the pan to the heat and bring the liquid to a boil, continuing to stir, and cook for 2 minutes. Add the lemon juice, dill weed, salt and pepper and peas, and boil briskly, uncovered, for 5 minutes, or until the peas are cooked to your taste.

NEW POTATOES WITH MINT

Patatítses me Thiósmo

With the first sprigs of mint that come out in my herb garden in the spring I flavor tiny new potatoes, a dish I remember having often in the islands. Use small young unpeeled potatoes whole if they are small enough, or if they are larger, cut in half. (*Serves 4 to 6.*)

2 *pounds small new potatoes*	*Pepper and additional salt to*
1 *tablespoon salt*	*taste*
¼ *cup melted salt butter*	¼ *cup chopped fresh mint*

Wash and scrub the potatoes to remove the dirt, but leave the skins on. Put them in a saucepan and cover them with water and add 1 tablespoon salt. Bring them to a boil, reduce the heat, then simmer covered until they are tender when pierced with a fork. Drain the water off the potatoes and keep them warm in the pan.

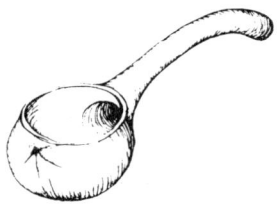

Melt the butter in a small saucepan, add it to the potatoes, season them with pepper and more salt if needed, and sprinkle the mint over them. Stir the potatoes gently with a wooden spoon to coat them with the butter and seasonings, and let them stand a few minutes before serving.

ARTICHOKES WITH TOMATOES

Anghináres me Domátes

An infinite number of dishes are prepared with artichokes, a vegetable used more frequently by city Greeks than village Greeks even though artichokes are raised in the villages. One typical way of preparing them is with the first fresh tomatoes of spring. (*Serves 4.*)

6 to 8 small artichokes or 4 large ones
1 lemon
⅓ cup olive oil
1 chopped medium-size onion
4 large peeled and sliced
tomatoes or 1 16-ounce can sliced tomatoes with their liquid
¼ cup chopped fresh dill weed
Salt and pepper to taste

Trim the artichokes by cutting off the stems, the tough outside leaves and the spiny tops of the tender inside leaves. Split them lengthwise in half (in quarters if larger artichokes are used) and scoop the fuzzy choke out of the center. Cut the lemon in half and rub the artichoke pieces with it to prevent them from browning. Heat the olive oil in a heavy skillet, add the artichokes and fry them over moderate heat until they are golden, then remove them from the skillet and place them on a paper towel to absorb the excess oil. In a casserole heat 2 tablespoons of the olive oil left in the skillet and cook the onion until it is soft; add the tomatoes, dill weed, salt and pepper, and simmer, covered, over low heat for 7 minutes. Add the fried artichokes, cover, and gently simmer for 25 to 35 minutes more or until the artichokes are almost tender, occasionally basting them with the tomato sauce. Add a little more water if it is needed for the artichokes to cook. If there is too much liquid left after cooking, reduce it by boiling it rapidly, uncovered, for a few minutes.

Cookies, Pastries and Pies

The vast collection of pastries and confections, *glyká* and *zaharotá*, with which the islanders indulge themselves are the best-known in all Greece. In every household any holy day is used as an excuse for making these sweets and on Easter great numbers of them are prepared by the housewives. Some of them are made in advance, like *kourambiéthes*, butter shortbread cookies that melt in your mouth the instant you bite into them. I remember the hours I used to spend helping my mother make them, crushing sugar and grinding it into powder by pounding it in a brass

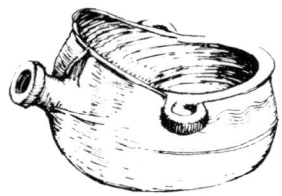

mortar and pestle, and dipping the baked and cooled *kourambiéthes* in blossom water and rolling them in the powdered sugar. Another loved sweet is *galaktoboúriko*, served to friends and the family and made the day before it is served so it will have time to absorb the syrup. It has a custard filling of eggs and spices that is baked in between thin sheets of buttered *phíllo* pastry. Less complicated for everyday, the easy-to-prepare dessert with the most natural ingredients is island cheese and honey pie, *meló-pitta nissiótiki*. It is made of soft, textured cheese and delicate-scented spring-blossom honey, and it has a most unusual taste and texture.

POWDERED-SUGAR COOKIES

Kourambiéthes

These white cookies covered with powdered sugar are tradition-ally baked in diamond shapes. To get the crumbling this cookie is known for, the dough must be not too firm and not too soft, and above all not overcooked. Its color should not change too much in baking. (*Makes about 20 to 22 cookies.*)

½ pound unsalted butter
¼ cup superfine sugar (found in boxes in American markets)
1 egg yolk
2 cups flour, sifted
1 teaspoon ouzo or brandy
½ cup ground blanched

almonds (optional) (page 269)
½ cup each confectioners' and superfine sugar com-bined, for rolling
¼ cup orange blossom or rosewater for dipping (found in drugstores)

Preheat the oven to 250°–275°. Let the butter stand at room temperature to soften, then beat it in a bowl with an electric or hand beater until it turns white. Mix in the sugar and the egg yolk and continue to beat until the mixture is creamy. Add the *ouzo* or brandy and optional almonds, and slowly add 1 cup of the flour, at first stirring with a wooden spoon until the dough starts to stiffen; then add the remaining flour and knead the dough with your hands until it is smooth. The dough should be a little bit on the soft side. Divide the dough in half and with your hands roll it into 2 12-inch-long ropes and cut them diagonally in 1-inch slices. Arrange the slices 1½ inches apart on an un-greased cookie sheet (they tend to spread) and bake them for 20 to 25 minutes or until their color changes to slightly gold. Re-move the cookies from the cookie sheet and place them side by side on a platter until they cool. Sift the confectioners' sugar onto a shallow plate, combine it with the superfine sugar, and put the blossom water in a bowl. Quickly dip the top of each cookie in the blossom water and then roll it in the sugar. Store the cookies in layers on a platter, adding powdered sugar between layers. *Kourambiéthes* last a long time.

CUSTARD-FILLED PASTRY

Galaktoboúriko

The marvelous custard filling makes this sweet pastry so refreshing, particularly when it is dribbled with syrup, cooled and sprinkled (if you wish) with rose- or orange-blossom water. (*Serves 10 to 12.*)

FILLING
4 cups milk
1½ cups sugar
¾ cup rice flour or farina
½ pound unsalted butter
8 medium-size eggs, separated
½ teaspoon powdered cinnamon
1 tablespoon grated orange peel (page 272)

PASTRY
½ pound unsalted clarified butter (page 269)
1 pound phíllo pastry

SYRUP
1½ cups water
¾ cup sugar
Peel of 1 orange

TO MAKE THE FILLING, combine the milk and 1 cup of sugar in a large saucepan and gradually stir in the rice flour or farina until it is diluted and smooth. Add the butter and set the pan over moderate heat, stirring constantly, until the mixture boils and thickens like a custard; then pour the mixture into a large bowl and let it completely cool. It will get thicker. Separate the eggs; add a pinch of salt to the whites and beat them until they peak but are not dry. Beat the egg yolks with the remaining sugar until they are light and creamy, and add both whites and yolks to the custard mixture by folding them in gently but quickly so as not to lose much air from them.

Preheat the oven to 350°. Generously brush the bottom and sides of a 9" x 13" x 2" pan with clarified butter, fit one of the *phíllo* sheets snugly in the pan, letting the excess hang over the edges; then brush butter all over it. Repeat the process until half the *phíllo* sheets are used, always buttering between sheets. Pour the custard filling into the *phíllo*-lined pan, spreading it evenly, and fold the hanging edges of *phíllo* in loosely over the filling to keep it from spilling out during cooking. Cut the remaining sheets of *phíllo* to fit the pan and place them one at a time over both the filling and the folded edges, always buttering between sheets. Bake for 35 to 45 minutes until the custard puffs and the top sheets of *phíllo* are golden brown. Let it cool (the top settles down considerably).

When the *galaktoboúriko* is cool, bring the syrup ingredients to a boil in a saucepan and remove any froth that collects on top, then reduce the heat to low and simmer for 15 minutes. Remove the syrup from the heat and pour it over the cooled *galaktoboúriko* immediately and cut the *galaktoboúriko* in squares with a sharp-pointed knife. When the *galaktoboúriko* is completely cool, put it in the refrigerator to chill. Sprinkle it with blossom water before serving.

ISLAND CHEESE AND HONEY PIE

Melópitta Nissiótiki

The cheese used for this 1-shell pie is *mizíthra,* soft, unsalted cheese that can be found in American markets under the Italian name "ricotta." I use American clover honey, which resembles the light Greek spring-blossom honey. While the pie is still hot it is puffed up and its consistency is light; but when it cools it settles down and its texture becomes more like cheesecake. It is delicious either way. (*Serves 12 to 15.*)

CRUST
1 cup unbleached all-purpose
   flour
1 tablespoon sugar

5 *tablespoons diced chilled*
   butter
Approximately 2 tablespoons
   ice water

FILLING
1 pound fresh mizíthra or
  ricotta cheese
½ cup sugar

½ cup honey
3 medium-size eggs, beaten
  lightly with a fork
1 teaspoon grated lemon peel

TO MAKE THE CRUST, sift the flour into a bowl and add the sugar and butter; if you are using unsalted butter, add a pinch of salt. Now work very quickly with your fingers, rubbing the flour and butter until the pieces of dough are about the size of white beans. Add ½ tablespoon of the ice water and mix it in with your hands, pressing inward from the sides of the bowl and up from the bottom. Add the remaining ice water, press the dough together, picking up the loose particles, and form the dough into a ball. Flatten the dough slightly, wrap it in waxed paper, and chill it for ½ hour.

Preheat the oven to 350°. Roll the dough out on a lightly floured board until it is about ⅛-inch thick and 1 inch larger all around than a 9-inch pie pan. Fold the dough in half and lift it into the pie pan, placing the fold at the center of the pan; then unfold it and line the pan with it. Turn the edges of the dough under and press them with your fingertips to make a fluted rim standing up about ½ inch above the edges of the pan to hold the filling when it rises. Set a slightly smaller pan inside the pie crust filled with enough dry beans to weigh the crust down and hold it in shape while it bakes. If you don't have another pan, line the crust with aluminum foil and weigh it down with the beans. Partially bake the crust for 10 to 15 minutes until it is slightly golden. Remove the crust from the oven and let it cool before removing the extra pie pan and beans.

TO MAKE THE FILLING, put the cheese, sugar and honey in a bowl and mix well. Add the eggs and lemon peel, mix well again, and pour the mixture into the cooled shell. Bake the pie at 350° for 45 minutes or until the surface is golden brown and cracks appear on it.

Puddings

When the weather warms up, the people in the islands promenade up and down the main street by the sea in the center of the city, where there are outdoor cafés and many little vending carts selling their goods by the side of the road. Some of the carts have *vitrínes*, a kind of glass cabinet that opens and closes from the top and contains little tin dishes of pudding bedded in crushed ice. People stop and buy them and eat the pudding right there to refresh themselves and then give back the dish. Those puddings, whose texture and fragrance are still in my memory, are *balezés*, made with milk and other flavorings and almost translucent, and *rizógalon*, a rice pudding that is one of the most popular puddings with Greeks for snacks. It is sold also in the cafés, always ice-cold and sprinkled with cinnamon.

RICE PUDDING

Rizógalon

Rizógalon is made in every home as well as in cafés and by vendors, with different variations. Sometimes it is eaten in the morning, sometimes between meals, and sometimes at the end of dinner as dessert. The rice used in the pudding is the short-grain variety that expands when cooked. (*Serves 4 to 5.*)

⅓ cup uncooked short-grain
   rice
1 quart milk
½ cup sugar

1 tablespoon grated lemon
   peel
Powdered cinnamon

Cover the rice with ½ cup of water and set it aside for 5 minutes. Combine the milk and sugar in a saucepan and bring them to a boil over moderate heat; add the rice with the water to the hot milk, and stirring continuously, bring it to a boil, then add the grated lemon peel. Reduce the heat and gently simmer the mixture until it is thick and creamy. If the liquid has evaporated before the rice is cooked, add a little hot water and cook a bit longer. Pour the pudding into individual dishes and chill; sprinkle with cinnamon before serving.

TRANSLUCENT PUDDING

Balezés

On the island of Mitilini, *balezés* is made by the well-wishing friends and relatives of a new mother, who take it to her after the fortieth day from her delivery, when they are permitted to see the newly born child. I make this pudding with less cornstarch than in the traditional island recipe and with the addition of unflavored gelatin, which gives it a lighter consistency. (*Serves 3.*)

1 tablespoon cornstarch
1 envelope unflavored gelatin
½ cup milk
5 tablespoons sugar

⅛ teaspoon almond extract
Ground blanched almonds
   (page 269) and pomegranate seeds (optional)

Dilute the cornstarch in ½ cup of cold water and soften the gelatin in another ½ cup water. Mix the milk with the sugar in a saucepan and stir in the diluted cornstarch, then bring the mixture to a boil over moderate heat, stirring continuously. Reduce the heat to low and cook for 1 minute, then remove the pan from the heat. Now add the gelatin and stir well until it dissolves, then add the almond extract. Pour the pudding mixture into individual serving dishes or a large shallow bowl and chill until it sets. Sprinkle with ground blanched almonds and pomegranate seeds before serving.

Fresh Fruits and Spoon Sweets

Hrisómilo, "golden apple" in Greek, is the juicy fruit of the apricot tree, which ripens in the latter part of spring. My mother always picked apricots with great care, making sure they were all of the same size and underripe — so they would all cook evenly and retain their shape — for her year's supply of whole apricot sweets in syrup. Very patiently she would thinly peel the skin off each

fruit with a small knife, pit it and stuff it with a blanched almond, then let them all soak in limewater to become firmer before cooking them. I remember that she stored the cooked apricots in a glass jar decorated on the outside with little enameled forget-me-not flowers, and when the jar was set to cool by the window the sun shining on it made it look like a jar full of gold.

Knowing that apricots are my favorite fruit, my husband planted two trees in the back yard of our New England house, and to our amazement they survived the freezing weather of the winter. One early spring one of the trees was full of blossoms, and in July the fruits were gold — much smaller than the ones in the islands, but just as juicy and sweet.

WHOLE APRICOT SWEETS

Hrisómila Glykó

Apricot sweets are offered in Greek homes as a welcome to guests — and are also used occasionally to sweeten oneself. They require a lot of elaborate preparation, but they are worth the effort if you like apricots, because preserved this way they last and last. Get firm, fresh apricots, not quite ripe, and unblemished. You can buy fresh apricots in the supermarket in spring. Limewater you can buy in drugstores.

2½ pounds fresh apricots (approximately 27 medium-size apricots)
Blanched almonds (page 269)
2 cups limewater

2 pounds (4 cups) sugar
2 cups cold water
Juice of 1 fresh lemon (4 tablespoons)
8 whole cloves

Use a small, clean screwdriver to pit the apricots. With its point inserted from the stem side, push the pit through the other end while holding the fruit firmly in your hand, being careful not to split the fruit or to puncture your hand. Peel the thin outer skin off each pitted apricot with a small paring knife and insert a blanched almond in the pit opening. Pour the limewater into a large earthenware bowl, add to it 2 cups of water, and soak the apricots in it for 2 to 3 hours; the limewater makes them firmer. Drain the apricots, rinse them twice in cold water, and put them to drain again in a colander.

Combine the sugar with the cold water in a large enamel or stainless-steel saucepan, bring the mixture to a boil, and remove with a metal spoon any froth that has collected on top. Reduce the heat and simmer for 5 minutes; add the well-drained apricots and cook them gently, uncovered, for 15 to 20 minutes, occasionally scooping the froth off the top. With a slotted spoon remove the apricots to a platter, then add the lemon juice and cloves to the syrup and boil it until large bubbles form on top. Return the fruit to the syrup and simmer for 1 minute; then remove the pan from the heat, cover it with a clean cloth, and set the apricots aside undisturbed overnight (6 to 8 hours). The next day, slowly simmer the apricots again over low heat until they look glazed and the syrup is thick or registers 210° on a candy thermometer. When the fruit and syrup are cool, transfer them to sterilized jars and seal them.

CREAMED APRICOTS

Hrisómila Peltés

Apricots have to be good and ripe to make *peltés*, a fruit dessert with almonds, sweetened with sugar then chilled and eaten. This dessert is served with clotted cream (*kaimáki*) in the islands, but I use whipped cream and it is just as good. The dried apricots that come in boxes in American stores are excellent for making the fruit pulp for this puree. (*Serves 4 to 6.*)

1 pound dried apricots
Sugar to taste
½ cup split blanched
almonds (page 269)
Whipped cream

Cover the apricots with cold water to 2 inches above them in an earthenware bowl and soak them overnight. The next day, transfer them with the water to an enamel or stainless-steel saucepan and simmer them gently, stirring occasionally, until they are soft. Puree the apricots with their juice through a strainer, using a wooden spoon. Return the puree to the saucepan, sweeten it with sugar to your taste, and add the blanched almonds. Bring the mixture to a boil over low heat until the sugar melts, stirring constantly to prevent the puree from burning on the bottom. Put the puree in small dessert dishes and set them in the refrigerator to chill. Top them with whipped cream just before serving.

SUMMER

Summer

In summer the islands are flooded with the strong light that makes the sea gleam in endless shades of blue and green and the small fields of ripe wheat look like gold. The leaves of the ancient, twisted olive trees shimmering in the light wind look silver and the pink and white blooms of oleanders brighten the ravines and scatter their fragrance in the clear air. No rains fall in the summer, and fog is unknown. This is the season that brings the most luscious vegetables to my island, vegetables that look like a painter's palette in the open marketplaces — deep purple eggplants, red tomatoes, green zucchini and cucumbers, and the green beans that shoppers snap to listen for the "click" sound of freshness.

Summer also is the time for salads and vegetables cooked with fresh herbs and olive oil; for tender veal cut in thin slices, then stuffed and rolled; for chopped meat made into meatballs and used with sauce in casseroles. Fresh fish of many kinds from the early morning catch are sold in the market or individually by fishermen from door to door, to be cooked for the midday meal the islands' favorite ways — fried and charcoal-broiled.

Fruits are the most abundant of all in summer, with sweet plums, peaches — white or yellow fleshed — many sizes of melons, grapes of all shades or purple, and seedless white grapes whose sweet, refreshing taste makes them the most popular of all.

Visiting the village farms under the cloudless summer sky, you see large patches of vegetables and watermelons, irrigated by ice-cold water from the windmills. The plentiful water runs through the little furrows in the black, rich soil hoed by the peasants so it can reach and refresh the plants, which look healthy even under the hot sun. Cucumbers taste so much better when just picked from the plant and eaten with a sprinkle of salt, and fresh tomato salad is most delicious prepared by the farmer with olive oil and herbs and served with wheat bread for lunch right there in the field under the shade of a fig tree. Then one can reach the fresh figs in the laden tree by just stretching the arm, to have a most memorable dessert.

Midsummer is the time of harvest and of the threshing of grains. As a child I loved this part of the season and always visited the village and my aunts at this time. They always took me to their *alóni,* threshing place, a flat area of cleared ground with a post in the middle to which animals are tied by ropes. With children on their backs to guide them, they go around in circles and thus slowly thresh with their feet the sheaves of wheat or barley. Winnowing is next, and it is beautiful to watch as the women take handfuls of the threshed mixture and, raising their hands very high against the wind, let it trickle down onto a canvaslike cover on the ground. The wind carries away the light straw and chaff, and the clean kernels of wheat or barley drop in mounds onto the cloth.

Harvesting the grapes takes place after threshing, late summer to autumn. Each family harvests its own vineyards, putting the bunches of grapes in willow baskets and carrying them by donkey to the village to be crushed in the family stamper, *linós,* and made into wine. The *linós,* an enclosed square stone trough with a spout in the front, is lined with bricks or large stones and is attached to the outside of the house and kept immaculately whitewashed. Grapes are dumped into it and children with washed feet jump on them and crush them, cheering, singing, and laughing. The must, or juices, runs red and sweet from the spout into a copper container called a *kasáni.* Mothers rush to make *moustoalevriá,* a sweet pudding made with some of the fresh must before the rest is put to ferment into wine in wooden barrels that have been washed with water scented with sage, pine needles, or mountain savory.

Summer is the season of happy times in the islands, with many weddings and fiestas taking place and everybody being involved and feeling alive — with lots of music, dancing and good food.

Appetizers

In the horseshoe-shaped harbor of the island Symi, there are colorful new Greek Revival houses built one above another up the stony hillside, and thousands of steps to climb up instead of roads. Fishermen untangle their nets and prepare their gear for the next trip to sea, while the *kaíki*, a boat with a high prow and many sails that looks like a contemporary of Columbus's *Santa Maria*, unloads its cargo of fresh food for the inhabitants of this barren fishing island who can't grow their own. There, in

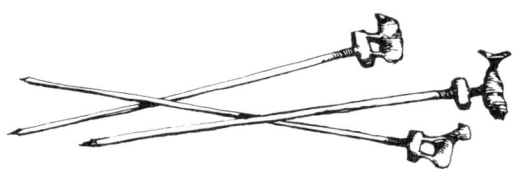

the little canopied outdoor cafés by the sea, people sit on rush-seated chairs sipping drinks and nibbling *mezéthes* with such a feeling of pleasure and peace as they watch the small waves hit the beach.

Some of these *mezéthes* are made from bits of meat and fish cooked skewered over red coals, spreading the barbecue aroma around the harbor. But the most refreshing of the summer appetizers are made from fresh or cooked vegetables dressed with lemon oil, *lemonólatho* (page 254), chilled and then eaten in flat bread, *pítta* (pages 235–236).

CUCUMBERS IN YOGURT SAUCE

Angúri me Yaoúrti

Very fresh and not overmature cucumbers should be used for this dish, and they must be finely cubed, with the excess liquid drained off before the cucumbers are mixed with the sauce. Sometimes the yogurt is strained through cheesecloth to give it a thicker consistency. This dish is served as either an appetizer or a salad. (*Serves 3 to 4.*)

2 small peeled cucumbers
½ cup plain whole-milk yogurt
1 mashed or pressed garlic

clove
¼ cup olive oil
Salt and pepper to taste
Flat-leaf parsley for garnish

Dice the cucumbers very fine into a small bowl and drain off the excess liquid. In another small bowl combine the yogurt, garlic, olive oil, salt and pepper. Stir them until they are well mixed, and gently fold in the cucumbers and chill. Garnish with parsley before serving.

EGGPLANT APPETIZER OR SALAD

Melintzanosaláta

Melintzanosaláta is very popular in the islands from the cities to the villages, and is made with eggplant, tomato, onion, and dressing. The eggplants are buried in the embers of the fireplace or brazier to cook, allowed to cool and then prepared. But you can also cook them in a kitchen oven; the eggplant then will cook faster and more evenly. Choose a firm, dark, shiny eggplant without dents. The stem should be green, indicating freshness. Close to the stem, where you find the whitest part (which is so delicious for this dish), the eggplant should be stout. (*Serves 3 to 4.*)

1 medium-size eggplant
1 large peeled and diced
   tomato
½ cup chopped fresh flat-leaf
   parsley

1 tablespoon mashed or
   pressed onion
⅓ cup olive oil
Juice of ½ lemon
Salt and pepper to taste

Preheat the oven to 350°. Puncture the eggplant with a knife to prevent it from exploding while it cooks, place it in a baking dish, and bake it in the preheated oven for about 1 hour. Then remove the eggplant from the oven and let it cool until it can be handled. Peel off the dark outside skin and dice the pulp inside into a bowl, straining off any excess liquid. Add the remaining ingredients to the bowl, mix, and then chill. Correct the seasonings before serving.

GRILLED MEAT ON SKEWERS

Souvlákia

In the past this food was found only during fiestas (*panighíria*), when it was sold in village coffeehouses or at small stands with hot charcoal burning in braziers just waiting for your order. Your choice of lean or fat pieces of lamb were threaded on skewers in front of you, then broiled, put in *pítta*, and sprinkled with fresh chopped parsley and chopped onion. Now, *souvlákia* stands are on practically every street corner, both on the mainland and in the islands, and *souvlákia* is a delicious snack for the local people and all the foreigners who pass through and the favorite food of my son Morgan when visiting Greece. (*Serves 4.*)

1 tablespoon fresh crushed or
   ½ teaspoon dried oregano
¼ cup olive oil
1 tablespoon lemon juice

1 teaspoon fresh onion juice
   (pressed) or 1 tablespoon
   finely chopped onion
1 pound lamb (from leg or

shoulder) *cut in ½-inch pieces*   *Salt and pepper to taste*

Crush the fresh oregano with a wooden bowl and spoon or mortar and pestle and mix it in a bowl with the oil, lemon juice and onion juice to make a marinade. Place the meat in the marinade and let it stand at room temperature for an hour, then drain the marinade off. Thread the pieces of meat onto 10-inch metal skewers and grill them over red-hot charcoal, turning them occasionally, for 5 to 10 minutes, depending on how hot the fire is. They will be done when they are nicely brown on the outside but still pink and juicy inside. Season with salt and pepper and serve.

FRIED WHITEBAIT

Maríthes Tiganités

Maríthes are small fish of various European species called "whitebait" in English. In America the fish closest to them in size are smelts, which are nearly always 2 to 5 inches long and sold in markets already cleaned and sometimes with their heads removed; but any small fish can be used for this recipe. Islanders are very fond of small fish. From the tiniest baby *maríthes*, they make delicious fish patties by mixing them into a pancakelike batter and dropping spoonfuls into hot olive oil to fry until golden. Larger ones are held together by their tails in fan-shaped bunches to be dipped also in batter and fried. (*Serves 4.*)

1 cup flour batter (*page 258*)   *Salt and pepper to taste*
1 pound whitebait or smelts   *Olive oil for frying*
  (*2 to 3 inches long*)   *Lemon wedges for garnish*

Prepare the flour batter and let it stand at room temperature for ½ hour. Gut and wash the fish, leaving the heads and tails on, and season them with salt and pepper to taste.

Pour enough olive oil into a skillet to cover the bottom by at least ¼ inch, and heat it over moderate heat until a haze forms on the oil. Holding 3 fish firmly together by their tails in a fan shape, dip them in the batter, and then drop them gently into the oil to fry until they are golden on both sides. Remove them with a spatula and serve them hot in bunches with lemon wedges.

Salads

Simple crisp salads, used throughout the summer in the islands, are made with combinations of fresh leafy greens in the beginning of the season. *Horiátiki*, peasant-style salad (known to Americans as "Greek salad"), actually eaten mainly in the city, is very colorful — the greens and other vegetables are topped with semisoft cheese and black olives — and it is served in the first part of the summer, with the midday meal. Later, as the weather gets hotter, the greens are replaced with tomatoes, green peppers, and cucumbers. Tomato salad, a favorite of the peasants, accompanies their lunches in the fields or their suppers at home throughout the hot days of the summer season.

PEASANT-STYLE SALAD

Horiátiki Saláta

This salad is made from two kinds of lettuce that differ in color and texture, and the leaves of each are cut differently; dark green romaine is sliced crosswise and Bibb lettuce is broken in pieces, and they are tossed and seasoned together in a large bowl. Then the remaining vegetables and other ingredients are arranged very carefully in layers and in contrasting colors on the greens, and the dressing is very evenly dribbled on top. The salad is placed in the middle of the table, and each person reaches with his fork to select from the bowl what he wishes to eat. (*Serves 6.*)

½ cup olive oil–vinegar salad dressing (pages 253–254)
1 head of romaine lettuce
1 head Bibb lettuce
Salt and pepper to taste
2 tomatoes cut in wedges
2 cucumbers, peeled in stripes (leaving some peel on), split in half lengthwise and sliced in half-moons
1 green pepper cut in thin rings
1 onion cut in thin rings
¼ cup coarsely chopped flat-leaf parsley
¾ cup coarsely crumbled fétta *cheese*
15 to 20 black Greek olives

Prepare the salad dressing and let it stand at room temperature at least 1 hour. Wash the lettuce leaves one by one under running cold water and dry them. Bunch together 3 or 4 romaine leaves at a time and cut them crosswise into ½-inch slices in a large bowl. Break the Bibb lettuce coarsely with your hands and toss it with the romaine and season them with salt and pepper. Then on top of the lettuce greens add in layers, lightly seasoning with salt between layers, first all the tomatoes, then all the cucumber, all the green pepper, onion, parsley, *fétta* cheese, and Greek olives. Drizzle the dressing over the salad and serve it immediately.

TOMATO SALAD

Domatosaláta

In the middle of summer when lettuce is not plentiful, the tomato, which is at the peak of its season, becomes queen of the salads. It is sliced in wedges and mixed with onions, a lot of flat-leaf parsley and, if available, thinly sliced cucumber and rings of green pepper. Then the salad is salted to make the tomato release its juices and mixed with the olive oil dressing to make a pungent combination. Wheat bread goes well with this salad. (*Serves 4.*)

4 large, firm ripe tomatoes
1 large green pepper sliced in
  thin rings
1 cucumber peeled in stripes
  (leaving some peel on),
  split in half lengthwise and
sliced in half-moons
1 onion sliced in thin rings
½ cup chopped fresh flat-leaf
  parsley
Salt and pepper to taste
⅓ cup olive oil

Wash the tomatoes, cut them in ½-inch wedges, and place them in a large salad bowl with the peppers, cucumber, and onion. Sprinkle on the parsley and salt and pepper, then pour the olive oil over the salad and toss it well to coat all the ingredients with the oil.

FRESH GREEN BEAN SALAD

Fasoulákia Fréska Saláta

The brilliant green color of this salad is achieved by cooking the small, tender beans quickly and uncovered, and the taste is enhanced if they are cooked at least 2 hours in advance and chilled. They are an excellent accompaniment to any fried or charcoal-broiled meat. (*Serves 4.*)

1 pound fresh green beans
2 tablespoons salt
¼ cup lemon-oil dressing
  (page 254)
1 large minced garlic clove
Pepper and additional salt to
  taste
1 tablespoon chopped flat-leaf
  parsley

Remove any ends and strings from the beans, leaving them whole. Bring 2 quarts of water plus 2 tablespoons salt to a vigorous boil and drop in the beans to cook uncovered over high heat until they are barely tender; be careful not to overcook them so they will not lose their fresh green color. Drain them and while they are still warm dribble them with the lemon-oil dressing, then sprinkle the minced garlic over them, season with salt and pepper, and put them into the refrigerator to chill. Sprinkle them with parsley before serving.

BOILED GREEN ZUCCHINI SALAD

Kolokithákia Vrastá Saláta

Fresh dill gives a delicate flavor to this salad, which is dribbled with lemon-oil dressing and served hot or cold. Small green zucchini about 3 inches long are best, and they should be fresh and firm. (*Serves 4.*)

2 pounds zucchini squash	*Pepper and additional salt to*
1 tablespoon salt	*taste*
¼ cup chopped fresh dill	*⅓ cup lemon-oil dressing*
weed	*(page 254)*

Wash the zucchini well but do not peel them, then cut the ends off and split them down the middle; if they are larger, quarter them. Bring 4 cups of water plus 1 tablespoon salt to a vigorous boil. Drop in the zucchini and boil them over moderate heat, uncovered, until they are tender. Drain the zucchini, place them in a bowl, and season them with the dill weed, salt and pepper. Pour the dressing over the salad, mix it gently, and serve warm or chilled.

Fish and Shellfish

Like unwinding lace, the foamy waves of summer hit the sandy or pebbled shores of the islands, where the fishermen stand in shallow waters hauling their nets in from the sea. Pulling the nets, called *tráta,* requires a lot of strength, but when the part that is full of colorful fish finally lands on the beach, you hear cheers and laughter for the good catch. The catch includes the beautiful red mullet (*barboúnia*), sea bream (*lithrínia*), bass (*sinagrítha*), porgies (*tsipoúra*), and of course the small whitebait (*maríthes*), which the islanders like to charcoal-broil or fry and eat with a salad.

Setting nets to trap the shrimp (*garíthes*) is more difficult work; they have been one of the favorite Greek seafoods since ancient days and there are many special ways of preparing them. Sweet-fleshed shrimp of different sizes are found all year round in the deep waters of the island of Astipalea and are caught by the fishermen from all the surrounding islands to be prepared — the larger ones, that is — in a casserole with fresh tomatoes and *fétta* cheese.

FRIED FISH

Psária Tiganitá

Fish fried in olive oil and served with lemon 'wedges is very popular all over Greece, particularly in the islands, whether you use fillets or small whole fish. The red mullet, a tasty fish, is almost always prepared this way; in America, mullet is available frozen in the fish markets, but any small fish will do as a substitute. Fillets of sea perch are also very good. The oil for pan frying should be hot before the fish is added, to prevent it from sticking, and there should be enough oil in the pan to half cover the fish. Fish is sufficiently cooked when the meat flakes easily when tested with a fork and is no longer translucent. You can also use a deep fryer for this recipe with good results. (*Serves 4 to 6.*)

2 pounds fresh fillets or small whole fish, like red mullet or smelts
Salt and pepper to taste
1 cup white flour for rolling

Olive oil for frying
Juice of ½ lemon
½ lemon cut in wedges for garnish

If small whole fish are used, scrape off any scales, and gut and degill the fish (pages 270–271), leaving the heads and tails on. Rinse the small fish or fillets thoroughly and pat them dry; season them with salt and pepper, and roll them in the flour, shaking off the excess. Put in a skillet enough olive oil to cover half of the fish when frying — in any case, not less than ½ inch — and heat over moderate fire. Add the fish and fry them until they are golden on both sides, from 7 to 10 minutes altogether. Remove the fish to a warm platter, sprinkle with a little lemon juice, and serve with lemon wedges.

CHARCOAL-BROILED FISH

Psári tis Sháras

The aroma of broiled fish fills the small cafés in summer. The fish are held over hot coals in doubled-over wire grills with handles called *sháres*, which the cook rotates over and over while basting the fish with lemon oil as they grill. The *shára* should be positioned about 2 to 3 inches over the charcoals when the fire is hot and lowered when the heat lessens, and care should be taken not to burn the skin. The fish is cooked when its flesh is no longer

translucent. You may use the broiler in your oven (it will take approximately the same amount of time to cook), taking the same care not to burn the fish, and basting it before and during cooking. (*Serves 4 to 6.*)

2 fish, 1½ to 2 pounds each
    (*sea bream, red snapper,*
    grouper or bass)
⅓ *cup lemon-oil dressing*
    (*page 254*)

Salt and pepper to taste
1 tablespoon chopped fresh or
    ¼ *teaspoon dry oregano*
    for garnish

Scale, gut, and degill the fish (pages 270–271), then rinse them and pat dry. Season the inside cavities with salt and pepper, rubbing it in with your fingers. Using a brush, baste the entire outside of the fish with some of the lemon-oil dressing and coat the grill with it. When the burning charcoal is hot, put the fish in the grill and hold the grill over the fire while turning it over and over, basting continuously until the fish are cooked, approximately 30 minutes, depending upon the thickness of the fish. Remove the fish to a platter, sprinkle with the remaining lemon-oil dressing, and garnish with oregano.

SHRIMP WITH FÉTTA CHEESE

Garíthes me Fétta

A popular dish in the islands that requires long preparation but tastes delicious is shrimp cooked on a bed of fresh tomatoes and herbs and topped with Greek *fétta* cheese. It can be prepared ahead of time and refrigerated until time to bake. If you live in an area where you can get fresh shrimp you are very fortunate; just shell and devein them and they are ready to cook. If you cannot find fresh shrimp, the quick-frozen ones from the fish market which come already cleaned are very good. First you must defrost them (see page 274); do not defrost them at room temperature or they will become limp and soggy. Serve with rice pilaf. (*Serves 4 to 6.*)

¼ *cup olive oil*
2 *pounds shelled shrimp or*
    2½ *pounds fresh shrimp*
    in their shells
Juice of ½ lemon (about 2
    tablespoons)
2 *peeled tomatoes thinly*
    sliced
¼ *pound thinly sliced* fétta
    cheese

SAUCE
¼ *cup olive oil*
1 *medium-size chopped onion*
4 *large peeled and diced*
    tomatoes
⅓ *cup dry white wine*
1 *finely minced garlic clove*
½ *cup chopped fresh flat-leaf*
    parsley
Salt and pepper to taste

TO MAKE THE SAUCE, heat the olive oil in a skillet and cook the onion over moderate heat until translucent, then add the tomatoes and the rest of the sauce ingredients and cook uncovered, stirring occasionally, until the sauce thickens, about 25 minutes. If you want a thicker sauce, stir in 1 tablespoon of flour diluted in 3 tablespoons water.

Preheat the oven to 450°. When the sauce is cooked, heat the olive oil in a large skillet until a haze forms in it, and quickly sear the peeled shrimp a few at a time for about 1 minute each; when they turn pink, remove them to a bowl with a slotted spoon. When the shrimp are all seared, pour the lemon juice over them and gently toss them to absorb it.

Pour the sauce into a pan 9" x 12" x 2" or any other shape and spread it evenly to cover the bottom. Put the shrimp in a layer on top of the sauce, the sliced tomatoes on top of the shrimp, and the *fétta* cheese on top of the tomatoes. Bake the casserole for 15 minutes or until the *fétta* begins to melt.

Poultry

When a summer wedding takes place in a small village, it usually starts on Sunday and continues for a whole week, and all the people there celebrate. Young men, singing and mingling with the girls, who are clad in their beautiful dresses, form the dancing circle of the fast *soústa* and other folk dances. Among the many foods served, there is a feast of chickens all cooked in different ways — with rice pilaf, or broiled with yogurt sauce, or stewed with the aromatic herb oregano. The feast is organized by the young unmarried men of the village and they go around door to door to collect chickens donated by friends and relatives of the groom. They bring them to the young unmarried girls, and with the help of the older women, they all prepare a festive table to which they invite the bride and groom as guests of honor.

In the islands a beautifully prepared chicken dish is considered the most appropriate thing to serve when unexpected guests arrive.

CHICKEN PILAF

Órnitha Piláfi

The bird usually used for this dish is a large, plump roaster, which is slowly simmered whole in sauce on top of the stove.

When it is cooked it is cut and separated into large pieces, and a tomato pilaf is made in its sauce. Served with stewed fresh green beans, it is a perfect meal for a large gathering of people. (*Serves 6.*)

1 4- to 5-pound roasting
  chicken
3 tablespoons olive oil
1 large chopped onion
6 large ripe tomatoes, peeled
  and diced

2 tablespoons tomato paste
¼ cup chopped fresh or ½
  teaspoon dry savory
Salt and pepper to taste
2 cups water
2 cups uncooked rice

Wash the chicken inside and out and pat it dry. Heat the olive oil in a heavy casserole over moderate heat and fry the chicken in it on all sides until it becomes light golden all over. Add the onion and cook uncovered until it becomes translucent; then add the tomatoes, tomato paste, savory, salt and pepper and cook for 3 minutes more. Then pour 2 cups of water into the casserole and cover it; when the water boils, reduce the heat and simmer until the chicken is tender but does not fall apart when tested with a fork, about 45 minutes to an hour. Remove the chicken from the pot onto a large platter to cool. Separate the legs and thighs into serving pieces, and pull the rest of the meat off the bones in large pieces. Add enough water to the casserole so that you have 4 cups of liquid, and bring to a boil, seasoning with salt and pepper. Return the chicken pieces to the sauce and add the rice, stirring until it boils; then cover the casserole, reduce the heat to low, and simmer slowly until the rice is cooked and the liquid is absorbed, about 25 to 30 minutes. Arrange the rice on a platter with the pieces of chicken in the center.

CHICKEN BREAST WITH HERBS

Órnitha me Arígano

Although in the islands this dish is cooked in a clay pot, slowly, over a wood fire, and with the herb oregano for flavor, it may be prepared as well on top of the stove in a heavy casserole with fresh tarragon in place of the oregano. Use whole breasts and cut them against the ridge of the breastbone, loosening the flesh and pulling it from the rib cage while you cut until the meat comes loose from the bone in one piece. The skin should be left on the meat. Serve with buttered noodles and a salad. (*Serves 6.*)

Meat from 3 whole chicken
   breasts
½ lemon
2 tablespoons olive oil
¼ cup white wine
⅓ cup hot chicken stock
   (page 255)

¼ cup chopped fresh flat-leaf
   parsley
2 tablespoons chopped fresh
   oregano or tarragon
1 mashed garlic clove
Salt and pepper to taste

Rub the meat with the ½ lemon, squeezing out the juice, and set the meat aside to absorb the juice. Heat the oil in a deep skillet over moderate heat and put the chicken breasts in skin-side down to fry until lightly golden, then turn them and fry them a few minutes on the other side. Pour the wine and then the hot stock over the chicken, add the herbs and garlic, season with salt and pepper, then reduce the heat to low and simmer the chicken uncovered until it is tender and the sauce is thick, about 20 minutes. If thicker sauce is preferred, mix in 1 table-spoon of flour diluted in 3 tablespoons water.

CHARCOAL-BROILED CHICKEN WITH YOGURT SAUCE

Órnitha tis Sháras me Yaoúrti

Your chickens become delicious when they are marinated in lemon-oil marinade for a couple of hours and then broiled over hot coals, and even more so when yogurt sauce is poured over them just before serving. For this recipe you may use either young broilers or fryers, 1½ to 3 pounds, split in half or quartered. Serve with a salad. (*Serves 4 to 6.*)

2 broilers or fryers, split or
   quartered

1 cup cold marinade for
   poultry (page 257)

1 cup yogurt sauce (page 59)

Marinate the chicken pieces in the marinade in the refrigerator for about 2 hours, then drain them and save the marinade. Prepare the yogurt sauce using ¾ cup of yogurt and set it aside.

Place the chicken pieces on the preheated grill over hot coals, taking care not to have them too close to the fire so that the skin will not burn. Turn the pieces over and over, basting them frequently with the marinade until the skin is golden and the meat loses its translucence. Remove the chicken to a platter, pour the yogurt sauce over it, and serve.

CHICKEN LIVERS WITH VINEGAR SAUCE

Sikotákia tis Órnithas Xithátá

A sauce of vinegar and thyme gives livers tanginess and good aroma. Only fresh, firm livers should be used. Serve with rice. (*Serves 2 to 3.*)

1 pound chicken livers
Flour for rolling
3 tablespoons olive oil
1 chopped onion
2 tablespoons red wine
  vinegar
½ cup hot chicken stock
  (page 255)

1 tablespoon flour, diluted in
  ¼ cup water
1 tablespoon chopped fresh
  thyme
Salt and pepper to taste
1 tablespoon fresh flat-leaf
  parsley

Cut the livers in half and discard any soft and discolored pieces, then rinse them with cold water, pat them dry, and roll them in flour. Heat the olive oil in a skillet over moderate heat and put in the livers a few at a time to sauté, turning them over and over until the red color disappears and they are brown on all sides, about 7 to 10 minutes. Remove the livers to a platter and keep them warm.

In the same skillet cook the onion until it is translucent; then stir in the vinegar, stock, diluted flour, thyme, salt and pepper, and cook until the sauce is thick, stirring constantly. Pour the sauce over the chicken livers, sprinkle with parsley, and serve.

Veal and Lamb

In the heat of the day the resinous aroma of pines coming from the valleys of evergreens reaches the village that sits at the foot of one island's highest mountain — a village very well known for its delicious lamb and veal, which come from the animals that feed in spring on the lush green mountainsides. On our summer visits we drive there on the steep mountain road where there is no sight of civilization and the only sound you hear is the murmuring of the cicadas and the goats' bells. There in the village *tavérna* under the grape trellis we have a delicious meal of meat broiled over an open charcoal fire, and when we depart we take with us some of the freshly dressed veal and lamb and prepare more elegant summer dinners at home. The veal we make into cutlets, which we stuff with ham and herbs and roll, or mince for making poached meatballs. The lamb we grind to use in casseroles or slice from the leg for pan-fried steaks.

POACHED MEATBALLS WITH EGG-LEMON SAUCE

Youvarlákia

The delicate flavor of this dish lies in the good quality of the veal and in the egg-lemon sauce added when the veal is cooked. It is also very good made with pork. It is served as a main dish with the sauce thick, or as soup when the amount of chicken stock called for here is doubled. Serve with a green salad. (*Serves 5.*)

1 chopped onion
5 tablespoons salt butter
1½ pounds ground veal or
    pork
½ cup uncooked rice
1 raw egg
3 tablespoons chopped fresh

flat-leaf parsley
Flour for rolling
2 cups chicken stock (page
    255)
Egg-lemon sauce II (page
    251)
Salt and pepper to taste

Add the onion to ½ cup water in a small pan and simmer it until it wilts and the water is absorbed; stir in 3 tablespoons of the butter until it melts and set the mixture aside to cool. Combine the onion, meat, rice, egg and parsley in a large bowl and blend them with your hands until the mixture is smooth. Take small amounts of the mixture, about 1 tablespoon each, and roll them between your palms to make balls, then roll the balls in flour and put them aside on a platter.

Pour the chicken stock plus the remaining butter into a casserole and bring it to a boil over moderate heat, then drop the meatballs in, a few at a time. Bring the liquid to a boil again, reduce the heat, and simmer until the balls are firm and cooked and the sauce is thick, about 30 minutes, occasionally shaking the pan or moving the balls around with a wooden spoon. Test the meatballs by cutting one in half; they are cooked when the rice in the middle is fluffy and moist. Remove the meatballs from the heat. Prepare the egg-lemon sauce and pour it over the meatballs in the casserole. Add salt and pepper. Heat again, but do not boil, and serve.

STUFFED ROLLED VEAL

Paraghemistá Thamalísia Roulá

The stuffing used traditionally for this dish is chopped pork with herbs, but I use boiled ham instead, cut in small pieces, which

gives the veal delightful flavor. You can ask the meatman to prepare cutlets from a leg of veal or you can use the fresh-cut ones
sold in the market. Serve with homemade noodles (page 239).
(*Serves 6.*)

VEAL ROLLS
¼ cup olive oil
1 chopped onion
½ pound finely cut boiled
    ham
1 mashed garlic clove
¼ cup chopped fresh flat-leaf
    parsley
1 tablespoon chopped fresh
    thyme
Pepper to taste

2 pounds veal cutlets, each
    about 5" x 3"
½ lemon
½ cup flour for rolling

SAUCE
½ cup dry white wine
½ cup chicken stock (page
    255)
¾ cup tomato sauce (pages
    248–249)
1 garlic clove, slit

TO MAKE THE STUFFING, heat 2 tablespoons of the olive oil over
moderate heat in a skillet and add the onion to cook until it becomes translucent. Remove the skillet from the heat and mix in

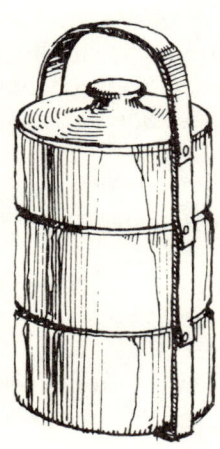

the ham, garlic, parsley, thyme, and pepper (do not salt if the
ham is salty), and set the pan aside.

Thin the veal cutlets by pounding them with a wooden mallet
on a board so that each is about ¼ inch thick and measures

about 5 inches by 3 inches, and place them side by side on a flat surface. Put 1 tablespoon of stuffing on the narrow end of each piece of veal and roll the meat all the way to the opposite end; tie both ends and the middle with string. Squeeze the lemon over the veal rolls and let them absorb it, and dip the rolls in the flour, shaking off the excess. Heat the remainder of the olive oil in a large skillet over moderate heat, add the rolls a few at a time to fry on both sides until they are lightly golden all around, then remove them to a casserole.

Add the sauce ingredients to the same skillet and bring the mixture to a boil, scraping the drippings from the skillet to mix with the sauce. Pour the sauce over the veal rolls in the casserole, cover, and simmer very slowly until the meat is tender.

LAMB STEAKS

Prizóles Arnioú

When marinated and then pan-fried or charcoal-broiled, lamb steaks are very tender and make a good meal for a hot summer day. If lamb steaks are not available already cut at your market, ask the meatman to cut them crosswise from a leg of lamb to the thickness of your choice. Serve with a peasant-style salad (pages 63–64). (*Serves 6.*)

1½ tablespoons crushed fresh or 1 teaspoon dry rosemary
1 cup olive oil
1 mashed garlic clove

½ cup dry red wine
1 leg of lamb, 5 to 6 pounds, cut in steaks
Salt and pepper to taste

Crush the rosemary in a wooden bowl or mortar and mix it with the olive oil, garlic, and wine to make a marinade. Put lamb steaks in a large pan and pour the marinade over them; let them stand at room temperature for at least 2 hours, then remove them from the marinade. Strain the marinade and save it in the refrigerator for another time.

Heat a heavy iron skillet over high heat; add the steaks 1 or 2 at a time, and sear them on both sides. Reduce the heat and cook the steaks a little longer, to your taste. Season them with salt and pepper before serving.

ZUCCHINI WITH LAMB

Kolokithákia me Arní

In the summer the squash plants in the village gardens are full of smiling yellow blossoms, which the villagers stuff with meat and rice and simmer in broth and eat. The little squashes are one of the first summer vegetables to arrive in the markets, and when they are cooked with chunks of lamb, they make a delicious main course for a family dinner. (*Serves 6.*)

¾ cup olive oil
*2 pounds lamb cut in walnut-
    size pieces*
1 diced onion
*6 medium-size peeled and
    diced tomatoes*
½ cup chopped fresh or 2

tablespoons dried dill weed
Salt and pepper to taste
*3 pounds small unpeeled
    zucchini about 3 to 4 inches
    long, ends cut off, and split
    lengthwise*

In a large saucepan heat ¼ cup of the olive oil over moderate heat and add the meat a few pieces at a time to brown on all sides. Return all the meat to the pan, add the onion and cook for a few minutes until it is translucent, then add the tomatoes, dill weed, salt and pepper. Cover and cook over moderate-low heat until the lamb is cooked but not falling apart, about 30 minutes. Preheat the oven to 350°. In a large skillet heat the remaining olive oil over moderate heat until it becomes hazy, then add the zucchini and sear them quickly on both sides until they are golden. Remove the zucchini and drain them on paper towels, and line a 9" x 12" x 2" pan with them, with the split side up, putting them snugly side by side to cover the bottom. Distribute the meat mixture evenly on top of the zucchini and bake for 20 minutes or until the zucchini are tender, being careful not to overcook them. Serve immediately.

EGGPLANT AND MEAT CASSEROLE

Moussaká

One of the ways Greeks prepare eggplant is in layers with meat sauce between and a crisp crust on top, called *moussaká*. This recipe, which came from my mother's Great-Aunt Franka, does not involve long preparation and has a lighter consistency and a better flavor than other recipes, because here the eggplant is baked fresh rather than fried first. Aunt Franka used to cook her *moussaká* in a covered tin-lined copper pan buried in hot charcoals; she loved *moussaká* and wanted to make it even on days when the outdoor oven was not lit, so she devised this method of baking in charcoal. In the kitchen oven, this dish can be baked in a regular nonaluminum 9" x 12" x 2" pan, uncovered to make the top crisp. The meat sauce can be prepared a day or two ahead and kept refrigerated, but once the eggplant is cut and assembled with the other ingredients it has to be cooked right away. Cooked *moussaká* can successfully be frozen and reheated, without defrosting, in a very low oven heat, about 200°.

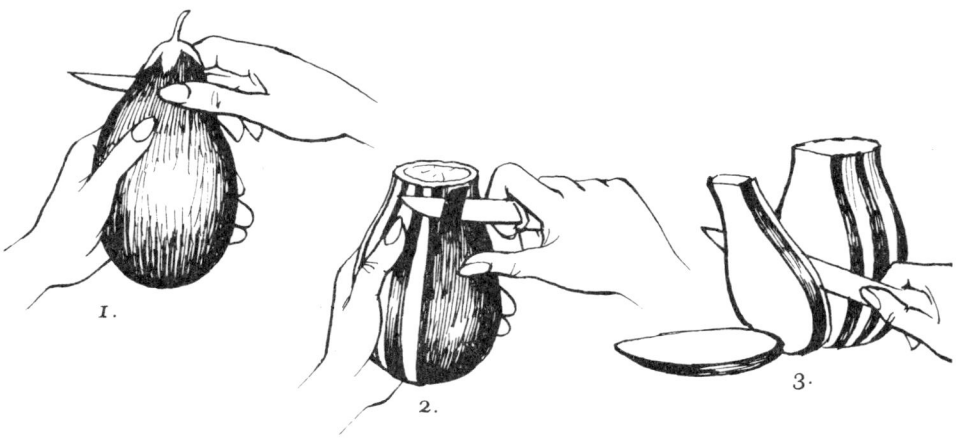

Pick fresh, firm, nonblemished, medium-size common eggplants and peel them in stripes like a zebra; the dark stripes that are left on will give enough but not too much of the eggplant taste. Because of the old superstition that eggplant was a poisonous fruit — it was once thought to be related to nightshade — people still have a tendency to soak eggplant forever in salty water, after which they supposedly squeeze out the poisonous, bitter juices by pressing it. Actually, you don't have to do this when eggplants are fresh — not only does it do them no good, it spoils their fine flavor; an eggplant gets bitter when it is bruised, and squeezing it after soaking bruises it. So just rinse the eggplant slices in a colander under tap water and proceed with the making of *moussaká*. Serve with a salad and a rice dish. (*Serves 8 to 10.*)

3 medium eggplants
½ cup bread crumbs
½ cup grated hard cheese
   (kephalotíri or Parmesan)
4 medium eggs

MEAT SAUCE
½ cup olive oil
1 medium-size chopped onion

2 pounds lean ground lamb
   or beef
2 cups tomato sauce (pages
   248–249) or 6 large peeled
   and diced tomatoes
½ cup chopped fresh flat-leaf
   parsley
2 garlic cloves slit in half
Salt and pepper to taste

TO MAKE THE MEAT SAUCE, heat the oil in a skillet over moderate heat and cook the onion until it is translucent but not brown, then stir the meat into the onions and cook until the red color of the meat disappears. Then add the tomato sauce or tomatoes, parsley, garlic, salt and pepper, and cook 15 minutes — longer for fresh tomatoes — or until the sauce is very thick and spreadable.

Preheat the oven to 350°. Partly peel the eggplants in stripes, slice them into ¼-inch or ½-inch-thick slices lengthwise, rinse the slices under cold water and drain them. Oil a 9″ x 12″ x 2″ pan and cover the bottom of it with half the eggplant slices, carefully cutting them to fit the bottom, leaving no gaps. Spread half the meat sauce evenly over the eggplant, then repeat the process with the remaining eggplant and sauce. Sprinkle the top with half the bread crumbs and half the grated cheese, then beat the eggs lightly with a fork until they are well mixed and spread them quickly and evenly on top. Sprinkle with the remaining bread crumbs and cheese, and set the casserole in the oven to bake for about 1 hour, or until the top is golden brown and the eggplant is soft (test it with a fork through the crust) and very little liquid shows when you tilt the casserole. The cooking time depends on the amount of moisture in the eggplant; if the top browns before the eggplant is cooked, place a piece of aluminum foil loosely over the casserole and continue baking. Cut in squares and serve.

Vegetables

There is a great passion among islanders for the vegetables of summer, whose variety captures their culinary imagination. The beautifully colored vegetables, admired for their excellent flavor, are grown in pockets of rich soil between the sea and mountains, and the housewives' march to the marketplace to get them fresh as they arrive from the village farms is a daily ritual. Zucchini squash, with their thin green skin, are cooked together with the feathery tops of dill weed and ripe tomatoes. With the royal purple eggplant, which comes in a variety of shapes and sizes, the islander traditionally makes *imám baildí* (swooning imam), which gets its name, so the story goes, from a gluttonous Muslim Turk who passed out after eating too much of the delicious dish. Fritters of sliced vegetables are served on a large platter covered with a thin garlic sauce, and make one of the lovely main dishes of the summer.

VEGETABLE FRITTERS

Tiganitá Skorthaliá

Prepare the fresh vegetables and fry them in good-quality olive oil — plain, rolled in flour, or dipped in batter. (*Serves 4.*)

2 large potatoes peeled and
cut crosswise in ¼-inch
slices
2 medium-size zucchini, sliced
crosswise in ¼-inch slices
2 green bell peppers, seeded
and cut in quarters
2 firm tomatoes, cut in ½-
inch slices

1 medium-size eggplant,
sliced lengthwise in ½-inch
slices
1 cup olive oil for frying
Flour for rolling or batter for
dipping (page 258)
Salt and pepper to taste
Garlic sauce (page 252)

If you are going to use batter, make it as on page 258; also make
the garlic sauce, and set them both aside. Salt the vegetables,
except for the potatoes, and let them stand for 5 minutes. Heat
½ the olive oil in a skillet over moderate heat until a haze forms
on it. Pat the potato slices to remove any moisture from them
and, being careful not to burn yourself from spatters, put them
into the oil a few at a time to fry on both sides until they are
golden. Then remove the potatoes from the oil to a towel to
absorb the excess oil. Proceed with the frying of the zucchini,
first rolling them in flour or dipping them in batter, whichever
way you have chosen; then do the same to the peppers, tomatoes,
and then the eggplant, frying one kind at a time and removing
it to paper towels to drain, adding oil to the skillet as needed.
Fry the eggplant last, because it has a tendency to absorb more
oil than the rest of the vegetables. Arrange all the fried vegetables on a platter, then stir the garlic sauce and pour it over
them, or serve the sauce separately in a bowl.

SAUTÉED SMALL WHOLE EGGPLANT

Imám Baildí

While the recipe for *moussaká* calls for the common egg-shaped
variety of eggplant, for this dish long and narrow ones are used
or miniature ones 3 to 6 inches long, which are found in many
markets here in America. (*Serves 3 to 4.*)

1 cup chopped fresh flat-leaf
parsley

3 finely minced garlic cloves
6 to 8 miniature eggplants

| 1 medium chopped onion | ⅓ cup olive oil |
| 4 to 5 peeled and diced ripe tomatoes | Salt and pepper to taste |

Mix the parsley, garlic and some salt and pepper and set it aside in a bowl. Wash the eggplants and cut off the green stems, and with a small knife peel off a thin strip of skin around the lengthwise circumference of each eggplant. Make a ½-inch slit in the exposed flesh on each side of each eggplant, about halfway through the eggplant, and stuff the slits with the parsley and garlic mixture. Heat the olive oil in a skillet over moderate heat and fry the stuffed eggplant on all sides for a few minutes until

the peeled strips are light gold in color. With a spatula carefully remove the eggplants from the skillet and place them side by side in a casserole. Remove any burned bits which may be left in the oil and sauté the onion in it until it is soft, then mix the tomatoes and let them both cook for 5 minutes over moderate heat. Season the tomato-onion mixture with salt and pepper, pour it over the eggplants in the casserole, set the casserole over low heat, and simmer it covered for 30 minutes, or until the eggplants are tender and the sauce is thick, occasionally shaking the pan from side to side to prevent the eggplants from sticking. Serve hot or cold.

STEWED ZUCCHINI

Kolokithákia Yahnistá

The long, narrow zucchini, a member of the squash family, has edible seeds, and when it is cooked becomes tender as marrow. (*Serves 4 to 6.*)

2 pounds small green
   zucchini, 3 to 4 inches long
¼ cup olive oil
5 chopped scallions

4 peeled and diced ripe
   tomatoes
½ cup chopped dill weed
Salt and pepper to taste

Wash and dry the zucchini, cut off their stems, and split them lengthwise in halves, or if they are larger, in quarters.

Heat the olive oil in a saucepan over moderate heat and sauté the scallions until they are soft, then add the tomatoes, dill weed, salt and pepper, and simmer covered for 10 minutes. Add the zucchini, stirring them in gently with a wooden spoon, and cook for 20 minutes over low heat until they are tender and the sauce is thick. Do not stir again during cooking, but instead shake the pan occasionally from side to side. If there is excess liquid from the vegetables, uncover the pan and boil to reduce it. Serve hot or cold.

STEWED FRESH GREEN BEANS

Fosoulákia Frésca Yahnistá

From villages to cities the green string beans are cooked the same way — stewed with tomatoes and onions and presented on the table as frequently as every other day. Occasionally lamb is added, and then the beans are served as a main dish with a bowl of rice pilaf. (*Serves 4.*)

1½ pounds fresh green beans
1 medium-size diced onion
½ cup olive oil
3 peeled and diced fresh
   large tomatoes

⅓ cup fresh coarsely chopped
   flat-leaf parsley
Salt and pepper to taste
¼ teaspoon cumin (optional)

Snip off the ends of the beans, cut them in half crosswise, rinse them under running cold water, and drain them. Put the onion in a saucepan, place the beans on top of the onion, sprinkle the olive oil over the beans, and let them sizzle over moderate heat for about 1 minute. Add the tomatoes, parsley, salt and pepper, and cook covered over moderate heat until the beans are tender. If the liquid evaporates, add a little water, but the sauce left with the beans when they are cooked should be thick. Add the cumin just before serving.

OKRAS

Bámies

My mother's way of preparing and cooking the okra is most fascinating and the best way I have found. Handling each pod

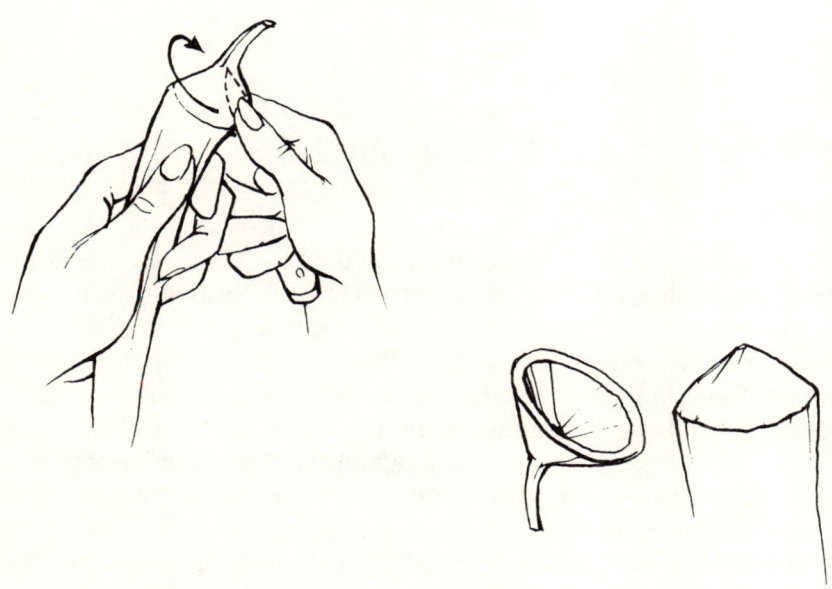

with care, first she rinses them under cold water and then spreads them out on a heavy cloth in the sun to dry. Then with a paring knife she peels the outer part off the head of each one, being careful not to cut into the seeds, or they will bleed and become glutinous when cooked. Each okra should be intact, with its juice sealed in. (*Serves 4.*)

⅓ cup olive oil
2 pounds trimmed fresh okra
Juice of 1 lemon
1 medium-size chopped onion
1 large garlic clove

4 large peeled and diced
  tomatoes
½ cup chopped fresh flat-leaf
  parsley
Salt and pepper to taste

Heat the olive oil in a skillet over moderate heat and put in the okras a few at a time to fry until they are lightly golden. Remove them from the oil with a slotted spoon and line side by side like sardines in layers in a saucepan. Sprinkle the lemon juice over them and distribute the onion, garlic, tomatoes and parsley evenly over them. Season them with salt and pepper and simmer covered over low heat, occasionally shaking the pan from side to side but never stirring the vegetables. When the okra is cooked, a small amount of thick sauce is left. Serve hot or cold.

STUFFED SUMMER VEGETABLES

Ghemistá

The many colors of the vegetables used — tomatoes, peppers, zucchini and potatoes — make this dish very festive to serve for a luncheon or to your family. The vegetables are stuffed with meat, rice, pine nuts and herbs and can be prepared hours ahead of time and kept in the refrigerator until cooking time, and they require hardly any attention while they cook. In the cities on the islands this dish is sent to the neighborhood oven to bake in the round, tin-lined copper pan (*tapsí*) in which they are prepared. But the vegetables can also be arranged in a 9″ x 12″ x 2″ pan and baked in the kitchen oven without the vegetables losing any of their flavor and color. (*Serves 4 to 6.*)

3 large green bell peppers
3 12-inch long zucchini
3 medium-size potatoes
3 large firm red tomatoes
1½ cups chicken stock (page
  255)

STUFFING
⅓ cup olive oil
1 chopped onion
1½ pounds ground lamb
½ cup chopped fresh flat-leaf
  parsley

1 cup rice
Pulp scooped out of the
   tomatoes to be stuffed
½ cup pine nuts

1 tablespoon tomato paste
½ cup cold water
Salt and pepper to taste

First prepare the vegetables, each group individually. Cut off the tops of the peppers, remove their seeds, blanch them for 5 minutes in boiling water, then remove them from the water and drain them. Cut off the stem ends of the zucchini and cut them crosswise in half. With a small paring knife scoop out all the pulp, being careful not to puncture the skin or break through the stem end, then blanch them in boiling water for 1 minute and drain them. Peel the potatoes and hollow out an opening in the middle of each one large enough for 2 tablespoons of stuffing, then blanch them for 5 minutes in boiling water and drain them; let them cool with the other vegetables. Slice the tops of the tomatoes almost off, leaving them hinged to serve as covers later on; then with a spoon scoop out the pulp and save it to be used in the stuffing.

Make the stuffing for the vegetables. Heat the oil in a skillet over moderate heat and add the onion to cook until it is wilted; stir in the chopped meat until it is all in crumbles, then add the rest of the stuffing ingredients. Stir the mixture with a wooden spoon and cook it uncovered over moderate heat for 10 to 15 minutes or until the water is absorbed, the rice is half cooked, and the mixture is thick. Remove it from the fire and let it cool.

Preheat the oven to 400°. Stuff the vegetables loosely, using a spoon, and arrange them in groups in a shallow pan, stuffing-side up, except for the zucchini, which should lie down snugly side by side. Pour the chicken stock into the bottom of the pan, cover the vegetables loosely with a piece of aluminum foil to prevent them from burning, and bake for 20 minutes; then remove the aluminum foil and cook 15 minutes longer. Let the stuffed vegetables cool slightly and transfer them to a platter; pour over them the broth left in the bottom of the pan and serve.

Cakes, Pastries and Cookies

The dry weather of the islands preserves some of the lonely oranges and lemons left over from the winter, when they ripen, so that they hang ripe on the shiny-leaved branches of their trees in among the new green fruit until the middle of summer. The thick and sweet-scented skin of these oranges is grated and used to perfume *ravaníe,* which village people so often serve at weddings and which, while it is being made, makes the kitchen smell like an orange grove. Less well defined are the smells of the mixtures of sweet meats and nuts in the pastry-shop kitchens of the cities, except when the dough of *kataífi* is prepared, which has a very distinctive aroma. With skillful hands the dough-maker mixes the thin batter to just the right consistency, then pours it into a many-fingered tin gadget with a small hole at the tip of each finger — it looks much like the colonial American candlemaker's mold. The batter falls thin like threads from the holes onto a large, shallow, hand-revolved copper pan heating on the coals. Almost as soon as the batter touches the hot pan, the doughmaker sweeps it out of the fire before it is scorched. Then the pastry dough, looking like shredded wheat but white, moist and pliable instead of dry, is ready to be assembled into the fabulous *kataífi.*

Cookies made from ground blanched almonds, *amigthalotá,* are prepared both in homes and in pastry shops. They resemble almond macaroons and are so delicious that they disappear quickly when children are around.

WALNUT CAKE

Ravanie

This cake made with basic ingredients and dressed with an orange-rum sauce is the housewife's favorite. For a lighter color, ground blanched almonds may be substituted for the walnuts. (*Serves 8 to 10.*)

ORANGE SAUCE
2 cups water
1¼ cups sugar
⅓ cup rum
2 orange slices ¼ inch thick, cut crosswise with the skin on

CAKE
2½ cups walnuts ground in a

blender or pounded with a mortar and pestle
10 finely ground zwieback or paximáthi (*page 273*)
8 large eggs, separated
⅔ cup sugar
2 tablespoons grated orange rind
¼ cup melted unsalted butter

Combine all the sauce ingredients in a saucepan and bring them to a boil, removing any dark foam from the top; then reduce the heat to low and simmer uncovered 10 to 15 minutes. Remove the sauce from the heat and set it aside to cool.

Preheat the oven to 350°. Mix the ground walnuts and zwieback or *paximáthi* together in a bowl and set it aside. Put the egg whites in a copper bowl with a pinch of salt and beat them with a hand or electric beater until they are firm and white but not dry. If you do not use a copper bowl, then add ½ teaspoon cream of tartar while beating to help them peak. Place the egg yolks in a large bowl and slowly add the sugar while beating, until the mixture becomes pale yellow and creamy. Fold the egg whites into the yolks with a large spatula, and slowly sprinkle in the walnut-zwieback mixture as you fold until the walnut-zwieback mixture is completely incorporated and the batter is light and smooth. Folding should be done fast to avoid loss of air from the eggs; you cut with the spatula from the center of the bowl down to the bottom and then up the side, while rotating the bowl. Then fold in the grated orange rind and finally the cool, melted butter. Pour the cake mixture into a well-buttered 9" x 12" x 2" pan and bake about 45 minutes, until the cake is golden and has pulled away from the sides of the pan. While the cake is still hot, strain the cooled sauce and pour it over the cake evenly. Then cut the cake in diamond-shaped pieces, let it cool, and place the pieces on a platter.

NUT-FILLED SHREDDED PASTRY

Kataífi

A cousin of *baklavá* is *kataífi*, a shredded pastry much loved for its consistency. It is made into individual small oblong rolls stuffed with spices and nuts, then baked, and while still hot it is moistened with a light syrup. The shredded pastry dough can be found fresh or frozen in 1-pound packages in Greek or Middle Eastern stores. Frozen dough should be thawed out in its container at room temperature the day on which it is to be used. (*Makes 22 rolls.*)

FILLING
1¼ *cups coarsely ground*
 walnuts
¼ *cup sugar*
1 *tablespoon powdered*
 cinnamon
1 *lightly beaten egg*

PASTRY
1 *pound* kataífi *pastry dough*

2 *sticks or ½ pound unsalted*
 butter, clarified (page 269)

SYRUP
3 *cups sugar*
2¾ *cups water*
1 *tablespoon lemon juice*
1 *tablespoon orange blossom*
 water or rosewater

TO MAKE THE FILLING, mix the walnuts, sugar and cinnamon together in a bowl, stir in the egg until the nuts are thoroughly moistened, and set the mixture aside.

Preheat the oven to 325°. Put the pastry dough on a flat surface and with your fingers try to loosen up the strands by gently shaking large handfuls of the dough. Spread each handful evenly on a board, put 1 tablespoon of the walnut filling in the center, and wrap the threads of dough tightly around to hide the filling, making an oblong-shape roll. Place the rolls side by side snugly in a 9″ x 12″ x 2″ pan, spoon the butter all over them, and bake them for 30 to 45 minutes until they are light golden.

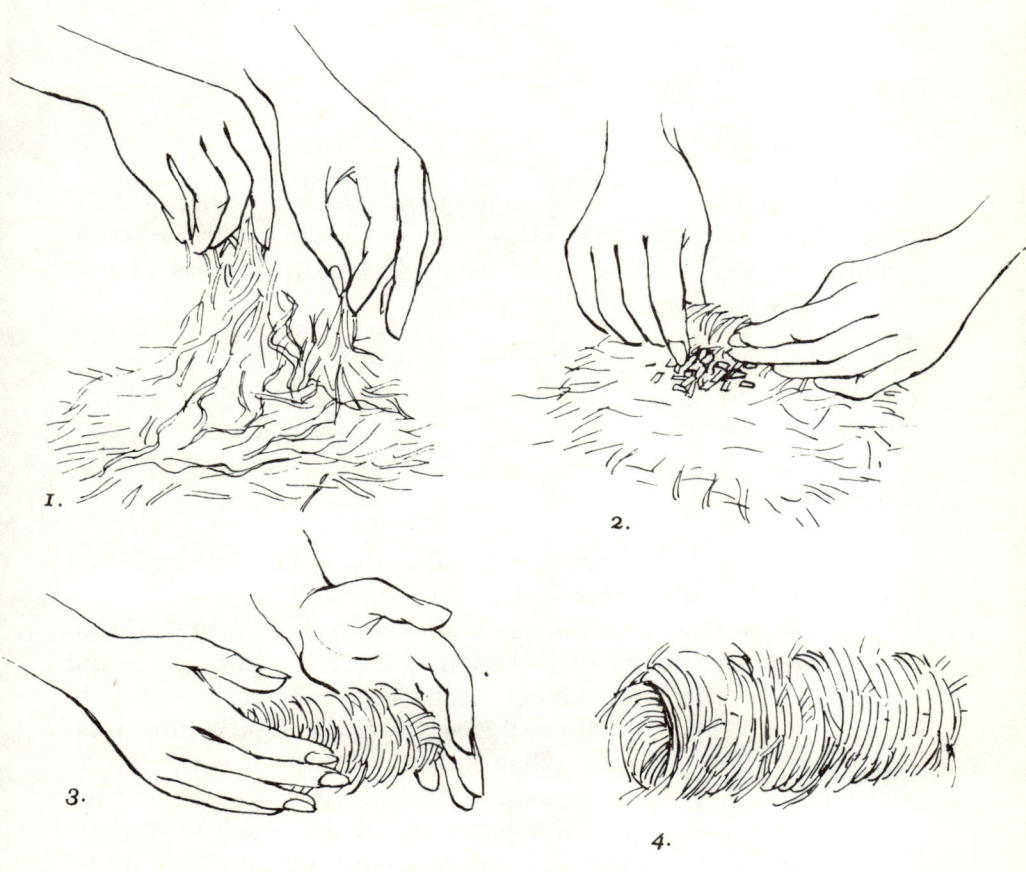

1.

2.

3.

4.

While the *kataifi* is baking, make the syrup. Combine the sugar, water and lemon juice in a saucepan and bring them to a boil over moderate heat. Remove any froth from the top of the syrup, reduce the heat to low, and simmer uncovered for 7 to

10 minutes. Remove the pan from the heat, add the orange blossom water (or rosewater) and set the syrup aside to cool.

When the *kataífi* are ready, remove them from the oven, and while they are still hot pour the cool syrup over them. Immediately cover the pan with a clean, heavy towel to trap the steam in and soften the pastry. Let the *kataífi* stand a day and serve at room temperature.

ALMOND COOKIES

Amigthalotá

Amigthalotá are very easy to prepare and keep beautifully if stored in a dry place. They can be served with tea, with ice cream and sherbets, or my sons' favorite way — with a glass of cold milk. (*Makes about 4 dozen cookies.*)

1 pound finely ground blanched almonds (page 269)	⅛ teaspoon salt
	⅛ teaspoon cream of tartar or lemon juice
¾ cup sugar	½ teaspoon almond extract
4 egg whites	

Preheat the oven to 275°. Mix together the ground almonds and sugar and set the mixture aside.

In a large bowl beat the egg whites with the salt added until they are fluffy, then add the cream of tartar or lemon juice and continue beating until the egg whites are stiff but not dry. Add the almond-sugar mixture to the egg foam a little at a time, folding it in with a spatula. When all the almond-sugar mixture is blended in, fold in the almond extract. Cut wax paper to fit the bottom of a cookie sheet and butter and flour one side of it, shaking off the excess flour. Place the wax paper buttered-side up on the cookie sheet and drop the cookie mixture on by teaspoonsful, allowing 2 inches in between cookies. Bake for 10 to 15 minutes or until the cookies turn rosy-colored, then remove them from the oven. Let the cookies cool slightly, then before they are completely cooled and hardened, remove them with a spatula from the paper to a platter.

Puddings

Puddings are the sweets that connect the cooking of many countries from East to West. Endless are the combinations, textures, and colors of these puddings, and the island ones range from the simple to the more elaborate. *Kréma karamélla,* a family favorite, is known by various names and served in various ways in many countries, but it is the same pudding throughout Europe and Asia Minor.

Another simple pudding, with a smooth purple texture, is the Greek *moustoalevriá,* made by the island villagers during the wine-making season with the freshly squeezed must of the grapes. This one my mother would make for all the children who took part in the stomping of the grapes to keep them happy and contented, because it is said that discontented or bad-tempered children will make sour wine.

CARAMEL PUDDING

Kréma Karamélla

(*Serves 6.*)

4 cups milk	*6 eggs plus 2 egg yolks*
½ cup sugar	*½ teaspoon salt*

Scald 3 cups of the milk and set it aside, keeping it warm.

Beat the eggs and egg yolks in a bowl until they are well mixed, then stir the remaining cup of milk into them. In a saucepan over moderate heat melt the sugar, stirring it continuously with a metal spoon until it becomes golden-brown syrup and starts to smoke. Remove it from the heat and stir in the warm milk, beaten-egg mixture and salt. Return the pan to the stove and cook over low heat, stirring constantly, until the pudding thickens. Pour it into small serving dishes, let them cool, and put them into the refrigerator to chill.

GRAPE-MUST PUDDING

Moustoalevriá

At the end of the summer, when the Concord grapes are ripe, I collect them from the stone walls and fences around our New England home, and with their juice I make this shiny pudding. If grapes are not available, use the unsweetened grape juice sold in local stores. (*Serves 6.*)

4 tablespoons cornstarch	*3 cups unsweetened grape*
4 tablespoons or more sugar	*juice*

Dilute the cornstarch with some of the grape juice in a small bowl and set it aside. Combine the sugar and the rest of the grape juice in a saucepan and bring them slowly to a boil for the sugar to melt. Mix in the diluted cornstarch and, while stirring constantly, bring the mixture to a boil again; then reduce the heat to low and cook for about 2 minutes until the pudding thickens.

Pour it into small serving dishes and chill.

Fresh Fruits and Spoon Sweets

Peaches and grapes, plentiful when in season, and piled in fruit baskets, are ever present on the tables, so that everyone coming in and out of the house can take one and refresh himself with its sweetness. Peaches, called "roses of China" in Greek, are sometimes cut in wedges and tossed with lemon juice and

sugar and served with thin shavings of ice mixed in. White seedless grapes just dusted with powdered sugar (which makes them look snow-frosted) are served at the end of an elegant dinner. Grapes are also picked one by one from their bunches, mixed with regular sugar in a large preserve pot, and left to bubble for the longest time without much attention given to make one of the spoon sweets that is a must in every Greek household in summer. When ready, the sweets are stored in jars for later use, but not before they are tested on well-buttered bread by each member of the family and given his or her approval.

FRESH PEACH COMPOTE

Rothákina Kompósta

Choose ripe but firm medium-size peaches. (*Serves 4 to 6.*)

2 pounds fresh peaches
Juice of 1 lemon (3 table-
spoons)

¾ cup granulated sugar
Finely crushed ice

Remove the skin from the peaches by dipping them first briefly in boiling water and then in cold. Split them in half lengthwise, remove the pits, and cut them in ½-inch thick wedges into a bowl.

Sprinkle the lemon juice and then the sugar over them and toss them gently to coat them well. Cover the bowl with plastic wrap and place it in the refrigerator for at least an hour. Serve in dessert bowl or glasses and top each portion with a tablespoon of finely crushed ice.

FROSTED GRAPES

Staphília Zaharoména

I love the white seedless grapes I find in the American markets. Their berries, larger, less sweet and slightly greener than the Greek ones, are best for this recipe when fresh — which can be determined from the greenness of their stems and their firm, unblemished fruit.

1 pound seedless white grapes
1 egg white

¾ cup confectioners' sugar

Rinse the grapes, in bunches, under cold water and let them

drain, then wipe off any moisture with a paper towel. Beat the egg white in a small bowl until it is frothy but not stiff and with a small brush or a small piece of clean cloth, dip into the egg white and coat each grape. Place the bunches on a wire cake rack over wax paper. Push the confectioners' sugar through a sieve over the grapes until they are well covered and put them, still on the rack, into the refrigerator to chill and for the sugar to set. Serve for dessert alone or with pastries.

GRAPE SPOON SWEET

Staphília Glykó

(*Makes approximately 1 quart.*)

2 pounds seedless white grapes	2 cinnamon sticks
1½ pounds sugar	1 tablespoon lemon juice

Remove the stems from the grapes and put the grapes in a colander. Wash them under cold running water and drain them. Then put the grapes, sugar and ¾ cup cold water in a large deep pot and cook over medium-low heat, covered, until the sugar melts. Add the cinnamon. Increase the heat to moderate, uncover the pot, and cook, occasionally stirring with a metal spoon and removing the froth that collects on top. Lower the heat if necessary to prevent the syrup from spilling over. Cook until the syrup is thick or the candy thermometer shows 220°. Pour in the lemon juice, remove the froth again, remove from the heat, cool and put in sterilized jars.

Ices and Beverages

Whenever I prepare cold drinks I think of the sparkling colors of the ones I used to get in the islands when my family went strolling with others on Sunday afternoon in the small park of the main square by the sea. The grown-ups always sat on the green-painted iron benches watching the fishermen pulling their hand lines in while the children played hide and seek behind the evenly sheared shrubs of the park. The drink vendors would appear in their white-starched jackets carrying their brass-trimmed glass containers of lemonade and cherry drink, which shone in the light of the setting sun and added color to the park. The children ran to buy *vissinátha*, a ruby-colored cherry drink with a delightful tartness, milky-colored *soumátha* made from almond juice and sugar syrup, and refreshing *lemonátha*, made from fresh lemons. As soon as the drink man left, the ice vendor would come, and the children would become very excited at seeing the many colors of the ices, which he would sell in paper cones and which, with their granular consistency, were so good to crunch on hot summer days.

Making ices at home used to take my mother long hours of work at the old-fashioned icebox of our city house. Using chipped ice from the block delivered to us early in the morning by the iceman and a lot of rock salt to make it colder, she would put the fruit mixture in cans and pack them in with ice to freeze, checking and stirring them every so often. Now I make it in the freezer very easily and serve it with *amigthalotá* (page 96) as a dessert for a summer meal.

PEACH ICE

Rothákino Serbéti

(*Serves 6.*)

1 tablespoon unflavored gelatin	2 firmly packed cups peeled and sliced fresh peaches
1½ cups water	3 tablespoons lemon juice
1 cup sugar	

Put the gelatin to soften in ¼ cup of the water in a small bowl and boil the rest of the water with the sugar in a saucepan for 5 minutes. Stir the soft gelatin into the sugar and water until it dissolves, and remove the mixture from the heat to cool.

Dip the peaches first into boiling water and then into cold to slip off their skins, then slice them and puree them in a blender or by rubbing them through a sieve. Add them to the sugar syrup and also add the lemon juice, and pour the mixture into refrigerator trays to freeze until mushy. Beat the half-frozen mixture with a fork and return it to the freezer until it is frozen but not solid. Serve in chilled glasses. If the peach ice freezes solid, let it stand at room temperature to soften slightly and then stir it again.

LEMON ICE

Lemóni Serbéti

(*Serves 10.*)

1 tablespoon unflavored gelatin	4 cups water
	2 cups sugar

| 1 tablespoon grated lemon | ¾ cup fresh lemon juice |
| rind | |

Put the gelatin in a small cup with ¼ cup of the water to soften. Boil the rest of the water in a saucepan with the sugar for 5 minutes, and stir in the soft gelatin until it dissolves. Remove the pan from the heat and mix in the lemon rind and juice, then pour the mixture into refrigerator trays and set them in the freezer until the lemon ice is almost frozen, stirring every hour with a fork. It will take about 4 hours almost to freeze. Spoon it into chilled glasses and keep it in the freezer until it is ready to be served.

Orange ice can be made the same way, using 1½ cups orange juice and 2 tablespoons lemon juice.

ALMOND DRINK

Soumátha

There is an island in the Aegean Sea with almond orchards covering the hills, so many in such a small place that when they are in bloom in the early spring the hills against the tall, savory-covered mountains look like a bride dressed in white. The best almonds that I can remember came from there, some with hard shells of different sizes and shapes and others with soft shells like peanut shells, so easy to break by hand to get to the sweet, meaty nut. Coming home from this island, where he used to go on business, my father always brought us — along with the other delicious products, goat cheese and cured pork — a bag of almonds. My mother shelled them and blanched them raw, before they were put out in the sun to dry, then ground them into a milky pulp and mixed them with sugar to make the syrup for *soumátha*. (*Makes 3½ to 4 cups syrup.*)

4½ cups water	ground almonds (page
4½ cups sugar	269)
1¾ cups blanched and finely	1 tablespoon almond extract

Combine the water and sugar in a saucepan and bring them to

a boil, stirring until the sugar has dissolved; add the ground almonds and cook the mixture for 20 minutes over moderate heat, stirring frequently and not allowing it to boil over. Remove the pan from the heat and let the mixture cool slightly. Line a strainer with a clean cheesecloth folded into 2 or 3 thicknesses and strain the almond syrup mixture through it, or make a bag with the cheesecloth, put the mixture in and tie the top, and hang it to drip over a bowl. When the almond syrup has completely dripped through the cheesecloth, place it in a pan, add the extract, and boil it for 5 minutes. The syrup should be thick enough to coat a spoon and make 3½ to 4 cups. Then pour the syrup into sterilized bottles and let it cool. Store it in the refrigerator. Make the *soumátha* drink by mixing 2 to 3 tablespoons syrup into a glass of ice water.

LEMONADE

Lemonátha

(*Makes 8 cups.*)

1 cup juice from fresh lemons   6 cups ice water
2 cups sugar

Strain the juice and combine it with the sugar and ice water in a pitcher. Stir until the sugar is completely dissolved and serve in chilled glasses with a sprig of mint.

AUTUMN

Autumn

The warm and gentle weather of autumn lures the city people to the beach, where they sit on the sandy shores in reverie watching the children trying to catch crabs and eels from the thousand holes of the pumice rocks that jut from the sea, left there by the volcanic eruptions of centuries ago.

People also hike at the foot of the herb-carpeted mountains, where birds feed on berries of the myrtle that resemble the high-bush blueberries, and ascend the ridges overlooking the magnificent olive groves and vineyards and search for the wild pear trees. The wild pears, a small fruit similar to that of the Seckel pear, are picked when still green although already aromatic, and are stuffed to ripen in the haybin, *aherónas*. The hay bin occupies one-fourth of the square village houses and is set off by wide boards that reach all the way to the ceiling; it holds the loose hay that is feed for the animals during the rainy months. When the pears are ripe, one follows their sweet smell to find them. Quinces, unlike the pears, are allowed to ripen on the moss-colored trees into large, light-yellow fruits, before they are made into compotes and into a spoon sweet with the fragrant flavoring of sweet geranium leaves.

Autumn is the time when village housewives prepare their food supplies for winter storage, first shelling the legumes from their sun-dried pods by paddling them lightly with a narrow, thick, wooden spatula. Next the dried figs, another supply for the chilly season, are roasted in outdoor ovens, then packed in baskets or large jugs with myrtle leaves between the layers, which give them an unusual flavor. Honey is collected again for the last time before the winter, thick and full of the pungent aroma of the thyme and the savory blossoms, whose nectar the bees brought home during the summer. The honey is stored in jars and sealed with wax.

The end of autumn is marked by *eleomaémata,* the gathering of the olives, an activity involving many people, with men climbing the trees to shake the olives loose with long thick sticks while women on their knees collect them from the ground with their fingers and fill the baskets. There is always lots of easy humor and good food. Of the cooked dishes people take with them to the fields and hills, some are made from mutton with newly dried beans and others from fresh vegetables of the season, like the much-loved fritters of cauliflower and pumpkin; and of course there are salads from the last of the garden tomatoes and peppers. After the olives are brought to the village, they are taken to the oil mill, but first the best ripe, black ones, *zoúppes,* are put in baskets with sea salt to cure them, and the hard, green, unripe ones are cracked and put in brine to become *tsakistés,* pickled olives.

At the oil mill the green olives are ground between two very large, flat, round stones turned by a blindfolded donkey, and are mashed, seeds and all, into pulp; then the pulp is poured onto large squares of heavy, handwoven wool cloth, which is folded around it like envelopes, then the envelopes are stacked and squeezed in a wooden press. The olive oil runs like a golden stream into a copper basin. The children roast dried figs or toast pieces of bread on the hot coals in the corner fireplace at the mill, dip them in fresh olive oil, and stuff them in their mouths. Fresh olive oil has an enticing smell that floats from the kitchen into the narrow streets of the village and makes everyone who passes by hungry.

Appetizers

Among the appetizers of autumn, many of which are made from
fresh and newly dried legumes of the season, are the great gifts
from the sea and the mountain forests. Mushrooms, wild and
large, which appear after the first rains on the edges of marshes

and in tree-shaded valleys, taste delicious marinated in lemon
and herbs. Uncle Panaghiotis, my mother's brother, who knows
how to make use of all of nature's gifts, always used to bring
some to us. To test their edibility, my mother would drop a silver
ring in the water in which the mushrooms had soaked overnight,

hoping that the ring would not tarnish. If it did not, then she could prepare them her favorite way and put them up in jars to last for a month. Octopus, fresh from the sea, when simmered for a long time in water and vinegar, becomes tender; then the white meat inside the tentacles is cut and sautéed in olive oil to make tasty bite-size pieces. Another favorite delicacy of the Greeks is lamb and veal brains, which are shaped into small patties, rolled in flour, fried and sprinkled lightly with lemon. Also, *tahinoróvitha* a superb dip with the gentle aroma of sesame seed paste, mixed with mashed chickpeas, chilled, garnished with fresh parsley and served in *pítta* bread.

CHICKPEAS AND SESAME SAUCE

Revíthia me Tahí

Crushed sesame seed paste — *tahí* — has a very distinctive taste and a beautiful smell. Greeks eat it during Lent especially because it has good nutritional value, sometimes mixing it with honey to give them more energy when they are fasting. When it is thinned out with some water and lemon juice and flavored lightly with garlic, it becomes a creamy sauce and can be used over vegetable and fish dishes. Here *tahí* is combined with cooked mashed chickpeas, which can be bought dried in local markets and supermarkets. *Tahí* is sold in Greek and Middle Eastern stores, at times with the name *tahini,* and also on the foreign food shelves in the supermarkets. (*Serves 4 to 6.*)

TAHÍ SAUCE	GROUND CHICKPEAS
3 tablespoons tahí *paste*	*1 cup cooked chickpeas (if*
1 tablespoon olive oil	*dried chickpeas are used,*
Juice of ½ lemon	*⅓ cup soaked overnight in*
½ cup water	*water)*
1 large mashed garlic clove	*Chopped fresh flat-leaf*
Salt and pepper to taste	*parsley to garnish*

TO MAKE THE TAHÍ SAUCE, combine the *tahí* and the olive oil in a bowl; mix in the lemon juice and slowly add the water while stirring constantly, until the mixture has turned white. When a little water is added to *tahí*, it has a tendency to thicken and even curdle, but more water will correct it; so be generous with the water and keep adding it until the mixture is almost milky white. Add the garlic and season with salt and pepper. Set aside.

Rinse the chickpeas, drain, and cover them again with fresh water. Simmer, covered, over moderate heat for 1 hour, or until they are soft, adding more water when needed. Drain the chickpeas and grind them through a food grinder or with a mortar and pestle or in a blender until they become a fine paste.

Combine the sauce and the ground chickpeas until well mixed, put in a bowl and garnish with some parsley in the center. Chill and serve.

FRIED BRAIN PATTIES

Mialá Tiganitá

Always buy brains through a reliable meat store to make sure of their freshness, which is vital to the success of this dish. When cooked with a minimum of seasoning, this dish is considered one of the great delicacies of home cooking in Greece. (*Serves 4.*)

4 lambs' brains or 2 calves' brains	*¼ cup olive oil*
1 tablespoon salt	*1 egg, slightly beaten*
2 tablespoons wine vinegar	*½ cup flour*
White pepper and additional salt to taste	*Juice of ½ lemon*
	Lemon wedges

Cover the brains with cold water and soak them for ½ hour. Very carefully peel off the outer, almost invisible, skin with your fingers; rinse the brains under cold water to remove any blood spots. Put them in a saucepan, cover them with fresh water, add salt and vinegar and bring gently to a boil over moderate heat. Remove the froth that may accumulate on the top of the water. Simmer for 12 minutes, remove from the heat, and let the brains cool in their own liquid. Drain them and cut them in ½-inch slices. Season with white pepper and more salt if it is needed. Heat the olive oil in a heavy skillet. Dip the slices of brain in the beaten egg, roll in the flour, then carefully place them in the hot oil to fry on both sides for a few minutes until golden. Sprinkle with lemon juice and serve with lemon wedges.

SAUTEED OCTOPUS

Ohtapóthi Áspro

When octopus is prepared with great fuss, as in this dish, it tastes remarkably like scallops. (*Serves 4 to 6.*)

3 pounds fresh or frozen octopus	*¼ cup olive oil*
3 tablespoons wine vinegar	*Juice of ½ small lemon*
	Salt and white pepper to taste

Wash the octopus. If it is frozen, defrost it in cold water first. Place it in a saucepan, cover it with cold water, and add the vinegar. Cover and bring to a boil slowly, and simmer for 45 minutes or until the octopus is tender. Remove from heat, cool, and drain. Under running cold water, strip and remove the outside skin and the little suction cups from the tentacles until only the white inside remains. Cut in ½-inch pieces. Heat the olive oil in a skillet and gently sauté the pieces until they are the color of light straw. Remove from the oil to a warm dish, sprinkle with lemon juice, season with salt and white pepper, and serve.

MARINATED MUSHROOMS

Manitária Marináta

In America, cultivated mushrooms are brought to the market by commercial growers, but in the islands one has to go to the mountain forests and pick one's own — first learning to distinguish the edible ones from the deadly. However, the small white fresh mushrooms sold in stores are safer to use than wild mushrooms, and very good prepared this way. (*Serves 8.*)

1 pound fresh mushrooms
½ cup olive oil
¼ cup fresh lemon juice
⅓ cup white dry wine
2 chopped scallions, white part only
¼ cup finely chopped fresh

flat-leaf parsley
Peel of ½ lemon
1 chopped stalk of celery
1 mashed garlic clove
2 tablespoons chopped fresh thyme
½ teaspoon pepper

Trim the stalks off the mushrooms, slice them in half if they are on the large side, and set them aside. Combine all the other ingredients in a saucepan, bring them to a boil, reduce the heat, and simmer uncovered for 7 minutes. Add the mushrooms to the marinade and stir them in with a wooden spoon; cover and simmer gently for 4 minutes, then uncover and cook for 3 minutes longer, occasionally stirring. Remove the pan from the heat and let the mushrooms cool in the marinade. To store, put in sterilized jars and keep refrigerated.

Soups

Whenever the autumn *meltémi,* the north wind, or *thramoun-dána,* the east wind from the Turkish mountains, sweeps the islands, bringing cool evenings, hot soups come into favor again. Soups like *psarósouppa nissiótiki,* a typical fish soup, are made of fish and other good things of the deep sea. To fishermen, this

soup is often a reward at the end of a hard day's work after they have hauled their nets into shore. But served to a family or guests, it is simply a delightful way to start a dinner. Another soup is made from tripe, cooked slowly for a long time, and others are made from bones, either lamb or veal, boiled to make a broth in which vegetables are sometimes cooked, too. *Phithés,* a very thin pasta sold in America under the Italian name of "vermicelli," is added to these meat broths to make a simple but very flavorful soup known to the islanders as *soúppa phithés.*

All these soups are served, with hot crusty bread, as a main or first course.

ISLAND FISH SOUP

Psarósouppa Nissiótiki

Like the fishermen, Greek housewives make this soup from the ferocious-looking red rockfish, called *scorpiós*, a fish well known for the delicious soups made from it. I use ocean perch, very similar to the Greek rockfish, which is found fresh or frozen in all American markets; other fish with firm, nonoily flesh can also be used. The head and bones of the fish make the stock in which the fillets are poached after the fish is strained. The fillets and bones can be bought separately, but if you use a whole fish, see page 271 for the way to fillet it. (*Serves 4.*)

2 to 3 pounds head, bones, and trimmings of perch or any other white-fleshed nonoily fish; and 2 pounds fillets, or 1 5-pound ocean perch
1 large peeled and quartered onion
1 large peeled and quartered potato
1 bay leaf
6 sprigs parsley with stems and leaves
3 fresh quartered tomatoes or 1 16-ounce can tomatoes with juice
⅓ cup olive oil
4 cups water
Salt and pepper to taste
Juice of ½ lemon

Put the bones, head and trimmings of the fish in a large pot with all the ingredients except the fillets and lemon juice. Bring quickly to a boil, removing any froth that collects on top. Cook for 25 to 30 minutes at a rolling boil, then remove the bones and head from the broth and discard them. Strain the broth through a fine sieve into a medium saucepan and puree the vegetables (force them through a strainer with a wooden spoon to release their juice and some of the pulp) into it. Correct the seasoning of the soup and bring it to a boil. Add the fillets and simmer for 10 to 15 minutes until the fish is cooked and flakes. Remove from the heat, add the lemon juice, and serve.

TRIPE SOUP

Soúppa Skembés

Patsantsíthika are restaurants that serve only tripe soup, which sometimes has knuckles mixed in. In the islands they are open early in the morning till late at night to serve the people on their way to and from work. Tripe — white, fresh honeycomb — is sold ready to use in American supermarkets, a time-saver from the old days when it took hours to scald and clean it. (See pages 141–142, tripe stewed with herbs.) (*Serves 3.*)

1 pound fresh tripe	*2 celery stalks, cut in thirds*
5 cups cold water	*Salt and pepper to taste*
1 peeled and quartered onion	*Egg-lemon sauce I (page 251)*

Wash the cleaned tripe thoroughly under running cold water. Cut in pieces approximately 1 inch square, put them in a kettle, and cover with fresh water. Bring to a boil quickly, then drain and cover them with 5 cups cold water and add the onion, celery, salt and pepper. Bring to a boil, then reduce the heat to low, cover, and simmer for 2 to 3 hours or until the tripe is tender, adding more water to the kettle as needed. Remove from the heat, take out the celery and onion, and make the egg-lemon sauce. Mix it gently into the soup and serve immediately.

BROTH SOUP

Soúppa Phithés

This soup is a very easy one to make when the broth is prepared ahead of time and kept refrigerated or frozen. (*Serves 4 to 6.*)

3 tablespoons olive oil	*1 mashed garlic clove*
1 small chopped onion	*Salt and pepper to taste*
1 cup peeled and chopped	*6 cups beef stock (page 256)*
tomatoes	*½ pound* phithés *or vermicelli*
¼ cup chopped fresh flat-leaf	Kephalotíri *or Parmesan*
parsley	*cheese*

Heat the oil in a skillet and cook the onion until soft but not brown. Add the tomatoes, parsley, garlic, salt and pepper and gently simmer until the mixture is thick. Rub it through a sieve into another saucepan, add the stock, and bring it to a boil. Break the *phithés* by crumbling it with your hands and add it to the broth. Cook over moderate heat, occasionally stirring, until the *phithés* has doubled in thickness and is cooked. Serve in bowls and sprinkle with cheese.

Salads

Vegetables that linger in the garden left over from summer, and the brilliant colored ones of autumn, make delicious salads enhanced by the distinctive flavor of the fresh olive oil Greeks always use. Tomatoes are sliced and alternated with *fétta* cheese and other vegetables and dressed with oil. Peppers, green or sweet red, are cooked buried in charcoal embers, then their almost invisible skin is removed and the peppers are made into salad. Yellow large onions, just unearthed and ready to be hung to dry, are chopped and combined with cooked kidney beans, so typical a salad of the autumn.

LAYERED SALAD WITH TOMATOES

Arathiastí Saláta me Domáthes

One of the long-lasting vegetables favored by the Greeks in their salads is the tomato, which stays in the garden until the winter arrives. Here it is combined with cheese and other vegetables in a salad that is delicious served with broiled meats or meat casseroles. (*Serves 6.*)

4 tomatoes, sliced crosswise　　　*1 diced onion*

2 seeded and slivered green
   bell peppers
¼ pound fétta cheese, thinly
   sliced in 2-inch pieces
10 to 15 black Greek olives

¼ cup chopped fresh flat-leaf
   parsley
Salt and pepper to taste
½ cup olive oil–vinegar
   dressing (pages 253–254)

In a deep glass bowl arrange in separate layers the tomatoes, onion, peppers, cheese, olives, and parsley, sprinkling each layer with salt and pepper. When all the vegetables are arranged, dribble the dressing over the salad, chill it for 1 hour in the refrigerator, and serve.

ROASTED PEPPER SALAD

Psités Pipperiés Saláta

Red and green peppers can be cooked in the kitchen oven or in

embers with the same results. Very crisp when fresh, they become soft and sweet when cooked. Use both colors combined for a beautiful salad. (*Serves 3 to 4.*)

4 peppers, green bells or
   sweet red or both
Salt and pepper to taste
¼ cup lemon–oil dressing

(page 254)
2 tablespoons finely minced
   fresh flat-leaf parsley

Preheat the oven to 400°. Wipe the peppers with a lightly oiled cloth, set them in a baking pan, and cook them in the oven until their skins darken and blister. Let them cool, then peel off with your fingers the transparent skin. Cut the peppers open, remove the seeds, and cut the peppers in strips. Put the strips in a shallow bowl, season with salt and pepper, pour the salad dressing over them, and sprinkle with the parsley. Serve this salad warm or cold.

RED KIDNEY BEAN SALAD

Kókkina Fassólia Saláta

If you are using dried beans, soak approximately 1 cup of them overnight in water to cover. Next day drain and put them in a saucepan with 6 cups of fresh water, and cook them slowly, covered, for ½ hour or until tender but not very soft, adding water if needed. When cooked, add 1 tablespoon salt, let stand 15 minutes, covered, and then drain. One cup of dried beans makes approximately 3 cups cooked. (*Serves* 6.)

3 cups cooked kidney beans
¾ cup chopped onion
1 cup chopped celery stalks
Salt and pepper to taste

*½ cup olive oil–vinegar
  dressing (pages 253–254)*
*¼ cup finely chopped fresh
  flat-leaf parsley*

Put the cooked beans in a large bowl, add the onion, celery, salt and pepper, and mix thoroughly. Pour the dressing over the salad and mix again, correct the seasoning, and sprinkle with the parsley. Serve warm or cold.

Fish and Shellfish

Halki, the island of my Great-Grandmother Mario, on my father's side, and a pirate's lair in the past, where beautiful women abducted during raids against the surrounding islands were kept, has high, bare mountains and scattered cactus, olive and fig trees on the dry hills in small clusters enclosed in high stone walls to protect them. But the sea surrounding this dry island is cobalt blue and full of fish, from which some of the island's best dishes come. *Psári plakí,* baked fish, is an old recipe that came to our family from this great-grandmother, a beautiful woman from an island known both for the beauty of its women and for its clear sea. *Platópsara,* a kind of flat fish, similar to flounder, abundant in this sea's waters, are caught from the sea bottom and make a delightful entrée when poached and served with garlic sauce. Mussels, plentiful in autumn and harvested from the rocks, are steamed in wine and become a delectable meal when crusty bread and a leafy salad accompany them.

BAKED FISH

Psári Plakí

Striped bass or any other white fish can be prepared this way. Have it scaled, gutted, and degilled (see pages 270–271 if you want to do it yourself), but leave the head on. Great care should be taken while the fish is baking not to puncture the skin, particularly while you are basting it. Also avoid putting bits of herbs or vegetables on the fish, which might burn and discolor the skin. The fish should look as handsome after cooking as before. (*Serves 4.*)

1 2- to 3-pound fish (striped bass, bluefish, red snapper, or pompano) gutted, scaled, and degilled
Juice of ½ lemon
2 large peeled and diced tomatoes

½ cup chopped fresh flat-leaf parsley
2 small minced garlic cloves
¼ cup dry white wine
¼ cup olive oil
Salt and pepper to taste

Preheat the oven to 350°. Salt the fish cavity, rubbing the salt in with your fingers. Place the fish in a well-oiled baking pan, 9″ x 12″ x 2″. Pour the lemon juice over the fish and set it aside. In a small bowl, combine the tomatoes, parsley, garlic, wine, olive oil, salt and pepper. Pour the mixture over the fish. With a wooden spoon gently push any bits of herbs or vegetables on top of the fish into the pan. Bake the fish 45 minutes, basting it occasionally with the pan juices. Serve with a peasant-style salad (pages 63–64).

MUSSELS STEAMED IN WINE

Míthia Krassáta

On the seacoasts of America, mussels hang in clusters on rocks and sand and wooden docks. They are much smaller than the Greek ones but just as tender. It takes time and several changes of water to prepare and scrub them, but only a few minutes to cook them. Use a wire brush or small knife to scrape them and remove their beards; then soak them in cold water for a few hours, drain, and rinse them several times. If the mussels are half open, press them between your forefinger and thumb. They should close; if not, they are not alive and should be discarded. (*Serves 4 to 5.*)

¼ cup olive oil
2 chopped scallions
2 tablespoons chopped fresh
    flat-leaf parsley
2 finely minced garlic cloves
1 tablespoon fresh or 1

teaspoon dry savory
⅛ teaspoon pepper
1 cup dry white wine
5 pounds cleaned blue
    mussels in the shell

Heat the olive oil in a large pan and sauté the scallions over moderate heat until they are soft. Add the parsley, garlic, savory, pepper, and wine, bring to a boil, and boil for 2 minutes; then add the mussels and bring to a boil again. Reduce the heat to moderate, cover, and simmer for 7 minutes, shaking the pot from side to side a few times until the shells open. Remove the pan from the heat, and with a slotted spoon transfer the mussels to a large, warm bowl. Then put the pan on high heat and boil the broth rapidly to reduce it to about 1 cup. Pour the broth through a sieve lined with cheesecloth (to catch any sand) over the mussels.

POACHED FILLETS OF FLOUNDER WITH EGG-GARLIC SAUCE

Platópsaro Brastó me Aliátha

The European sole, a tasty fish, is often poached whole and covered with egg sauce flavored with garlic. I use instead the fillets of flounder that are available in local markets or bone the ones my husband brings home from fishing (pages 270–271). This dish is especially delicious when the fillets are surrounded with small new boiled potatoes, dressed with butter and finely minced parsley. (*Serves 6.*)

¾ cup egg-garlic sauce
    (pages 252–253)
2 pounds flounder or

sole fillets
1½ cups fish stock (pages
    256–257)

Prepare the egg-garlic sauce, cover, and set aside.
    Place the fillets in a skillet and over them pour the fish stock; bring the liquid to a boil, cover, reduce the heat to moderate, and

cook for 5 minutes or until the fish flakes when tested with a
fork. Remove the fillets from the liquid to a warm platter and
over them pour the egg-garlic sauce, and serve.

Game Birds and Chicken

Over the gently rolling hills of the islands, flocks of partridges and other wild birds hide under the purple savory bushes. During the shooting season in autumn, sportsmen return with their catches of these birds fastened to their belts in bunches, and give the women long and elaborate work to pluck and clean them. The partridges are stuffed with *pergúri*, cracked wheat, seasoned lightly with herbs, and baked in the oven, while the small birds are skewered whole and roasted over hot coals to make a most rewarding meal. Domesticated birds such as chicken are also eaten in this season, prepared less elaborately — just rubbed with lemon and herbs, and roasted in the oven with potatoes to make a Sunday meal.

SMALL BIRDS SPIT-ROASTED

Paulákia stin Soúvla

Small birds, after being trapped and killed, are plucked and grilled on skewers over coals and served at many village cafés with cheese or fried eggs on the side, a delicacy in Greece since ancient times. The birds are dipped in boiling water to loosen the feathers, which are pulled out by hand (pages 269–270). The

head and feet are cut off, and the bird is then gutted and washed.
(*Serves 4.*)

12 birds
Salt and pepper to taste
¼ cup olive oil

½ teaspoon dried thyme
Juice of ½ lemon

Rub the birds with salt and pepper and thread them on a metal skewer with an inch of space between birds. Combine the olive oil, thyme, and lemon juice in a bowl and beat lightly with a fork till well mixed, then baste the birds with the mixture. Grill over the charcoal fire 7 to 10 minutes, turning often to cook all sides and basting frequently. Instead of grilling, the birds can be fried in hot olive oil after they are seasoned with salt and pepper.

ROAST STUFFED PARTRIDGE

Pérthika Ghemistí tou Foúrnou

Folk songs of the islands compare the beauty and grace of a young girl with those of the partridge. Beautiful and in great abundance, partridge are considered very tasty when prepared as they do on Rhodes. Allow 1 partridge per person, since the bird weighs barely a pound. Pluck and clean them (pages 269–270), reserving their livers. Marinate them in cold wine marinade (pages 257–258) at least 24 hours and drain. (*Serves 6.*)

6 marinated partridges
Olive oil to baste

STUFFING
½ cup olive oil
1 large chopped onion
Chopped livers from the partridges
1 cup fresh chopped mushrooms

1 cup diced celery
1 cup cracked wheat
3 cups chicken stock (page 255)
2 tablespoons tomato paste
1 teaspoon dried powdered thyme
¼ teaspoon pepper
Salt to taste

Heat the olive oil in a skillet or saucepan and sauté the onion until soft. Mix in the livers and cook over moderate heat till their red color disappears; then add the mushrooms and celery and stir for 1 minute. Add the cracked wheat, chicken stock, and tomato paste, and stir with a wooden spoon until the paste dilutes and mixes well with the rest of the mixture. Season with the thyme, pepper and salt, cover, and simmer for 25 minutes or until thick. Let the stuffing cool.

Preheat the oven to 400°. Stuff the partridge cavities and sew them closed with a needle and heavy thread. Turn the wings under and tie the legs together with a string. Arrange the birds in a large oiled roasting pan or casserole, side by side with breasts up, baste them with olive oil, and roast them for 10 minutes. Then baste them again and turn them to roast on one side for 15 minutes; baste again and roast them on the other side for 15 more minutes. Finally, with breasts up, and basting frequently, roast them again until the legs can easily be pulled away from the body. Transfer carefully to a warm platter and serve.

OVEN-BAKED CHICKEN

Órnitha tou Foúrnou

This uncomplicated way of preparing a one-dish meal is very popular with housewives who don't want to spend all day in the kitchen. (*Serves 6.*)

1 5-pound plump roasting chicken	2 peeled carrots, split in half
½ lemon	3 tablespoons olive oil
1 peeled and quartered onion	5 to 6 medium peeled
Salt and pepper to taste	potatoes, cut in quarters or
3 stalks of celery, cut in half crosswise	thick wedges
	1½ cups water

Preheat the oven to 375°. Wash the chicken inside and out and rub it with the lemon, squeezing the juice all over the bird, then let the chicken stand to absorb the juice. Stuff the onion quarters in the cavity of the chicken, and rub the outside of the chicken with salt and pepper. Layer the celery and carrots in the bottom of a roasting pan to keep the chicken from sticking to the pan and also to give flavor to the juices. Place the chicken on top of them, and with your hands rub some olive oil on it. Toss the potatoes with salt and pepper and arrange them around the chicken. Dribble over them the rest of the olive oil and pour the water in the bottom of the pan. Cover the whole pan with foil, making a hole in the top for the steam to escape, and bake the chicken ½ hour. Uncover it and cook ½ hour longer, adding more water if needed, until the chicken and potatoes are cooked.

Mutton

Mutton is prized among the Greek people for its versatility and robust taste — especially in the autumn, when it is at the height of its flavor. It used to be the only meat available in the fall, and on Saturdays, the day the fresh meat was brought to market, the Greek housewives would buy a whole leg of mutton. This would furnish enough meat for a family in a variety of dishes for several days in the week, with some meatless dishes eaten in between. Many dishes are made of mutton cut up in large chunks and cooked with either giant white beans or chickpeas, or stewed alone in a thick sauce with spices. Ground mutton is used in fillings for pasta and rice casseroles, and the bones are used to make rich broth for soups. In the American markets one can find good cuts of young mutton that lend themselves to many ways of cooking numerous dishes for both everyday meals and special celebrations.

GIANT DRIED WHITE BEANS WITH MUTTON

Ghíghes me Arní

Flavorful dishes are prepared with chunks of mutton, a hint of garlic, the spice of cumin, and the almost forgotten dried vegetables, which stay silent in your kitchen cupboard for a long time. Giant dried white beans, similar to the large lima beans, and *revíthia,* chickpeas, can be found in local markets in 1-pound packages. (*Serves 6.*)

1 pound giant dried lima beans	*2 diced stalks of celery with tops*
½ cup olive oil	*3 tablespoons tomato paste*
2 pounds mutton from the leg or shoulder, cut in 2-inch chunks	*1 large mashed garlic clove*
	1 teaspoon ground cumin
	Salt and pepper to taste
1 chopped onion	*1½ cups water*

Put the beans in a medium-size pan, add 4 cups cold water, and slowly bring to a boil. Remove from the heat, cover, and set aside to soak for approximately 30 minutes, then drain.

Heat the olive oil in a skillet, fry the meat a few pieces at a time over moderate heat until golden brown, and with a slotted spoon remove the pieces to a heavy casserole. In the same skillet, fry the onion to a blond color and add it with the oil to the meat. Now add the celery, tomato paste, garlic, cumin, salt, pepper, and 1 cup of water. Cover and simmer for ½ hour. Add the drained beans and ½ cup more of water, cover and simmer, adding more water if needed, until the meat and beans are tender — about 30 minutes. (Chickpeas are cooked the same way, but they have to be presoaked overnight. Use ½ pound of dry chickpeas covered with 4 cups of fresh water, and instead of cooking the meat first alone, put the chickpeas into the casserole with the meat to cook together from the start.)

BAKED PASTA WITH MEAT SAUCE

Pastítsion

A Greek version of pasta is this casserole made with thin spaghetti or short macaroni and chopped meat and a simple white sauce over it. Adapted into the Greek cuisine from the Italians who ruled the islands for many years, it is one of the well-known

dishes in Greece, and popular for entertaining young people.
(*Serves 8.*)

MEAT SAUCE
¼ cup olive oil
1 chopped onion
2 pounds ground lean meat
  (lamb, mutton, beef)
2 cups tomato sauce (pages
  248–249) or 1 16-ounce can
¼ cup dry white wine
¼ cup chopped fresh flat-leaf
  parsley
1 mashed garlic clove
Salt and pepper to taste

FOR THE PASTÍTSION
1 pound thin spaghetti or

short macaroni, cooked
  according to the package
  instructions
5 tablespoons melted salt
  butter
2 tablespoons fine bread
  crumbs
4 medium eggs, lightly beaten
  with a fork
Meat sauce (see above)
3 cups white sauce (page
  250)
3 tablespoons grated
  kephalotíri or Parmesan
  cheese

TO MAKE THE MEAT SAUCE, heat the olive oil in a large skillet and sauté the onion over moderate heat until soft. Add the chopped meat to it and cook until it crumbles and all redness disappears. Now add the tomato sauce, wine, parsley, garlic, salt

and pepper and stir until it thickens, and then remove from the fire and set aside.

TO PREPARE THE PASTA, drain the cooked pasta in a colander, rinse under warm water, and transfer to a large bowl. Add 4 tablespoons of butter and the eggs and toss the pasta until it is well coated.

TO ASSEMBLE THE CASSEROLE, preheat the oven to 350°. Butter with the remaining one tablespoon the bottom and sides of a 9" x 13" x 2" or 9" x 14" x 2" pan and sprinkle lightly with bread crumbs to coat it. Spread half of the pasta evenly in the pan, sprinkle with 1 tablespoon of the cheese and cover it with half of the meat sauce. Repeat with the remaining pasta and another tablespoon of cheese and the meat sauce, then smooth the top down with the back of a spoon. Now pour on the white sauce and spread it to cover the top and the corners. Sprinkle with the remaining cheese. Bake for 45 minutes or until the top is lightly golden. Cut in squares and serve with a green leafy salad.

BAKED LAMB IN PAPER

Arní tou Hartioú

This tasty way of cooking pieces of leg of lamb with each wrapped package served individually is widely used all over Greece. It is delicious with a side dish of potatoes and salad. (*Serves 6 to 8.*)

1 5- to 6-pound leg of lamb, cut crosswise in serving pieces
Juice of 1 large lemon
3 garlic cloves
½ teaspoon salt

½ cup olive oil
Pepper
½ pound thinly sliced kephalotíri or any semihard cheese

Preheat the oven to 325°. Sprinkle the pieces of meat with the lemon juice and set them aside on a large platter to absorb it. Mash the garlic with the salt in a mortar or a wooden bowl and rub both sides of each piece of meat with it; then oil the pieces generously and season them with pepper. Cut parchment or any porous paper to make 2 pieces for each piece of meat, large enough to wrap around and secure. Place half of the paper on a damp, flat surface and oil the tops with a brush. Place each piece of meat, with a slice of cheese on top of it, in the center of the oiled paper, fold the paper over the meat, and twist the edges tightly together. Then wrap each piece in an unoiled piece of paper and tie the package once around with string. Place the packages in a baking pan, cheese-side up, and bake them for about an hour. Remove them from the oven, let them cool slightly, cut off the string, and remove the outer layer of paper. Serve the meat still wrapped in the oiled paper.

Furred Game

Deer still roam the mountain forests of my native island, called by the ancients Elafousa, "island of deer." They are hunted together with rabbits during the government-regulated hunting season in late fall and winter, and at this time venison and the meat of other wild animals are available to people through hunter friends and relatives who sell or share their game. The meat of running game animals has a certain flavor and toughness most people don't favor; and for this reason, after the game is gutted it should be properly aged with the skin still on. Then it is skinned, cut up, and marinated before being cooked, to become tender and take on a good aroma. Rabbit needs to be marinated at least 24 hours in the refrigerator, venison 2 days, and wild boar even longer. In America many kinds of game meat can be found in special game-meat stores; it is supplied by game farms or hunters, already aged, cut up and packaged for making a delicious roast or stew.

ROAST SADDLE OF VENISON

Eláfi ston Foúrno

Serve with any vegetable or rice dish. (*Serves 6.*)

Cold marinade using red wine
  (page 257)
1 5- to 6-pound trimmed
  saddle of venison
¼ cup olive oil or lard

¼ pound salt pork cut in
  strips
1 cup water
1 tablespoon flour
Watercress for garnish

Prepare the marinade in an earthenware or glass bowl. Put the saddle of venison in the marinade, cover the bowl with wax paper or plastic wrap, and let it stand in the refrigerator for 2 days, turning the meat over several times in the marinade. Then remove the venison from the marinade and pat it dry. Save the marinade.

Preheat the oven to 375°. Heat the olive oil or lard in a large, heavy skillet over moderate heat until it becomes hazy, and brown the meat on all sides, then transfer it to a heavy, oven-proof casserole, pour the oil from the skillet over it and cover the meat with the strips of salt pork. Place the casserole in the oven and bake the venison approximately 1 hour — for rare meat — basting it a few times with the fat from the pan.

While the meat is cooking, make the sauce. Put the saved marinade with its vegetables in a saucepan and set it over high heat to bring it to a boil. Remove with a spoon the froth from the top of the marinade and discard it, add 1 cup of water to it and bring the marinade to a boil again. Reduce the heat to moderate and simmer the mixture, covered, until the vegetables are tender and the liquid remaining with them measures about 1 cup. Strain the marinade and set it aside, and discard the vegetables.

When the venison is done, remove it to a platter and keep it warm. Drain off all the fat from the casserole the venison was cooked in, except 2 tablespoons, set it over the stove on moderate heat, and stir in the flour and the strained marinade, mixing to scrape the drippings from the bottom of the casserole to mix with the liquid until it thickens, then put it into a gravy boat. Garnish the venison with watercress and serve the sauce with it.

RABBIT COOKED IN MARINADE

Lagós stin Sálmi

Serve with potatoes or rice and a salad. (*Serves 6.*)

*Cold marinade using white
  wine (page 257)
1 4- to 5-pound rabbit cut up
  in serving pieces
¼ cup olive oil*

*1 garlic clove
1 bay leaf
Salt and pepper to taste
1 tablespoon flour diluted in
  ¼ cup water*

Make the marinade in an earthenware or glass bowl, put in the pieces of meat, then cover the bowl with wax paper or plastic wrap and set it in the refrigerator for 24 hours, turning the meat 2 or 3 times in the liquid. Remove the meat from the marinade and pat it dry with a towel. Strain the marinade and set it aside, discarding the vegetables. Heat the olive oil in a heavy casserole over moderate heat and fry the pieces of meat in it on all sides until they are golden. Drain the excess oil out of the casserole and pour the strained marinade over the meat. Bring the liquid to a boil, remove the froth from the top, add the garlic and bay leaf, reduce the heat to low, and simmer the meat covered for an hour or until it is tender when tested with a fork. Correct the seasoning, thicken the sauce with the diluted flour, and serve.

Liver, Kidney, Sweetbreads and Tripe

In the islands many delicious dishes are prepared with the innards of the meat animals, which in this country are neglected. Sweetbreads, the most prized of all the innards, becomes a most delectable dish when parboiled and then braised with vegetables. Heart, kidney, and liver, cooked with wine and vinegar, fill the kitchen with their aroma, and tripe, if it is cooked slowly and for a long time, turns from its tough, rubbery consistency to a delightful, succulent, chewy meat. All are served as main dishes with vegetables or salads and rice. All the innards used for the recipes below should be very fresh and can be ordered through the meat department at your local stores.

LAMB KIDNEYS, HEART AND LIVER

Endósthia Arnioú

(Serves 6.)

3 pounds of a combination of lamb kidneys, heart, and liver

⅓ cup olive oil
1 chopped onion
1 cup dry red wine

3 tablespoons red wine vinegar	2 mashed garlic cloves
2 tablespoons tomato paste	2 bay leaves
	Salt and pepper to taste

Remove the outside, opaque skin of the kidneys, split them in half lengthwise, and cover them in water and 1 tablespoon of the wine vinegar to soak for 15 minutes. Drain and rinse the kidneys under cold water, remove any white substance in them, and cut in quarters. Split the heart in half. For both the heart and the liver, discard any fat present, cut in 1½-inch pieces, rinse and pat dry. Heat the olive oil in a heavy casserole and fry the pieces of innards over high heat for about 15 minutes, stirring often, until their moistness evaporates and they start to sizzle. Mix in the onion and cook for 1 minute, then add the wine, rest of the vinegar, tomato paste, garlic, bay leaves, salt and pepper, and stir with a wooden spoon. Reduce the heat to low, cover, and simmer for 2 hours. Check it occasionally and add a little water if the liquid is reduced. There should be a thick gravy left with the cooked meat.

BRAISED SWEETBREADS

Glykáthia

To prepare the sweetbreads, soak them in cold water for at least 1 hour and drain them. Place them in a saucepan with 1 tablespoon wine vinegar, bring them to a boil, and simmer for 1 to 5 minutes according to the size of the sweetbreads. Drain them and refresh them in cold water. Carefully remove and discard the membranes connecting the lobes of the sweetbreads with your hands, then place the sweetbreads on a flat surface and press with a plate to flatten them before they cool. (*Serves 4.*)

¼ cup olive oil	5 sprigs fresh flat-leaf parsley
1 chopped onion	2 tablespoons dried or a few
1 cup diced carrots	sprigs fresh thyme
1½ cups diced celery	2½ pounds sweetbreads,
½ cup dry white wine	boiled and cleaned as above

Preheat the oven to 350°. Heat the olive oil on the stove in a heavy casserole, stir in the onion, and cook it until golden; then add the carrots and celery and cook over moderate heat for 5 minutes, occasionally stirring. Add the wine, parsley, thyme, salt and pepper and stir until well mixed. Place the sweetbreads on top of the vegetables, cover, and simmer for 20 minutes. Put the casserole in the oven, uncovered, and bake 45 minutes — basting frequently and turning the sweetbreads once so that they will brown on both sides — until they fall apart easily when tested with a fork. Transfer the sweetbreads to a warm platter, strain the vegetables and juice through a sieve, pressing through with a wooden spoon, and pour their juice over the sweetbreads and serve.

TRIPE STEWED WITH HERBS

Skembés Yahnistós

Fresh, clean tripe is sold in the supermarkets, but it is not to be confused with the pickled variety, which is also sold over the counter. When using this fresh tripe, rinse it well and drop it in boiling water for 1 minute to get rid of any preservatives used, then drain well and cut in 1½-inch pieces. Another type of fresh tripe, this one unprepared, can be ordered from Greek or Italian markets. More effort is needed to clean it (page 274), but it has a better flavor because preservatives are not used. (*Serves 4.*)

¼ cup olive oil	¼ cup chopped fresh thyme
1 chopped onion	1 bay leaf
2 pounds fresh tripe, cut in 1½-inch pieces	1 cup chicken stock (page 255)
2 tablespoons tomato paste	Salt and pepper to taste
1 mashed garlic clove	

Heat the olive oil in a heavy casserole and add the onion to cook until brown. Stir in the pieces of tripe and cook over high heat for 5 minutes. Add the rest of the ingredients and enough water to just cover the meat, and bring to a boil. Reduce the heat to low and simmer covered, adding water a little at a time when needed, until the tripe is tender, about 3 to 4 hours. The sauce left with the cooked meat should be thick.

Vegetables

One can always tell autumn has arrived by the festive look of the white village houses brightened by orange pumpkins on the edges of the flat roofs against the blue sky — placed there to preserve them for the months to come. The kind of pumpkin with moist, sweet flesh, used in America to make pumpkin pies, in the islands is fried in olive oil to make one of the best dishes of the squash family.

Another autumn arrival is the red-speckled shell beans, called *barboúnia* in island Greek, which are my favorite of all beans. Mature but not quite dry, these beans are shelled and cooked with fresh tomatoes and seasonings. In autumn, a transitional time for vegetables, the last of the summer garden vegetables — the second or third sowing, called *épsima* — and the newly grown fall and winter vegetables, combined or separately, make the pleasant dishes the season is known for.

CAULIFLOWER FRITTERS

Kounoupíthi Tiganitó

Tempting fritters are made from that enormous flower, the cauliflower, and they taste even better when cold. No autumn picnic basket is without them. First the cauliflower is cored and the green leaves are removed. Then the foamy white part is split in half lengthwise, placed in a saucepan base-side down, and covered with water and 1 tablespoon salt. It is then brought to a boil and simmered, covered, until it is almost tender but not falling apart. Then it is drained and cooled. (*Serves 3 to 4.*)

Flour batter for dipping
  (*page 258*)
1 medium head of cauliflower
  (*prepared as above*)

Olive oil for frying
Salt and pepper to taste
Juice of 1 lemon (*optional*)

Prepare the batter and let it stand at room temperature for 1 hour. Slice the cauliflower in ½-inch pieces down to its stem and press the pieces gently in your palms to flatten them. Heat the olive oil poured ¼ inch deep into a skillet. Holding each piece of cauliflower by the stem, dip it in the batter and carefully place it in the oil, being careful not to burn yourself from the splashing oil. Fry on both sides until lightly golden, remove to a dish lined with paper to absorb the excess oil, correct the seasonings, and serve hot or cold with a sprinkle of lemon juice.

STEWED SHELL BEANS

Barboúnia Fasólia Yahnistá

The beans inside are red-speckled, like their pods. When they are shelled and cooked while still fresh, they acquire a certain delicate tanginess that they lack when allowed to dry completely. The plants are very easy to grow in the garden; and the beans mature all at once at the end of the summer. They are also available at some supermarkets and farm stands under the name of shell beans. (*Serves 6.*)

3 pounds of beans (*weighed*
  in their shells)
⅓ cup olive oil
2 large chopped onions
4 large peeled and diced

tomatoes or 1 16-ounce can
  tomatoes with juice
½ cup chopped fresh flat-leaf
  parsley
Salt and pepper to taste

Shell the beans, put them in a colander, and rinse them under running cold water. Heat the olive oil in a saucepan, add the onions and cook over moderate heat until soft. Add the beans, tomatoes and parsley, and season with salt and pepper. Cover

and simmer for 35 to 45 minutes or until tender, stirring occasionally and adding water when needed. Cooked beans should have a small amount of sauce left with them. Serve with charcoal-broiled meats.

FRIED PUMPKIN

Kókkino Kolokíthi Tiganitó

The small sugar pumpkin is often cut in sections shaped like the thin crescent moon and fried. Split the pumpkin in half, remove the seeds, slice vertically in ½-inch to 1-inch sections. Peel off the tough outside skin and cut the slices in half if they are too long. This dish makes a sweet side dish for any meat. (*Serves 6.*)

1 small-size sugar pumpkin,
    prepared as above
Salt and pepper to taste

Flour for rolling
Olive oil for frying

Salt and pepper the pumpkin pieces and let them stand for 5 minutes, then roll them in flour and shake off any excess. Heat olive oil poured ¼ inch deep into a skillet, and fry the floured pieces of pumpkin on all sides until golden brown. Drain the excess oil on paper and serve.

STUFFED TOMATOES

Domátes Ghemistés

Tomatoes are almost always present in one form or another on a Greek table; when stuffed with meat and rice, they are served as a main course. Because they are cooked in olive oil, these plain, rice-stuffed tomatoes can be eaten hot or cold with a side dish of cheese and olives. (*Serves 6.*)

8 firm ripe tomatoes
½ cup olive oil
1 chopped onion
1 cup uncooked rice
½ cup pine nuts
1 mashed garlic clove

¼ cup chopped fresh flat-leaf parsley
¼ cup chopped fresh dill weed
Salt and pepper to taste

Slice the tops almost off the tomatoes, leaving them hinged on to be used as covers when the tomatoes are stuffed. Scoop the pulp and seeds out of the tomatoes; chop the pulp and seeds and set them aside. Put the tomatoes upside down to drain. In a skillet heat half of the oil and fry the onion until it is golden. Mix in the tomato pulp and seeds and cook over moderate heat for 1 minute. Now add the rest of the ingredients and 1 cup of water; mix, cover, and bring to a boil. Reduce the heat, and simmer until the rice is almost cooked, about 20 minutes. Remove the rice mixture and let it cool so that you can just handle it.

Preheat the oven to 375°. Fill the tomato shells with the rice mixture and cover each with its lid. Arrange the stuffed tomatoes side by side in a baking dish that has been oiled with the remaining olive oil and pour ½ cup of water in the bottom of the pan. Bake for 30 minutes. Serve either hot or cold.

MIXED VEGETABLE STEW

Tourloú-Briáni

When a farmer and his family go to the fields early in the morning, they just take along a clay pot, cutlery, bread, a little olive oil in a small jug, and seasonings. Water is always available on the farm, and so are twigs and wood for a fire, and so are vegetables. Before too long, the pot is resting in between two large stones over the wood fire and seasoned vegetables are bubbling together to make the tasty dish called *tourloú*. (*Serves 6.*)

½ cup olive oil
1 large peeled and sliced
  onion
2 medium-size, peeled eggplants, cut in 1-inch cubes
3 medium-size zucchini, cut
  in ½-inch slices
2 large celery stalks, cut in

½-inch pieces
4 large ripe peeled and diced
  tomatoes
½ cup chopped fresh flat-leaf
  parsley
2 mashed garlic cloves
Salt and pepper to taste

Heat the olive oil in a large saucepan and cook the onion until soft but not brown. Stir in the eggplant and cook for 2 minutes, mixing with a wooden spoon. Add the zucchini, celery, tomatoes, parsley and one of the garlic cloves. Stir the vegetables gently, cover the saucepan, and cook over low heat for 40 minutes, occasionally shaking the pot from side to side to prevent the vegetables from sticking to the bottom. Season with salt and pepper to taste and add the other garlic clove. Simmer 10 minutes longer (if there is too much liquid, cook uncovered) or until the vegetables are cooked to your taste. *Tourloú* is served hot or cold.

Cakes and Pastries

A cause for a big family celebration is the return of relatives from faraway lands, or the birth of a son, or the marriage of a daughter, all of which always start with a big feast that ends with Greek sweets in fanciful shapes. In the villages platters full

of deep-fried twists called *katiméria* are laced with honey syrup and served at large gatherings, but traditionally they were made for a reward at the end of a big family project such as making wine, threshing grain, or gathering olives. In the city, when housewives take an afternoon coffee hour to exchange visits and gossip, little squares of lemon-scented cake are served. They are called *lemonópitta* and have a tart sugary crust very delicious with tea or coffee. Throughout the year, in the cities and villages alike, christenings take place; and the food served on such occasions is prepared by the best cooks among the women relatives. The sweets served include *plakoúndes,* nut-stuffed pastry rolls which, because of their long, easy-to-hold shape are much loved by the children.

DEEP-FRIED TWISTS

Katiméria

This old village recipe remains basically unchanged from when it was used by peasants of long ago when they took time to rest in between projects and to enjoy the fruits of their labor in the sweet taste of the *katiméria.* (*Makes a platterful of twists.*)

2 *whole eggs, plus 4 egg yolks*	1 *teaspoon baking powder*
2 *tablespoons sugar*	*Oil for frying*
2 *tablespoons olive oil*	
⅓ *cup orange juice*	HONEY SYRUP
1 *tablespoon grated fresh*	1 *cup honey*
orange peel	1 *cup sugar*
3¼ *cups flour, sifted twice*	1 *cup water*

Put the whole eggs, egg yolks, and sugar in a bowl and beat until the mixture is light and creamy, about 2 minutes with an electric mixer at medium speed. Then stir in the olive oil, orange juice, and orange peel with a wooden spoon until they are well blended with the egg mixture. Sift the flour with the baking powder and slowly add it to the mixture, stirring continuously until the dough stiffens. With your hands knead the dough, adding any remaining flour, until it is smooth. The dough should be a bit sticky and not very stiff. Divide the dough in half and roll each half with a rolling pin on a well-floured board covered with a pastry cloth into a circle ⅓ of an inch thick. With a small sharp knife cut the rolled-out dough in strips ½ inch wide and 3 inches long, and tie each strip in a loose knot. Heat about 2 inches of oil in a deep skillet or heat an electric deep-fryer to 375° or 400°;

drop in 10 to 15 pastry twists and when they rise to the surface of the oil, move them around with a slotted spoon so that they will become lightly golden all over. Remove the twists from the oil to a deep bowl and drench them with honey syrup (see below). Eat hot or cold.

Combine all the syrup ingredients in a saucepan and boil uncovered over moderate heat for 3 minutes. Let the mixture cool slightly and pour over the twists.

LEMON CAKE

Lemonópitta

I usually double this recipe and bake in two pans, so it will not be too thick, because it freezes beautifully cut in small squares and layered on a platter between sheets of waxed paper. When needed for serving, the squares take but 2 minutes to defrost. (*The single recipe makes a 9" x 12" x 2" cake.*)

7 tablespoons unsalted butter	1½ tablespoons grated lemon
¾ cup sugar	peel
2 medium eggs	
½ cup warm milk	TOPPING
1½ cups sifted flour	½ cup fresh lemon juice
1½ teaspoons baking powder	1 cup sugar
¼ teaspoon salt	

Preheat the oven to 350°. Cream the butter thoroughly in a bowl and gradually add the sugar while beating. Beat the eggs until light and creamy and with a spoon fold them into the butter and sugar. Stir in the milk with a wooden spoon, then slowly the flour, baking powder and salt combined; add the grated lemon peel and mix it in well. Pour the batter in a well-greased 9" x 12" x 2" pan and bake 25 minutes.

Just before the cake is ready to come out of the oven, squeeze 1 or more fresh lemons to make ½ cup of juice and add it to the sugar to barely moisten but not melt the sugar. Remove the pan from the oven, spoon the mixture evenly over the hot cake, and return it to the oven to bake 5 minutes longer so that the juice will penetrate through the cake and the top will be dry. While it is still warm cut it into small squares with a sharp, pointed knife. Let it cool, remove it from the pan, and place it on a platter.

NUT-STUFFED PASTRIES

Plakoúndes

There are as many varieties of fillings as there are shapes among the desserts made from *phíllo,* a thin pastry dough found in this country in Greek and Middle Eastern grocery stores. *Plakoúndes*

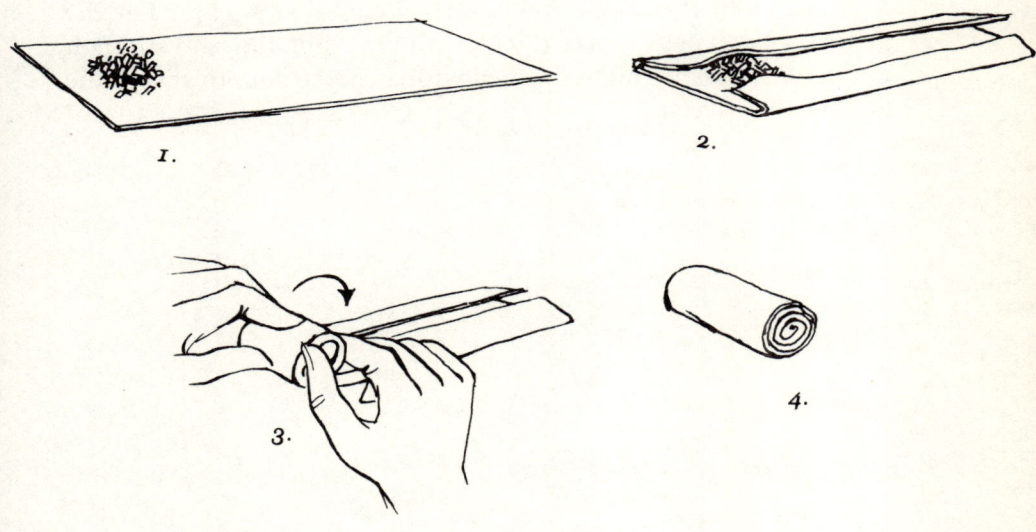

are stuffed with cinnamon and spiced ground almonds, rolled in *phíllo* in the shape of a cigar, then syruped at the end of the baking time. (*Makes 30 to 40 plakoúndes.*)

1 pound phíllo *dough*
1 pound clarified unsalted
   butter (page 269)
baklavá *syrup*

FILLING
3 egg yolks
1 pound ground almonds
1 teaspoon nutmeg

1 tablespoon powdered   ¼ cup sugar
    cinnamon

Beat the egg yolks lightly with a fork. Combine the other ingredients for the filling in a bowl, stir in the egg yolks until well
mixed, and set the mixture aside.

Preheat the oven to 325°. Spread the layers of *phíllo* on a board
and cut them in 5-inch strips. (See page 273 for how to work
with *phíllo*.) Place 2 layers of strips of *phíllo* on a flat surface
and brush them with the clarified butter. Put 1 tablespoon of
filling at one end of the strip, fold in the sides to keep the filling
from escaping, and roll it down to the other end to make a cigar
shape. Arrange the rolls side by side in a well-buttered 9″ x 12″ x
2″ baking pan, brush the tops with any remaining butter, and
bake for 30 minutes or until golden. Prepare a syrup for *plakoúndes* as in the recipe for *baklavá* (pages 213–214). Let the
syrup cool and pour it over the *plakoúndes* while they are still hot.
Let them stand overnight covered with a cheesecloth to absorb the
syrup before serving.

Fruits and Spoon Sweets

Quinces remind me vividly of my childhood in the city. My mother would take me with her to the market, where from the many grades of quinces displayed she would choose the ripest for preparing the many sweets of autumn. For her compote she would pick the largest, and for the spoon sweets the yellowest, and would smell each one at least twice before deciding to keep it. I remember the full basket we carried home and showed off to the rest of the admiring family, and sitting in the garden on a low stool under the lemon tree, where I would help wipe off the fuzz of each quince with a towel to expose the shining yellow skin. With her quick, small hands my mother would peel and core the quinces, cut them in quarters, and drop them into a large earthenware bowl of acidulated water to keep them from turning brown. Quinces, uneatable when raw, with off-white flesh and stiff, semitart taste, became tender when cooked in pieces with sugar in a compote. And in the spoon sweet, full of delicate perfume, the tiny pieces glowed like amber after they were cooked. The peels my mother saved, boiled in water, and strained. Then she mixed the juice with sugar and cooked it for a long time to make jelly, which she set to harden in shallow cut-glass dishes. This became another quince sweet that my brothers and I so rapturously devoured.

QUINCE COMPOTE

Kithóni Kompósta

(*Serves 6 to 8.*)

Juice of 1 lemon
6 medium-size quinces or 3
   pounds of quinces

2 cinnamon sticks
3 cups sugar

Remove the fuzz from the outside of the quinces by rubbing them with a cloth or washing them under running cold water. Cut them in quarters and remove the core, but do not peel. As you clean them, drop them in a bowl of water with the juice of 1 lemon added to it, then drain when you are ready to cook them. Put the quinces in a saucepan with 3½ cups of cold water and the cinnamon sticks, bring to a boil, reduce the heat to moderate, and cook covered until the quinces are tender. Remove the pan from the fire, mix in the sugar, and cook 10 to 12 minutes longer or until the color changes to amber. Let the mixture cool and transfer to a deep glass bowl. Chill and serve.

QUINCE SPOON SWEET

Kithóni Glykó

Some of my American friends eat this with butter on muffins or bread for breakfast. (*Makes 3 to 4 pint jars.*)

3 pounds quinces
5 fresh sweet geranium leaves
   or 2 cinnamon sticks

4 cups sugar
Juice of 1 lemon

Remove the fuzz from the outside of the quinces and peel the outside skin thinly. Split the quinces in half, core them, and dice them. Put them in a saucepan with ½ cup of cold water (the saucepan should be large enough to allow for the puffiness that the fruit and sugar reach when boiling). Slowly cook the diced fruit, covered, until tender. Remove the pan from the heat and mix in the geranium leaves or cinnamon sticks and the sugar, then raise the heat to moderately high and cook uncovered until the syrup thickens, removing any froth that collects on the surface. When the back of a metal spoon dipped in the syrup becomes coated, stir in the lemon juice; then cook a little longer. The sweet is done when a drop of syrup forms a pearl shape in a glass of cold water. Pour the syrup into sterilized jars and store.

PEARS IN SPICED WINE

Appíthia se Krassí

Pears, like the quinces, ripen in the autumn. Their subtle flavor can be enhanced by cooking them whole in spiced red wine. The fruit absorbs the red color and becomes a beautiful as well as delicious dessert. (*Serves 6.*)

6 firm pears	*2 cinnamon sticks*
2 cups dry red wine	*3 cloves*
1 cup sugar	*Peel of 1 lemon*

Peel but do not core the pears, leaving the woody stem on, and set them aside. Heat the wine in a saucepan large enough to hold all the pears. Stir in the sugar, cinnamon, cloves and lemon peel, and simmer uncovered for 3 minutes. Arrange the pears stem up in the pan and baste with the wine sauce. Cook the pears slowly, continuously basting, until they are tender and translucent. Remove them to a glass bowl. Reduce the syrup over high heat until it thickens and pour it over the pears. Chill and serve.

Confections

On early autumn mornings vendors carrying sweets, from breads to confections, in baskets or glass-covered trays shout to praise the freshness of their wares as they wander through the narrow, sandstone-arched streets of the old city. The steaming hot breads and the other sweets scatter their aroma: the mixture of sweetness and roasted nuts of the unmistakable *pastélli* candy, and the smell of the mastic (an aromatic sap of the mastic bush) or rose (oil extracted from rose petals mixed with water) that only the *loukoúmi,* the so-called Turkish delight, could have. Adults as well as children enjoy the crunchiness of *pastélli,* candy similar to American peanut brittle, and the jellylike softness of the powdered-sugar-coated *loukoúmi.*

SWEET DELIGHT

Loukoúmi

A *loukoúmi* is served to a child speared on a silver fork resting crosswise on top of a glass of water. He or she dips the *loukoúmi* to sweeten the water and then slowly drinks it while eating the sweet. (*Makes 15 pieces.*)

2 cups granulated sugar
½ cup corn syrup
⅓ cup cornstarch plus 3
   tablespoons extra for
   dusting
3 cups water
⅛ teaspoon ground mastic or
   1 tablespoon rosewater

2 tablespoons fresh lemon
   juice
Nuts (optional)
Red or yellow food coloring
   (optional)
Confectioners' sugar for
   rolling

Put the granulated sugar and the corn syrup in a large saucepan and over moderate heat bring it to a boil, stirring constantly; cook for 30 seconds and set it aside to cool. Dilute the cornstarch with the water in another saucepan, and slowly, over low heat and stirring, cook the mixture until it is thick. Quickly mix the cornstarch into the syrup and bring it slowly to a boil, continuously stirring to prevent lumps from forming. Reduce the heat to very low and cook uncovered, stirring every so often until the candy thermometer registers about 220°. Add the mastic or rosewater, lemon juice, food coloring and the nuts and stir. Pour the hot mixture into a 4″ x 8″ x 2″ pan lined, bottom and sides, with a clean, heavy kitchen towel heavily dusted with cornstarch. Shake the pan to spread the mixture evenly and dust the top with cornstarch. Cover it with a cloth and let it stand until the next day. Then cut it in 1½-inch squares with a sharp knife, roll the pieces in confectioners' sugar, and store them in boxes, where they will keep for weeks.

GLAZED ALMOND CLUSTERS

Pastélli

This is a recipe my sweet-toothed son, Ted, often makes at home on rainy days. Use shelled almonds with or without skins, spread them in a pan, and toast them in a 350° oven for 5 minutes, being careful not to burn them and shaking the pan repeatedly. Remove the almonds to a dish and let them cool.

1 cup roasted almonds
2 cups sugar

Juice of ½ lemon

Butter a pan or shallow platter and arrange the almonds to cover the dish evenly. Cook the sugar and lemon juice in a saucepan over moderate heat, stirring continuously until the sugar melts. First it will become lumpy and then it will melt into a thin syrup, which should be poured over the nuts immediately. Let the nuts and sugar set and cool, but before the candy gets hard, wet the edge of a sharp knife and mark it off in squares. When the candy is cold enough to handle, follow the marked lines and break it into pieces, then wrap them in wax paper and keep them in a dry place.

Hot Beverages

On the islands great emphasis is put on hot breakfast drinks, particularly by Greek mothers who don't want to let anybody get out of the house before warming up with something hot to drink. Breakfast used to be the most complicated meal in our house when I was growing up, especially during the school season in the autumn, when each member of the family liked something

different to drink. My father always had coffee in a little demitasse cup, which he drank *métrios* (medium sweet); only my mother could prepare it for him the way he wanted it. My middle brother loved hot tea with a lot of sugar in it, while my younger brother's favorite was plain hot milk with sugar. I drank *kakáo* (hot chocolate), unsweetened powder for which could be bought in the little *bakáliko* (grocery store) around the corner. My oldest brother had a more elaborate drink called *krókos*, which was supposed to give him strength and put flesh on him. To make it my mother beat egg yolks and sugar in a cup until they were pale, pale yellow, then she added hot milk and he drank it immediately.

HOT MILK DRINK

Salépi

Salépi is the pulverized root of a woodland orchid; it can be bought in America in Greek and Middle Eastern stores. It makes a delicious breakfast and bedtime drink similar to malted milk. (*Serves* 2.)

2 cups milk	*2 tablespoons* salépi *powder*
2 teaspoons sugar	*Powdered cinnamon*

Heat the milk in a saucepan, add the sugar and *salépi,* and beat with a fork or a whisk until the mixture is foamy. Cook over moderate heat, stirring continuously, for 3 to 7 minutes or until the mixture thickens. Pour into cups and sprinkle with cinnamon.

HOT CHOCOLATE

Kakáo

Over the years cocoa has found its way to Greece in many different forms. It used to be sold in nibs (cocoa beans broken into small pieces), or ground into a powder with or without sugar, as it is now found in local stores in both Greece and America. Greeks mix cocoa with milk and top it with *kaimáki,* which is similar to clotted cream; whipped cream can also be used. Do not let the milk boil after the cocoa is added or it will become oily and lose its fine flavor. (*Serves* 2.)

¼ cup hot water	*2½ tablespoons unsweetened*
2 tablespoons sugar (*or more,*	*cocoa powder*
to taste)	*2 cups milk*

Whipped cream

Add the hot water to the sugar in a saucepan and mix until the sugar dissolves. Stir in the cocoa and mix well, and add the milk, stirring well. Heat again (but do not boil), still stirring constantly. Remove immediately from the heat, pour into cups, and top with whipped cream.

FROTHY EGGNOG

Krókos

A really nourishing breakfast beverage, and excellent also for warming up on cold days. (*Serves 1.*)

1 egg yolk
2 teaspoons sugar (or to
   taste)

1 drop vanilla (optional)
1 cup hot milk

Put the egg yolk, sugar, and vanilla into a mug. Beat this mixture with an ordinary teaspoon in a circular motion until the yolk is thick and pale. Slowly add the hot milk, stir, and serve immediately.

WINTER

Winter

The strong wind that blows before and sometimes after the winter rains is the kind children like to walk against and let themselves go in, almost to be lifted by it. Sudden rainfalls end abruptly with the clearing of the sky and sunshine that makes the fruit-laden citrus trees on the island's hills glisten. Winter weather in the Greek islands is not so very cold, but is chilly, and disliked by the islanders, who hurry through the streets wrapped in woolen clothing, complaining and hoping that the end of this season is near.

In some of the smaller islands, where rain is the main water supply for the dry summer months, the people welcome the showers that fill their cisterns. But on fishing islands, the same weather fills with dismay the young men who stand idle waiting for the storm to subside so they can return to the sea, while the older fishermen take the time to repair their nets and tell sea stories to the fascinated children who gather around them.

December rains benefit the grain-sown fields in the villages but keep the people indoors. Men, left with not much to do, spend hours in the *tavérna* fingering their worry beads, *kombolóy*, drinking tea and coffee, and discussing politics, while the women visit each other and busy themselves with weaving, embroidery, and cooking, and the children play. Aromas of winter food fill the houses with the smells of the full-bodied soups cooking on the wood fire, the kabobing of all sorts of meat, and the roasting of chestnuts in the continuously burning fire or charcoal brazier. Other smells of the winter are the freshly baked breads hanging from the beams of the ceiling in a basket, and the dry legumes cooked with or without meat, and the earthy meat stews simmered slowly with the fresh winter vegetables, which make the most delicious one-pot meals.

During Christmas and New Year's the activity of the village increases as though everybody has just woken up from a long sleep. People busily prepare for this joyous season, which includes many customs left to them from a pre-Christian era, such as the slaughtering and dressing, by the man of the family, of pigs raised during the summer and the women deciding which delicate and tasty pork dishes they are going to prepare for the feast of the holy days, an occasion involving everybody, old and young. Holiday baking is another of the lovely traditions, similar to that of the Americans, where grandmother, mother and daughters spend days making cakes, and cookies with beautiful designs. These are stuffed with walnuts and then dipped in hot honey and lemon syrup, whose fresh smell lingers in the house for days.

The city is more alive with activity than the villages are, particularly on the eves of Christmas and New Year's, when the whole city wakes up to the sound of children in the streets going from door to door singing traditional holiday carols. On New Year's Eve family and friends join in a big feast that ends with card games. This is the only time that the family allows the children to play cards; at other times, card-playing by children is considered bad luck. On the first day of the New Year, after lunch, the *vasilópitta*, a cake with a gold piece inserted in the dough before it is baked, is cut in equal pieces according to the number of members of the family and served; whoever finds the gold coin in his piece of cake is the lucky one in that household for the rest of the year.

Appetizers

Winter appetizers, unlike those of other seasons, are made of things that the housewife puts aside to have always on hand, such as brine cheese, made at the height of the milking season in March. While still fresh, some is put in earthenware jars and

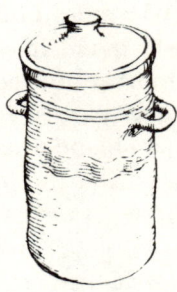

covered with brine, which is sometimes mixed with whey, to be used through the fall and winter. The same cheese is dried and grated as topping for dishes or is simply fried in pieces in olive oil to make *saganáki*.

Fish roe, *taramá*, is another of the winter appetizers my mother always prepared with great patience, murmuring her favorite song while crushing and working in with care each ingredient in the wooden mortar and pestle. And sun-dried octopus which my father would skewer and cook over red coals in the *mangáli,* a charcoal burner used to warm the rooms of the house in the winter. The flavors of these appetizers blend very well with the dry red Greek wine called *proúsko,* and the aniset-flavored aperitif *oúzo,* which are often served when guests drop in.

FISH ROE DIP

Taramá

Taramá, a Greek delicacy, is the roe of the red mullet, a fish that is very plentiful in the Aegean Sea. This roe has a salmony color, and when prepared with oil and lemon becomes a very zesty dip called *taramosaláta.* In this country it comes packed in jars and can be found in Greek markets; for this recipe you need the Greek product, *taramá;* do not use any other kind of fish roe. Since it is preserved in salt, you have to add bread that has been soaked in water and squeezed out, to cut the saltiness, and you can use more bread or lemon and olive oil than this recipe calls for to make it to your taste. It is very important to use a wooden mortar and pestle or a wooden bowl and spoon to crush the little teeny eggs, rubbing them between the wooden utensils; afterward, a blender may be used to work in the other ingredients. The trick is that the longer *taramá* is worked with wooden utensils, the better it tastes in the end. (*Serves 4 to 6.*)

½ loaf stale Greek or Italian bread
½ jar (4 ounces) taramá (mullet roe)
¼ cup cold water

½ cup olive oil
Juice of 1 large lemon
1 teaspoon very finely minced onion
1 parsley sprig for garnish

Soak the stale bread thoroughly and squeeze out the excess water with your hands. Cut off and discard the crust, and pick off small white pieces to make approximately 1 ½ to 2 cups. Put the *taramá* in a wooden bowl and with a wooden spoon or pestle crush the little eggs well, as described above. Slowly mix ¼ cup cold water in with the roe and add the pieces of bread a few at a time while crushing the fish eggs and mixing them with the bread until they are well blended. Alternately add small amounts of olive oil and lemon, still mixing, until all the olive oil and lemon have been added and the mixture is smooth and has a light salmon-pink color. Then mix in the onion, transfer the mixture to a bowl, and chill. Before serving, garnish the *taramá* with a sprig of parsley on top and place the bowl on a platter with small pieces of toast or *pítta* around it.

STUFFED SAUSAGES

Matiés e Saffáthes

Before the big Christmas meal, a fat sausage with a very unusual and delicious flavor is served for an appetizer. It is made from ground pork, rice and spices stuffed in a casing and tied in sections, first boiled and then fried. I was delighted to discover that casing comes frozen in America and can be ordered through the meatman at the markets. (*Serves 6.*)

Casing
Olive oil for frying

STUFFING
1½ *pounds ground pork*
¼ *cup uncooked rice*
2 *large mashed garlic cloves*
2 *teaspoons ground cumin*

½ *teaspoon grated orange peel* (*page 272*)
½ *cup chopped fresh flat-leaf parsley*
1 *slightly beaten egg*
½ *teaspoon pepper*
Salt to taste

Put all the stuffing ingredients in a large bowl and blend and knead them until the mixture is smooth. If frozen casings are used, defrost them under running cold water or overnight in the refrigerator, and if they are long, cut them in 15-inch pieces; run cold water through them to rinse them, then let them drain. Tie one end of each casing with heavy thread and stuff the pork mixture loosely in, using a spoon or a sausage stuffer, and tie the open end. Then tie the stuffed casings in 3- to 4-inch sections and place them in a saucepan covered with cold water. Cook the sausages over moderate heat 1 to 1½ hours, remove them from the heat, let them cool in their own broth, then drain them and pat them dry with towels. Heat the olive oil over moderate heat in a skillet and fry the sausages all around until they are golden. Serve them hot, a chain to each person.

OCTOPUS IN WINE

Oktapóthi Krassáto

During the winter, dried octopus is very popular all over Greece, including the islands, and is sold in all markets, hanging with their tentacles spread out; if you are not used to them, the sight will probably frighten you. Men on their way back from work occasionally buy one to bring home to cook for appetizers. The tentacles are cut in pieces, speared on skewers like marshmallows, and roasted over hot charcoals in a brazier, which gives them a wonderful flavor. Dried octopus, when soaked overnight in water, becomes soft and can be cooked for a stew, very slowly with wine and herbs until it is tender. It is hard to find in America so I use fresh or frozen, which is available in American fish markets and sometimes in supermarkets, with the same good results. (*Serves 6.*)

3 pounds fresh or frozen octopus meat
1 cup dry red wine

¼ cup olive oil
1 bay leaf
Salt and pepper to taste

If you are using frozen octopus, let it defrost overnight in the refrigerator. Rinse it under running cold water and remove any bones and ink, then cut the meat into small pieces; when small, octopus can be left whole.

Put the octopus in a saucepan with 1 cup of water, cover the pan and bring the water to a boil, then reduce the heat to low and simmer until the water is almost all absorbed. Remove the saucepan from the heat and add the wine, olive oil, bay leaf and salt and pepper, then cover it and return it to the stove and simmer again until the octopus is tender and the sauce is thick. Serve hot or cold.

PORK ASPIC

Pihti

An aspic, which is made from the feet, head, knuckles and some bones of a pig, is particularly popular around the Christmas season, when the pigs are slaughtered. The pieces are put in a large pot with water and spices and cooked slowly for hours, and sometimes overnight, over very low heat. Then the meat is deboned, the broth is strained, and both are mixed with lemon

juice. The meat and liquid are then put in small earthenware dishes that are placed in a hanging screen cupboard and set in the wind to cool and become aspic. And that is what the village people call *pihti*.

To make the broth, I use fresh pig knuckles and feet, which are available in American markets and meat stores, and any other pieces of pork and bones, and to cool and set the aspic I use the refrigerator. (*Serves 4 to 6.*)

3 pounds pork meat and bones	3 split garlic cloves
(knuckles and bones plus	Peel of ½ lemon
any other pieces of meat)	Salt to taste
3 bay leaves	Juice of 2 lemons
10 peppercorns	

Put the meat and bones in a large pot and cover them with 7 cups of water. Add the spices and lemon peel and bring the liquid to a boil, removing the froth that will collect on top of the liquid just before it boils, and boil 10 minutes or until the liquid is clear. Cover the pot, reduce the heat to low, and simmer for at least 4 hours or until the meat falls off the bones. Remove the meat and bones from the broth, then remove the meat from the bones, discard the bones, and cut the meat into small pieces. Strain the broth and season with salt, then return the pieces of meat and the broth to the pan, bring the broth to a boil, and cook over moderate heat for 5 minutes. Stir in the lemon juice, remove the pot from the heat, put the broth and pieces of meat in small serving dishes, and chill in the refrigerator until the aspic jells. It will keep for 1 week.

SPINACH TRIANGLES

Spanakotrígona

Fillings of many kinds can be prepared to stuff thin *phíllo* dough to make the pastries that Greeks use for appetizers and first courses. Made in triangle shapes and baked until golden and crisp, small pastries are ideal for parties and picnics. (*Makes 2½ to 3 dozen.*)

½ pound phíllo *pastry dough*   *Olive oil for brushing*
Spinach filling (page 37)

Prepare the spinach filling and set it aside to cool. Preheat the oven to 350°.
Cut the *phíllo* into 3″ x 10″ or 3″ x 12″ strips (page 273). Using the strips in double layers, put 1 tablespoon of filling at the end of each strip and fold it in triangles, as you would a flag, all the way to the other end (see page 11). Place the triangles on an oiled cooking sheet or pan, brush their tops with oil, and bake them for about 15 to 20 minutes or until they are golden. Serve them hot from the oven.

FRIED CHEESE

Saganáki

Kephalotíri, a semihard cheese, is usually grated and used to flavor various dishes, but when it is sliced and fried by itself in olive oil, it makes a delicious appetizer to be eaten on thinly sliced wheat bread.

kephalotíri	*Thinly sliced wheat bread*
Olive oil for frying	*Fresh lemon juice (optional)*

Cut the cheese into chunks ½ inch thick and 1 inch square. Pour into a skillet enough olive oil to cover the bottom ⅛ inch deep, heat it over moderate heat until a haze forms, and fry the pieces of cheese on each side until they are golden. Place the pieces of cheese on bread, sprinkle them with lemon juice, and serve them hot.

Soups

The islands' hearty winter soups are perfect for warming up at lunch or dinner during the cold months. Full-bodied, they make a meal by themselves with crusty bread, often accompanied by

cheese and olives. Most of the soups are made from legumes and winter vegetables, sometimes with macaroni, noodles or rice added at the end of the cooking period.

Fakkí, an old ancestor of our Greek soups, very delicious and thick, today is still made with those tiny round legumes, lentils, and cooked with olive oil and spices. *Fasoulátha,* bean soup, is a dish that a farmer's wife will cook early in the morning and take to her husband in the field; with crusty bread, *fasoulátha,* a yellow onion and some radishes, together they sit under an olive tree and have lunch. *Soúppa lahanikí* is a brew of hearty vegetables and one I always prepare for the family when we go to the country; wonderful soup to have after a long walk or skiing.

Leftover soups can be refrigerated a few days and reheated; they thicken in the refrigerator and need to be thinned with water. All these soups are delicious with crusty bread.

LENTIL SOUP

Fakkí

Lentils, which come in red, green and brown, are very popular throughout Greece in the winter months. The lentils found in American stores are the easy-to-cook type that need no presoaking. (*Serves 4 to 6.*)

1 pound dried lentils	½ cup olive oil
1 coarsely chopped medium- size onion	3 tablespoons tomato paste Pepper to taste
2 chopped celery stalks, including tops	Salt to taste 1 tablespoon wine vinegar
2 minced garlic cloves	(optional)

Put the lentils in a 2-quart saucepan, cover them by 3 inches with water, and add the onion, celery, garlic, olive oil, tomato paste, and pepper. Cover the pan and bring the mixture to a boil, then reduce the heat to moderate and cook for 30 minutes. Check the soup occasionally and add more water if necessary, but it should be fairly thick. Just before serving add the salt and 1 tablespoon wine vinegar if you wish.

BEAN SOUP

Fasoulátha

Dried white bean soup is the Greek national dish and is found in homes from the cities to the villages from late fall through the winter. Use the little white pea beans found in American markets and soak them overnight for faster cooking. (*Serves* 6).

1 pound white pea beans	*½ cup olive oil*
1 large chopped onion	*3 tablespoons tomato paste*
1 cup diced celery, some tops	*Pepper to taste*
included	*Salt to taste*
4 diced carrots	*1 teaspoon ground cumin*

Drain the presoaked beans, put them in a large soup kettle or pot, then add enough fresh water to cover them by 3 inches. Add the remaining ingredients except for the salt and cumin and bring them to a boil. Reduce the heat, cover the pot, and simmer the soup until the beans are tender, adding water as needed to keep them just covered. Add the salt and cumin just before serving.

WINTER VEGETABLE SOUP

Soúppa Lahaniki

This colorful soup is made with carrots, cabbage, celery, potatoes and two kinds of cooked dried beans. When the soup is cooked, each vegetable retains its own texture, and the flavor of each is merged into the broth. The beans can be cooked ahead of time and refrigerated. (*Serves 6 to 8.*)

⅓ cup dried white pea beans	*½ cup diced potatoes*
⅓ cup dried red kidney beans	*½ cup small uncooked*
Half a small head of cabbage,	*macaroni*
shredded	*2 crushed garlic cloves*
1 cup peeled and diced carrots	*1½ teaspoons dry savory*
1 cup diced celery	*Salt and pepper to taste*
1 16-ounce can tomatoes with	*½ cup olive oil*
liquid	*1 slice white bread, cubed*
2 quarts water	

Cover the beans with water, each kind in a separate pan, to soak overnight; ⅓ cup of dried beans will make approximately ½ cup cooked beans. Drain the beans, cover them again with fresh water, and in separate pans cook them slowly until they are tender, adding more water if needed. The cooking time varies from 35 to 45 minutes, depending upon the age of the beans.

Put the cabbage, carrots, celery and tomatoes in a large pot, add 2 quarts water, then cover the pot and bring the vegetables to a boil. Reduce the heat to moderate and cook the vegetables for 20 minutes, then add the beans, potatoes, macaroni, garlic and savory. Season the soup with salt and pepper and cook it 20 to 25 minutes longer until the potatoes and macaroni are soft. Heat the olive oil in a small saucepan and brown the cubed bread in it until it is crisp, then add both the bread and oil to the soup. Stir it well, remove it from the heat and let it stand covered 5 to 10 minutes before serving. If the soup is thicker than you wish, add a little water and heat it. With the soup serve a bowl of grated hard cheese, either *kephalotíri* or Parmesan, to be sprinkled on top.

Salads

Accompaniment to any meal of fried fish or hearty stew meat can be the winter salads of the islands, made mostly of cooked vegetables, except for cabbage left raw and cut very fine and dressed with olive oil and vinegar, or lemon if you prefer, always served with bread hot out of the oven.

BEET AND ONION SALAD

Pantzária me Kromíthi Saláta

Beets were very popular with the ancient Greeks but are not very much used by islanders today. I have seen beets prepared only two ways — either as a hot or cold salad with dressing or pickled in brine and cut thin in pretty patterns. Beets make a delicious winter salad cooked carefully and prepared with onions and olive oil–vinegar dressing. (*Serves 4.*)

½ cup olive oil–vinegar dressing (pages 253–254)
1½ to 2 pounds medium-size beets
1 tablespoon vinegar

1 tablespoon salt
1 large diced onion
Salt and pepper to taste
½ cup chopped fresh flat-leaf parsley

Mix the olive oil–vinegar dressing and set it aside. Pull the leaves and stalks off the beets with your hands (do not cut their bases or they will bleed when they are cooking), then scrub them under cold running water to remove all the sand. Place them in a pan covered with cold water plus 1 tablespoon each of vinegar and salt and bring them to a rapid boil over high heat. Reduce the heat to medium and cook the beets, covered, until they are tender, then drain them. Slip the skins off them by rubbing them with your fingers, then slice them in ¼-inch slices crosswise into a bowl and add the onion and salt and pepper. Pour the olive oil–vinegar dressing over them, sprinkle them with parsley, and then mix gently. Serve either warm or cold.

HOT POTATO SALAD

Patatosaláta

This delicious salad can be served hot as a main dish or as an accompaniment with any meat or fish dish. Use nonbaking potatoes of medium size and make sure that you do not overcook them. (*Serves 4.*)

2 pounds potatoes
1 tablespoon salt
Pepper and additional salt to
    taste
½ cup olive oil–vinegar
    dressing (pages 253–254)

5 peeled and chopped
    scallions, green parts
    included
½ cup finely chopped flat-leaf
    parsley

Mix the olive oil–vinegar dressing and set it aside. Scrub the potatoes to remove any grit and sand, leaving the skins on. Place them in a saucepan in enough cold water to cover them, add 1 tablespoon salt, and bring them to a boil. Then reduce the heat to low and simmer them covered for 25 minutes or until they are tender when pierced with a fork, then drain them. While they are still hot, peel them and cut them in thick wedges (quarters if they are small) into a warm bowl; season them with salt and pepper, add the dressing and scallions and toss them gently with a wooden spoon. Let the potatoes stand for a few minutes to absorb the dressing, then sprinkle them with the parsley and serve them hot.

CABBAGE SALAD

Lahanosaláta

A crisp cabbage salad is a welcome change in the winter from the usual cooked vegetables, particularly if the cabbage is fresh, white and firm and shredded very fine and then tossed with onion-flavored dressing. (*Serves 4.*)

⅓ cup olive oil
2 tablespoons red wine
   tarragon vinegar
¾ teaspoon sugar

1 small firm cabbage
Salt and pepper to taste
1 onion, peeled and cut in
   slivers

To make the dressing, combine the oil, vinegar and sugar in a medium-size bowl and mix them vigorously with a wooden spoon for 1 minute. Then the dressing should stand for at least ½ hour at room temperature.

Cut the core out of the cabbage, remove and discard the outer leaves, cut the cabbage head in half and shred it; then slice thin slivers across the halves with a knife or a cabbage shredder. Place the shredded cabbage in a bowl and season it with salt and pepper; toss the cabbage with your hands, bruising it by gently squeezing it so that it can absorb the seasoning. Add the onion and dressing to the cabbage, toss it with forks until thoroughly mixed, and serve.

Fish

In the summer, fish are split in half, heavily salted, and dried slowly in the island's hot summer sun for the winter months when fishermen have to keep away from the sea and fresh fish is not plentiful in the markets. When it is soaked in many changes of water, dried fish becomes sweet; but to make *bakaliá-ros yahnistós*, a stewed cod dish, or cod fried and covered with garlic sauce for *bakaliáros tiganitós*, we used to get dried salt codfish, imported from other countries and sold in the stores during

winter. The small supply of fresh fish available in this bad weather season consists of smelts, whitebait, many kinds of rockfish and eels.

Eels' ability to disappear swiftly into the holes in the volcanic sea rocks makes catching them a challenge and a sport. My brothers loved to catch eels when we were children, and I remember when they tried to pry them out of their holes with long, curved, hooked contraptions they made out of wire, and then grabbed them just at the right place on the back of the head to avoid their painful bite. With their close-grained flesh, eels are a delicacy to all Greeks and they make delicious meals fried or stewed with herbs. These fish dishes go well with boiled greens and potatoes.

STEWED CODFISH

Bakaliáros Yahnistós

Because of its strong saltiness, dried codfish has to be soaked in water 24 hours in the refrigerator and the water changed several times. Then the sweet meat is stewed or fried, the islanders' favorite ways of preparing it. In Greece dried cod is sold whole, each one weighing from 3 to 7 pounds or even more, and can be found that way in Greek and Middle Eastern stores of America. But in American fish markets and supermarkets, dried cod is sold already cut in pieces in small wooden boxes or packages, and it is not as dry or salty as the other style, so needs to soak less time. (*Serves 6.*)

2 *pounds salted codfish*	*¼ cup chopped fresh flat-leaf*
3 *tablespoons olive oil*	*parsley*
3 *coarsely sliced onions*	1 *bay leaf*
2 *tablespoons tomato paste*	*Pepper to taste*
diluted in ¾ cup water	

Cut the codfish in serving pieces, soak it as described above, then rinse it and pat it dry.

Heat the olive oil over low heat in a casserole and sauté the onion until it is soft but not browned; add the diluted tomato paste, parsley, bay leaf and pepper and cook the sauce uncovered over moderate heat for 10 minutes. Place the pieces of cod in the casserole with the sauce and simmer covered for 25 minutes, occasionally basting, until the cod is cooked and flakes.

FRIED COD WITH GARLIC SAUCE

Bakaliáros Tiganitós Skorthaliá

(*Serves 6.*)

2 pounds soaked salted cod   Garlic sauce (*page 252*)
Flour batter (*page 258*)   Olive oil for frying

Cut the codfish in serving pieces, soak it as described above, then rinse it and pat it dry. Mix the flour batter and let it stand ½ hour at room temperature. Make the garlic sauce and set it aside. Dip the pieces of cod in the batter and leave them on a platter for a few minutes.

Heat the olive oil in a skillet until a haze forms, using enough to cover the bottom of the pan by ¼ of an inch, then carefully fry the pieces of cod over moderate heat, turning them to brown on both sides. Remove them to a warm platter. Stir the garlic sauce and pour it over the fried cod and serve.

FRIED EEL

Héli Tiganitó

On Christmas Eve in the islands, eel, stewed or fried, is traditionally served to the family. Eel of many sizes can be found fresh or frozen in American fish markets. Fresh eel should be gutted and skinned before it is cooked (page 270). (*Serves 3 to 4.*)

2 pounds skinned eel   Flour for rolling
Salt and pepper to taste   Olive oil for frying
1 egg   Lemon wedges for garnish

Cut the eels in pieces 3 inches long, then place them in a saucepan, cover them with boiling water, and let them stand for 8 to 10 minutes. Then with a slotted spoon remove them to a platter and season them with salt and pepper. Beat the egg slightly with a fork, dip the pieces of eel in it, roll them in flour, and set them aside. Cover the bottom of a skillet with ¼ inch of olive oil and heat it over moderate heat until a haze forms. Place the pieces of eel in it and fry them for 5 minutes, turning them to brown evenly on all sides. Remove them from the oil and serve them hot with lemon wedges.

STEWED EEL

Héli Yahnistó

A pot of eel stewed with herbs is a very satisfying meal when served by the fireside on a winter's evening. This is one of the

few Greek stews to which tomato is not added; the chunks of eel are stewed instead in white fish stock to retain their whiteness. (*Serves 4 to 6.*)

2½ pounds skinned eel (page 270)	*1 mashed garlic clove*
3 tablespoons olive oil	*1 bay leaf*
1 chopped medium-size onion	*¼ teaspoon ground dry sage*
2 tablespoons flour	*¼ cup chopped fresh flat-leaf parsley*
1½ cups fish stock (pages 256–257)	*Juice of ½ lemon*
	Salt and pepper to taste

Cut the eel in 3-inch pieces and set them aside.

Heat the olive oil in a casserole and add the onion to cook until it is soft but not browned. Stir in the flour until it is absorbed by the oil, being careful not to burn it, then slowly add the fish stock, stirring continuously, until it boils. Add the garlic, bay leaves, sage, parsley and lemon juice and season with salt and pepper; then put in the pieces of eel and simmer covered for 20 minutes over low heat or until the eel is cooked and white. Put the eel on a warm platter, strain the sauce and pour it over the eel, and serve.

ISLAND MARINATED FISH

Psária Marináta

In the past, the few times that fresh fish was available during the winter in the islands, people bought it in big quantities, which they cooked and preserved in a strong marinade sauce so that they could keep the fish a long time and use it up slowly. This method has been used since ancient times and is still in use today in villages where refrigeration is not available. In the cities, however, fish is marinated this way today primarily because people like it so much. Small fish like large smelts and whitebait are used, cleaned and left whole. (*Serves 5.*)

3 pounds smelts or whitebait
Salt and pepper to taste
Flour for rolling plus 3 tablespoons
Olive oil for frying

3 cloves finely minced garlic
1 cup hot water
½ cup white or red wine vinegar
1 teaspoon dried rosemary

Clean, gut and degill the fish leaving the heads on (pages 270–271); then rinse them under running cold water, season them with salt and pepper, and let them stand at room temperature for 10 minutes. Then dip them in flour and tap them to shake off the excess. Put enough olive oil in a skillet to cover the bottom at least ¼ inch deep, heat it over moderate heat until a haze forms, and fry the fish a few at a time until they are golden on both sides. Remove them to a deep clay or earthenware bowl and keep them warm. Strain the remaining oil from the skillet into a saucepan and over moderate heat sauté the garlic until it is light gold. Add 3 tablespoons of flour and stir constantly until the flour is absorbed by the oil, then slowly add 1 cup of hot water and bring it to a boil. Continuing to stir, add the vinegar and rosemary and season with salt and pepper to taste. Simmer the sauce uncovered for 5 minutes. Pour the sauce over the fish in the earthenware bowl and serve hot or cold.

Poultry

When a chicken no longer lays eggs regularly, it ends up in a pot cooking slowly to make a rich Greek island stew, *órnitha kapamá,* a red-all-over dish cooked in the outdoor oven, or *órnitha stiffáto,* a light-colored dish cooked with white wine and herbs. Such birds, from 1 to 5 years of age, would be called fowl in this country; they have a good flavor for soups and stews. But I find young, tender chickens tasty and available throughout the year in American markets, so I substitute them for the fowl and that cuts the cooking time considerably.

STEWED CHICKEN IN TOMATO SAUCE

Órnitha Kapamá

This easy-to-prepare chicken dish has good flavor and color. The chicken is seared in olive oil, then cooked on top of the stove in a heavy casserole. Either dry red or dry white wine can be added along with herbs to make the sauce, which mixes with the juices of the bird and thickens by the end of the cooking. Tomato paste or tomato sauce is used, since tomatoes are not available in the winter in most parts of Greece and in America are not at their best. Serve with stewed potatoes (page 206). (*Serves 4 to 6.*)

1 plump 3- to 4-pound chicken
Salt and pepper to taste
⅓ cup olive oil
1 chopped onion

½ cup dry red wine
3 tablespoons tomato paste
    diluted in ½ cup water
½ teaspoon dry oregano

Cut the chicken in serving pieces, then wash them, dry them, and rub salt and fresh pepper all over them. Heat the olive oil in a large skillet over moderate heat and fry the chicken pieces until they are golden on both sides, then transfer them to a heavy casserole. Discard from the skillet all but 2 tablespoons of the oil, in which you sauté the onion until it is translucent but not brown; then add it to the casserole. Add the remaining ingredients, cover the casserole, and simmer over moderate heat for 1 to 1¼ hours, checking occasionally so that it does not overcook.

CHICKEN WITH ONIONS AND WINE

Órnitha Stiffáto

This chicken dish is prepared in the same way as the dark classic *stiffáto* of beef, but its flavor is more delicate and its color is light. This recipe is traditionally made with fowl, but I use a fryer or a roaster; if stewing chicken (fowl) is used, then it should be cooked longer than the time given in this recipe. Serve with rice and braised celery. (*Serves 4 to 6.*)

1 4-pound chicken
Flour for rolling
¼ cup olive oil
½ cup dry white wine
1 mashed garlic clove

1 teaspoon dry thyme
2 tablespoons chopped fresh
    flat-leaf parsley
Salt and pepper to taste
20 small white peeled onions

Cut the chicken in serving pieces, then wash them, pat them dry with a towel, roll them in flour and shake them to remove the excess. Heat the olive oil in a skillet to moderate heat and fry the chicken pieces on all sides until they are lightly golden, then remove them to a large casserole and set it aside. Discard from the skillet all but 3 tablespoons oil, and to it add the wine, stirring to loosen the chicken drippings to mix with the oil and wine. Then mix in all the remaining ingredients but the onions and put them in the casserole with the chicken. Simmer them covered for 30 minutes. Then add the onions and simmer covered for 30 minutes longer until both the chicken and the onions are cooked.

TURKEY WITH GREEK STUFFING

Thiános Ghemistós

The flavor of Greek turkeys is excellent because the birds are fed organically and left to roam loose, but they lack plumpness and juiciness when compared with American turkeys. Cooked mostly during the winter and served at special family gatherings, they are stuffed with an elaborate and rich mixture of meat, nuts and sherry-soaked raisins combined with herbs whose flavor pervades the whole stuffing. For a more simple stuffing, see page 195.

1 12-pound turkey
Juice of 1 lemon

STUFFING
3 tablespoons olive oil
3 tablespoons chopped onion
The chopped turkey giblets
¾ pound fresh ground pork
¾ cup uncooked rice
½ cup pine nuts
⅓ cup seedless dark rai-

sins soaked in sherry
½ cup chopped fresh flat-leaf
*   parsley*
2 teaspoons dry powdered
*   sage*
Salt and pepper to taste
1 cup water
Olive oil for basting
1 to 2 tablespoons flour for
*   gravy*

Wash the turkey inside and out and dry it thoroughly with towels, then rub it with lemon juice all over, inside and out, and set it aside to absorb the juice while you are preparing the stuffing.

To make the stuffing, heat the olive oil in a large skillet over moderate heat and cook the onion until it is translucent; then add the giblets and cook, stirring constantly, until their red color has disappeared. Add the ground pork and, stirring constantly, cook it until it crumbles. Now, one at a time, add the remaining stuffing ingredients and cook the mixture uncovered over moderate heat until the water is absorbed and the rice is half cooked, about 15 minutes. Remove the stuffing from the heat and let it cool. Preheat the oven to 425°.

Stuff the turkey cavity loosely and sew it up with thick thread; if there is any stuffing left, stuff the neck cavity and skewer closed. Turn the tips of the wings under to make a platform for the bird and tie the legs together with string. Oil the bottom of a roasting pan, place the turkey in it breast-up and baste the bird all over with the olive oil. Cover the pan and roast the turkey in the oven for ½ hour, then reduce the heat to 350° and continue roasting about 2 to 2½ hours, or until the legs pull away from the body easily. Remove the turkey to a warm platter.

To make the gravy from the pan juice and drippings, heat the roasting pan on top of the stove over moderate heat until the drippings sizzle, then add the flour, stirring until it is absorbed by the drippings. Add 1½ cups hot water and, stirring constantly, let the gravy boil until it becomes thick. Correct the seasoning and serve the gravy hot with the turkey and the stuffing.

Pork and Beef

The custom of sacrificing a pig in the ancient Greek winter festivals has been carried through the centuries and is present today in the slaughtering of the pig during the Christmas festivities. The pigs, which were raised from little piglets by each village family during the summer, are kept away from the houses, on

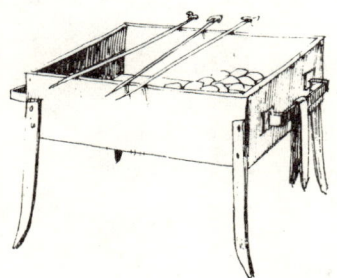

the outskirts of the village and under the shade of an oak tree, *pouthoukloméno*, leashed or tied by the front leg and fed twice a day by the children as part of their household chores. They grow fast into hogs and by Christmas are ready to be slaughtered. Winter is the time of the year when pork is good and plentiful and the only season when it is eaten in Greece, while in America it is available year round and can be bought fresh on all meat counters.

Cattle raising is impractical in the islands because of the mountain terrain, and the few cows are used for farm labor, mainly plowing fields, so they are highly valued by the peasants. The few dishes that do call for beef are winter ones, and the good tender beef available in America makes these Greek dishes more delicious.

Dark beef stews go well with buttered homemade egg noodles (page 239), while pork stews go better with rice.

PORK-STUFFED CABBAGE LEAVES

Lahanodolmáthes

Pork and cabbage, a winter food combination in many other countries besides Greece, is enjoyed by almost everyone for lunch or dinner. The cabbage leaves are individually stuffed with a mixture of pork, rice and herbs, which can be done a few hours ahead of time, and then cooked in meat stock. When reheated, leftovers still retain their delicious flavor. The head of cabbage used should be fresh but not very firm, so that the leaves will come off easily and without breaking. (*Serves 4.*)

1 medium-size head of cabbage
2 tablespoons olive oil
1½ cups chicken stock (page 255)

STUFFING
1½ pounds lean ground pork

½ cup uncooked rice
½ cup chopped fresh or 1 tablespoon dry dill weed
1 slightly beaten egg
3 finely chopped scallions
3 tablespoons tomato paste
Salt and pepper to taste

Remove the coarse outer leaves of the cabbage and set them aside. Cut out and discard the core from the base of the head, then plunge the whole cabbage, core-side down, into a large saucepan with a large amount of boiling water and cook it uncovered for 10 to 15 minutes. Remove the head to a colander and run cold water over it to cool it, then take off the cabbage leaves one by one and cut off the thick stems and discard them, leaving just the pliable part of the leaves to stuff. In the same boiling water cook the coarse outer leaves of the cabbage for 5 minutes, then remove them and line the bottom of a casserole dish with them so that if the pan scorches the stuffed leaves will not burn.

To make the stuffing, combine all the ingredients in a bowl and mix and knead with your hands until the mixture is smooth. Then take a cabbage leaf in your palm and place 1 to 2 tablespoons of stuffing (depending on the size of the leaf) in the middle of it; fold the sides in over the stuffing and then roll the leaf tightly from the stem end toward the tip of the leaf. Stuff all the leaves and then arrange them in a casserole snugly side by side in layers, with the tips of each roll tucked under, until all the stuffing and cabbage leaves are used. Pour the olive oil and chicken stock over them, place a small plate on top of the last layer and push the rolls down a bit, cover the casserole, and simmer the rolls for 45 minutes to an hour. Serve with egg-lemon sauce III (page 251) or with lemon juice.

PORK WITH CELERY AND EGG-LEMON SAUCE

Hirinó me Séllino Avgolémono

Pork stewed slowly in wine and herbs is typical of winter dishes in the islands. Celery hearts, at their best in winter, are added to the stew, and egg-lemon sauce stirred in at the end of the cooking gives the dish a delicate, piquant flavor. (*Serves 4 to 6.*)

¼ cup olive oil
2 pounds lean pork cut in
   walnut-size pieces
1 large chopped onion
½ cup dry white wine
½ cup chicken stock (page
   255)
2 tablespoons flour stirred into

½ cup water
1 large mashed garlic clove
2 tablespoons chopped fresh
   flat-leaf parsley
Salt and pepper to taste
6 celery hearts
Egg-lemon sauce II (page
   251)

Heat the olive oil in a skillet over moderate heat and brown the pork pieces a few at a time, removing them as they are done with a slotted spoon into a casserole; when the pieces are all browned, pour the olive oil from the skillet with the meat. Place the casserole over moderate heat, then add the onion and stir it for 1 minute; then pour in the wine, chicken stock and diluted flour, and add the garlic, parsley, salt and pepper; stir the mixture until it boils, then reduce the heat to low and simmer covered until the meat is almost cooked, 45 minutes to an hour.

Wash the celery hearts and split them in half the long way, then place them in the casserole on top of the meat and baste them with the meat juices. Cover the casserole again and simmer the meat and celery until both are tender, or about 30 minutes, then remove the casserole from the heat. Prepare the egg-lemon sauce and stir it gently into the pork and celery, then reheat but do not boil the mixture. Serve immediately.

PORK STEW WITH LEEKS AND OTHER VEGETABLES

Hirinó me Prássa

At the end of the winter the leeks arrive, green and fresh, and they can be prepared in many ways: either alone, first blanched and then dipped in batter and fried; or sautéed in a meat stock; or stewed with pork and other vegetables — a dish with a beautiful combination of colors that can be served for lunch or dinner. (*Serves 4 to 6.*)

¼ cup olive oil	1 cup diced carrots
2 pounds lean pork cut in	1 cup diced celery
walnut-size pieces	Salt and pepper to taste
2 tablespoons flour stirred into	1 large mashed garlic clove
½ cup water	6 leeks

Heat the oil in a large casserole over moderate heat and lightly brown the pork. Stir in the flour and water plus 1 cup of water, stirring continuously until it boils, then reduce the heat and simmer covered for 45 minutes. Mix in the carrots, celery, salt, pepper and garlic, cover the casserole again, and simmer for 10 minutes. Wash the leeks, especially between the greens to remove the grit, and cut them crosswise in 3-inch-long pieces. Place the leeks on top of the meat and vegetables, baste them with the meat juices, and without stirring let them cook covered until they are tender.

ROAST STUFFED SUCKLING PIG

Gourounópoulo e Hiráki Ghemistó

When a "name day" or a christening is celebrated there is always a big feast with relatives and friends. A name day is the celebration of the Christian name of a person on the day dedicated to the saint who has the same name. The Greek Orthodox religion dedicates each day of the year to a different saint. If it is the season when piglets are available, one is stuffed and roasted in the outdoor beehive village oven. Roasted in your kitchen oven, however, a suckling pig will turn out golden brown and with the same delicious flavor. You will need a large but not too deep roasting pan.

In America, piglets, usually 1½ to 2 months old and weighing 10 to 15 pounds, can be ordered through your meatman. For stuffing use the Greek one on page 189 or use this one, which I am fond of but which is not Greek at all but rather very American, given to me by my mother-in-law. Roast pig is delicious served with carrots or any of the braised vegetables. (*Serves 12 to 15.*)

1 piglet, about 12 pounds
3 tablespoons olive oil for basting
2 tablespoons flour
Salt and pepper to taste
Parsley sprigs, 1 apple or orange, and sliced olives for garnish

STUFFING
1 loaf of day-old sliced white bread (1 pound)
1 large chopped onion
3 chopped celery stalks
4 tablespoons salt butter cut in small pieces
1 tablespoon dried thyme
Salt and pepper to taste

To make the stuffing, remove the crust from the bread and shred the white part by hand in small pieces. Put the ingredients in a large bowl, mix them together, and set aside.

Preheat the oven to 350°. Wash the pig inside and out with cold water, pat it dry, and with your hand rub the cavity with salt and pepper, then fill it loosely with the stuffing. Close the cavity with skewers and lace it with twine or sew it with string. Place the pig in a crouching position by pulling the front and back legs forward and tying them and put it in the roasting pan stomach down. Brush olive oil all over the pig and with a sharp knife make a few short and shallow cuts in the pig's back to let the fat escape during roasting. Put a block of wood into the pig's mouth to keep it open. Cover the ears with foil so they will not burn, and pour 2 cups of water in the bottom of the pan. Roast the pig in the oven, basting with olive oil occasionally, until the meat is tender, about 3 to 4 hours. If the skin browns too fast, cover it with aluminum foil until the last half hour of cooking, then uncover it and let it become crisp.

Remove the cooked pig to a warm platter. To make gravy from the drippings, first skim the fat off the juices in the pan, then on top of the stove, heat the juices until they sizzle, scraping the drippings off the bottom of the pan to mix with the rest of the juices. Stir in the flour until it bubbles and add 2½ cups water, stirring constantly. Cook the gravy until it thickens. Then season it with salt and pepper and keep it hot.

Before serving the pig, remove the foil from the ears and the wood from the mouth. Garnish the platter with sprigs of green mint or parsley and place an orange or apple in the mouth and pieces of olives in the eyes. Serve with the gravy.

BEEF STEW WITH ONIONS

Stiffáto

This beef stew is strictly a winter dish in Greece. It is cooked with whole onions, wine and herbs, and fills the house with its rich aroma while it is cooking. My grandmother used malt vinegar instead of wine and my mother still uses it, but I have found that a combination of the two makes the stew not so heavy. A tender cut of beef is not required for this dish, and in fact would fall apart during the long, slow cooking that gives the dish its special flavor; prime chuck without much fat is very good. The important thing is to sear the meat and seal in the juices, which will be released again but not until the meat has cooked for a while with the wine and herbs. This way, the meat stays tender and juicy. (*Serves 6.*)

½ cup olive oil
2 pounds rump or chuck cut
  into walnut-size pieces
2 pounds peeled small whole
  onions
2 peeled garlic cloves

3 tablespoons tomato paste
  diluted in ½ cup water
1 cup dry red wine
2 tablespoons wine vinegar
2 small bay leaves
Salt and pepper to taste

Heat the olive oil in a deep skillet (the oil is hot enough when a small cube of bread dropped into it turns color) and brown the pieces of meat nicely on all sides a few at a time, then remove them with a slotted spoon into a heavy pot. Fry the onions in the same oil until they are brown, then remove them into a bowl and set them aside. Put the garlic, diluted tomato paste, wine, vinegar, bay leaves, salt and pepper into the skillet and boil the liquid briefly. Remove the skillet from the heat and add the mixture to the beef; then bring the beef and liquid to a boil, reduce the heat to low, and simmer for 35 minutes tightly covered. Add the onions to the meat and simmer covered for 30 minutes longer until both the beef and the onions are cooked and the sauce is thick. If the sauce is not thick enough, remove the cover and simmer it a few minutes longer to reduce it. Remove the bay leaves before serving.

MEAT SAUSAGES IN WINE SAUCE

Souzoukákia

The smooth texture of these spiced meat sausages is achieved by repeatedly grinding the beef and then kneading it vigorously by hand. It is an interesting recipe that consists of fried meat shaped into sausages and simmered in a sauce into which their flavor is released. Because I can prepare it ahead, it is one of my favorite dishes for entertaining — particularly since the preparation is elaborate; all that is needed for serving is reheating, which should be done very slowly and with a little water added to the sauce. (*Serves 6.*)

½ *loaf stale white Greek or*
  Italian bread
2 *pounds finely ground lean*
  beef
3 *lightly beaten eggs*
2 *finely minced garlic*
  cloves
¼ *cup chopped fresh flat-leaf*
  parsley
2 *tablespoons grated*
  kephalotíri or Parmesan
  cheese

1 *teaspoon ground cumin*
Salt and pepper to taste
1 *cup flour for rolling*
1 *cup olive oil for frying*

SAUCE
2 *cups tomato sauce (pages*
  248–249)
1 *slit garlic clove*
1 *bay leaf*
¾ *cup dry red wine*
Salt and pepper to taste

Soak the stale bread in water and squeeze it hard with your hands to remove the excess. Cut the crust off the bread and pick

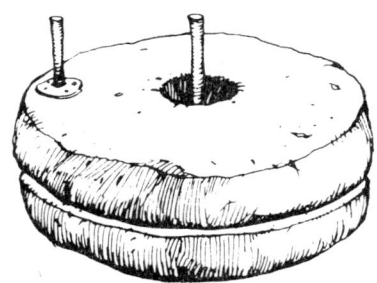

1 cup of small pieces of the white part. Put the meat and the bread in a bowl and mix them together thoroughly, then add the eggs, garlic, parsley, cheese, cumin, salt and pepper, and knead the mixture with your hands until all the ingredients are smoothly blended. Take 1 egg-size piece of the mixture, roll it between your palms into a 2-inch-long sausage shape, dip it in flour, and shake it to remove the excess flour. Repeat the process until you have used the mixture up.

Heat the olive oil in a skillet until a haze has formed on it and fry the sausages on all sides until they are evenly brown all over. Remove them with a slotted spoon to a bowl and set them aside.

To make the sauce, take 2 tablespoons of olive oil from the skillet and put it in a heavy casserole, then add the tomato sauce, garlic, bay leaf, wine, salt and pepper, and over moderate heat boil the ingredients briefly. Remove the casserole from the heat, add the sausages to the sauce and return the casserole to the heat. Simmer for 30 minutes, occasionally shaking the casserole from side to side. Serve in the casserole or in a large serving dish.

STUFFED BEEF ROLL

Vothinó Rouló me Ghémisi

This is a typical winter Sunday dinner dish in the islands that is served with homemade pasta in bows and ribbon shapes that take hours to prepare by hand and are made the day before; but commercial spaghetti and macaroni also go very well with it. The beef is a flank steak rolled with a lightly seasoned pork stuffing, then fried and cooked in a sauce with wine added, until it is tender. (*Serves 6.*)

2½ to 3 pounds flank steak
Flour for rolling
2 tablespoons olive oil
1 chopped onion
3 tablespoons tomato paste
*   diluted in ¾ cup water*
1 bay leaf
Salt and pepper to taste
½ cup dry red wine

STUFFING
1 pound ground pork
1 mashed garlic clove
2 tablespoons chopped fresh
*   flat-leaf parsley*
1 lightly beaten egg
2 tablespoons dry sherry
Salt and pepper to taste

TO MAKE THE STUFFING, blend all the ingredients together in a bowl and knead them until the mixture is smooth.

Spread out the flank steak and remove any bits of loose fat. Place the stuffing on one end of the meat, roll it up tightly like a jelly roll, and with a strong string tie the roll lengthwise and at ends and the middle. Dredge it in flour and tap it to shake off the excess.

Heat the oil in a heavy casserole until a haze forms and place the beef roll into it to fry until it is evenly brown all over, then remove the roll to a platter. Stir the onion into the oil and cook over moderate heat for about a minute, then add the diluted tomato paste, bay leaf, salt, pepper and wine. Cover the casserole and when the liquid boils rapidly, return the beef roll to it and simmer it, covered, over low heat, basting the meat occasionally with the sauce until it is tender, about 2½ hours, Remove the beef roll to a warm platter, let it cool slightly, remove the strings, then slice it crosswise and spoon some of the sauce over the slices. Put the remaining sauce in a gravy boat to serve with the meat and over any pasta you serve with it.

BEEF AND POTATOES

Patátes me Kréas

The potato is a basic ingredient for a variety of dishes, but beef and potatoes is a classic combination used all over Greece in the winter. Cooked with tomato sauce and herbs, the potato acquires a rich color that contrasts beautifully with the boiled greens served with it. (*Serves 6.*)

2 pounds beef chuck	*2 tablespoons crushed fresh*
¼ cup olive oil	*or 1 teaspoon dry savory*
1 chopped onion	*¼ cup chopped fresh flat-leaf*
3 tablespoons tomato paste	*parsley*
diluted in ¾ cup water	*Salt and pepper to taste*
1 mashed garlic clove	*2 pounds potatoes*

Cut the beef into walnut-size pieces and dry each piece thoroughly. Heat the olive oil in a casserole until it forms a haze and brown the beef on all sides a few pieces at a time. Remove them with a slotted spoon to a bowl. When all the meat is brown return it to the casserole, then add the onion and cook, stirring, for 1 minute. Then add the diluted tomato paste, garlic, savory, parsley, salt and pepper, and cook for 15 minutes, still over moderate heat. Add about ½ cup more water to the casserole, stir, and simmer covered for ½ hour longer, or until the meat is almost cooked. Peel the potatoes and cut them in thick wedges; small potatoes may be cut into quarters. Mix them gently into the casserole with a wooden spoon, then cover and simmer until they are tender. Do not stir again so as not to break the potatoes; instead, shake the pan from side to side occasionally and add more water if needed. When the meat and potatoes are cooked, a small amount of sauce will be left.

Vegetables

I remember my aunt's farm in the winter when it was full of the large bud shapes of cabbages and cauliflowers and the many shades of green feathery and leafy tops of the root vegetables all encircled by a high brush fence to keep out the strong winds of the winter and spring. Together we walked through the olive grove path and jumped from boulder to boulder to cross the narrow, rain-filled river that ran like a shiny snake dividing the village fields in half. We would gather vegetables and fill our basket with red beets, orange carrots and tender, translucent bulbs of fennel, then bring them home to use in many ways with meat in stews and soups or boiled by themselves, being careful not to overcook them to preserve their color and texture when preparing them.

BRAISED FENNEL

Márathron e Finóchio Sigopsiméno

Tender stalks of anise-flavored fennel taste very good eaten raw with just a sprinkle of salt, but when prepared the Greek islands way they are a delicious side dish to serve with any meat. And the fresh green feathery tops of fennel may be used to flavor sauces for fish. (*Serves 4 to 6.*)

3 *large fennels*	1 *mashed garlic clove*
3 *tablespoons olive oil*	*Salt and pepper to taste*
1 *chopped onion*	2 *to 3 tablespoons grated*
½ *cup chicken stock (page*	*kephalotíri or Parmesan*
255)	*cheese*

Remove the fibrous outer fennel stalks and trim off and discard the cores and feathery tops, leaving only the tender middle stalks. Cut the bulbs in quarters, or in half if they are smaller, wash them thoroughly under running cold water in between the stalks to remove any dirt, and drain them. Heat the olive oil in a deep skillet or casserole over moderate heat and sauté the fennel and the onion until the fennel becomes translucent, about 5 to 7 minutes. Add the chicken stock, garlic, salt and pepper to the fennel, reduce the heat to low, cover and simmer for 20 minutes or until the fennel is tender. Remove the pan from the fire, sprinkle the fennel with cheese, and cover the pan for 2 minutes for the cheese to melt, then serve it hot.

BRAISED CELERY

Séllino Sigopsiméno

The celery family, including knobs and roots, can be eaten raw, or cooked with chicken stock and served with pork dishes. There are different kinds of celery in this country and the most frequently used ones are heart celery, jade-green in color, and pascal celery, dark green and unblanched. For the recipe below use pascal celery. (*Serves 4 to 6.*)

2 *bunches celery*	*255)*
1 *tablespoon salt*	*Pepper and additional salt to*
3 *tablespoons olive oil*	*taste*
1 *chopped onion*	2 *tablespoons chopped fresh*
1 *chopped carrot*	*flat-leaf parsley*
¾ *cup chicken stock (page*	

Remove the core and outer fibrous stalks from each bunch of celery and trim off the leafy tops, leaving the stalks 6 to 8 inches long, then quarter them and rinse them under running cold water. Put them in a saucepan with enough cold water to cover them plus 1 tablespoon of salt, bring the water to a boil and blanch them for 5 minutes, then drain off the water. Heat the olive oil in a casserole and sauté the onion and carrot over moderate heat until they are limp and lightly golden. Put the celery on top of the sautéed vegetables, pour in the chicken stock, add salt and pepper, and bring the stock to a boil. Reduce the heat to low and simmer the vegetables for 30 to 45 minutes covered, or until the celery is tender. Remove the celery to a warm dish, then strain the other vegetables from the casserole and force them with a spoon through a sieve. Pour the strained vegetables with the juice over the top of the celery, sprinkle with parsley, and serve hot.

CARROTS

Karóta

The tough, woody texture of Greek carrots keeps people from eating them raw; instead they are cooked in soups or boiled just until they are tender and served with hot dressing for a delicious side dish with meat or fish. Tender, fresh carrots can be found all year round in American markets, have a more delicate flavor than the ones found in Greece, and are delicious when prepared this way. (*Serves 4.*)

1 pound fresh carrots
3 tablespoons salt
½ cup lemon-oil dressing
  (page 254)
1 teaspoon sugar

Pepper and additional salt to
  taste
2 tablespoons chopped fresh
  flat-leaf parsley

Peel the carrots with a paring knife instead of scraping them and cut them into 1″ x ⅓″ pieces. Drop them into 6 cups of boiling water to which 3 tablespoons of salt have been added and cook them over high heat for 25 minutes or until they are tender.

Drain the carrots and transfer them to a warm platter or bowl and set them aside.

To make the hot dressing, put the lemon-oil dressing, sugar, salt and pepper into a small saucepan, and while mixing, heat just to the boiling point. Then pour the hot dressing over the carrots, sprinkle them with parsley, and serve them hot.

CAULIFLOWER STEW

Kounoupíthi Yahnistó

The beautiful vegetable cauliflower of the cabbage family is often added to meat stews or blanched and dipped in batter and then fried. But cooking cauliflower with tomatoes or tomato sauce brings out a delightful tanginess in its flavor. Fresh cauliflower has a foamy white center surrounded with dark leaves; for the recipe below, the leaves are discarded with the core and the white part is separated into flowerets. (*Serves 4.*)

1 medium-size head cauliflower
3 tablespoons olive oil
1 chopped onion
1 16-ounce can tomatoes with juice or 1 8-ounce can tomato sauce or 1 cup

homemade tomato sauce (pages 248–249)
¼ cup chopped fresh flat-leaf parsley
1 mashed garlic clove
Salt and pepper to taste

Split the cauliflower in half, separate it into flowerets, and slice about ½ inch into the thick part of each stem with a knife so the stems will cook evenly with the tops.

Heat the olive oil in a casserole, sauté the onion until the pieces are soft and translucent, add the tomatoes or tomato sauce, salt, pepper, parsley and garlic, and cook for 5 minutes over moderate heat. Then place the cauliflower flowerets on top of the tomatoes, baste with the liquid, and simmer covered over low heat for 15 to 20 minutes; instead of stirring, shake the pan from side to side a few times to prevent it from scorching. Cooked cauliflower should be tender but not very soft.

SWISS CHARD

Séfklo Xerosímisis

The chard, with its loose dark green leaves and mild tender ribs, has long been a popular green in the Greek diet. It slightly resembles spinach with a subtler flavor, is full of vitamins, is the easiest thing to grow in the garden, and is sold in American markets during most months of the year. The tender stalks can also be cooked separately from the leaves and served with your favorite dressing, but cooked together they have an interesting consistency. Boiled, drained, and dressed with *xerosímisis* (cubes of bread fried in olive oil), is one of the ways islanders most frequently prepare this green. (*Serves 4.*)

2 pounds Swiss chard
2 tablespoons salt
½ cup olive oil
1 slice white bread, cubed

Pepper and additional salt to taste
Juice of ½ lemon

Cut off the stalks and the leaves at the base of the chard, remove any strings from them, then wash each leaf and stalk separately under running cold water. Drop the leaves and stalks in a large pot of boiling water with 2 tablespoons of salt added and cook them uncovered, occasionally turning them over, for 15 to 18 minutes or until the stalks are tender but not soft. Drain them well and place them in a bowl. To make the *xerosímisis*, heat the olive oil over moderate heat until a haze forms. Add the cubed bread and when the bread turns color pour it with the oil over the cooked Swiss chard. Correct the seasoning and sprinkle with lemon juice before serving.

STEWED POTATOES

Patátes Yahnistés

During the winter, potatoes prepared one way or another are part of almost every Greek meal. In this dish regular nonbaking potatoes are peeled, cut in thick wedges, seared until they are golden and crusty and then cooked in tomato sauce. (*Serves 4.*)

2 pounds nonbaking potatoes
¼ cup olive oil
1 chopped onion
3 tablespoons tomato paste
  diluted in ¾ cup water

¼ cup chopped fresh flat-leaf
  parsley
1 mashed garlic clove
Salt and pepper to taste

Cut the peeled potatoes in thick wedges or quarters, depending on the size, wash them, and set them aside to drain.

Heat the olive oil in a casserole, add the potatoes — which should be thoroughly dry — a few at a time and sear them quickly over high heat until golden brown. When the potatoes are all browned, return them to the casserole, stir in the onion with a wooden spoon, and cook for 1 minute, then add the diluted tomato paste, parsley, garlic, salt, pepper and 1 cup of water. Cook the potatoes over low heat with the cover tilted for the steam to escape, occasionally shaking the pot from side to side to prevent them from scorching. Add more water if it is needed from time to time; at the end of the cooking a small amount of sauce should be left with the potatoes.

CHICKPEA PATTIES

Revithokeftéthes

This very old village recipe, my favorite as a child and liked by everyone, is eaten hot or cold, for lunch or dinner and in between meals, and is made from dried chickpeas, cooked, mashed, spiced, shaped in patties, and fried in olive oil. In America chickpeas are available in Greek and Middle Eastern stores and now are carried in supermarkets. A mortar and pestle are used in the villages to pound the cooked chickpeas, but a meat grinder can be used and takes less time. (*Serves 4.*)

1 cup dried or 3 cups
  precooked chickpeas
1 peeled medium-size onion

1 peeled and boiled potato
Salt and pepper to taste
1 egg

*½ cup chopped fresh flat-leaf   Flour for rolling
   parsley   Olive oil for frying*

If you are using dried chickpeas, cover them with cold water and soak them overnight, then drain them, rinse them in cold water, and put them in a saucepan with 4 cups of fresh cold water. Cover the pot and bring the water to a boil, then reduce the heat to low and simmer the chickpeas for 1½ hours or until they are soft, and drain them. Put the cooked chickpeas through a meat grinder together with the onion and the potato, season the mixture with salt and pepper, and add the egg and the parsley. Blend them in well until the mixture is smooth. Shape the mixture into small patties and roll them in flour, shaking off the excess. Heat the olive oil in a skillet and fry the patties over moderate heat until they are golden on both sides, and serve.

LENTILS WITH NOODLES

Fakómatso

The combination of legumes and pasta is very popular among the poor, but is also used during the Lenten season by everybody throughout Greece. Brown and green lentils are used, with homemade noodles to give this dish a special flavor and fullness. (*Serves 4 to 6.*)

*Egg noodles (page 239)   1 teaspoon dry savory
2 tablespoons salt   1 chopped onion
8 tablespoons olive oil   1 mashed garlic clove
1 cup brown or green lentils   Pepper and additional salt to
2 tablespoons tomato paste   taste*

Follow the recipe on page 239 to make the noodles using only 2 eggs and 1 yolk. Boil 3 to 4 quarts water with 2 tablespoons of salt and 2 tablespoons of the olive oil added to it, drop the noodles in and boil them 10 minutes. Drain them and set them aside.

Put the lentils in a saucepan, add enough water to come 2 inches above them and add the tomato paste, savory, onion, garlic, remaining olive oil and pepper. Bring the lentils to a boil, reduce the heat and cook them covered over moderate heat until they are tender. Mix the cooked noodles into the lentils gently with a wooden spoon and season the mixture with salt to taste. Add a little more water if it is needed, bring the mixture to a boil again, stirring, then simmer it over low heat, covered, for 5 minutes longer. Serve hot.

WHITE BEANS WITH PASTA

Fasoulomakárouna

Cooked thick, this recipe can be served as a main dish. But it tastes equally good when served as a soup with more water added. White pea beans and small macaroni, called *ditalini*, are used in this dish and both can be found in American markets. (*Serves 4 to 6.*)

1½ cups dried white pea
   beans
1½ tablespoons tomato paste
½ teaspoon dried savory
¼ cup olive oil
2 split garlic cloves

2 tablespoons chopped fresh
   flat-leaf parsley
1 cup uncooked macaroni
Salt and pepper to taste
Grated cheese

Cover the beans with cold water, soak them overnight and drain them, then put them in a saucepan with 3½ cups of fresh cold water, add the tomato paste and savory, and bring the beans to a boil. Reduce the heat to low and simmer them covered until they are soft.

Heat the olive oil in a small skillet and sauté the garlic and parsley 1 minute, being careful not to burn them, then add them with the oil to the beans. Stir the mixture and add the macaroni, salt and pepper, and cook, covered, over moderate heat, stirring occasionally until the macaroni is tender. Sprinkle with the grated cheese and serve immediately.

Cookies, Pastries and Cakes

Treasured recipes of sweets that have been in families for many generations are prepared during the holidays of Christmas and New Year's by every household everywhere in Greece. It would not be Christmas without the *phinikia,* sweet spiced dough cookies prepared in great quantities and given to relatives and friends. And they send back theirs in equal amounts in return.

The traditional New Year's cake brings a lot of excitement to a household with children because of the belief that the one who finds the gold piece will have good luck all through the year. *Vasilópitta,* St. Basil's cake, is another name for it. St. Basil is the Greek Santa Claus who comes on New Year's Day instead of Christmas and brings candy to the children.

More sophisticated are the pastries made from paper-thin *phíllo* dough with nuts and syrups, prepared in homes and in pastry shops and served sometimes on name days.

SWEET SPICED BARS IN LEMON-HONEY SAUCE

Phiníkia

Lemon and honey soak these spiced and nut-filled cookies, which have been pressed on cut glass of different patterns before being baked to give them the festive look of Christmas. Mixing the dough is easy, but extra hands are needed for the rolling, stuffing and syruping of *phiníkia;* it is a good project before the holidays with family or friends and neighbors, which is what I usually do when this kind of baking is involved. They are the favorite cookies of my youngest son, Burton, and because they last so long he never runs out of them. (*Makes 4 dozen.*)

FILLING
1½ cups finely chopped
   walnuts
1 large or 2 small eggs
⅓ cup sugar
1 teaspoon ground cinnamon

SYRUP
2 cups honey
1 cup water
Juice of 1 lemon

DOUGH
2 cups refined olive oil or
   corn oil

2 cups sugar
½ teaspoon baking soda
1 cup freshly squeezed orange
   juice
2 tablespoons grated fresh
   orange peel
1 tablespoon ground
   cinnamon
1 tablespoon ground nutmeg
3 teaspoons baking powder
7 to 7½ cups sifted all-
   purpose flour

TOPPING
½ cup finely chopped walnuts

Mix all the filling ingredients together in a bowl and set them aside. Mix all the syrup ingredients in a 2-quart saucepan and set that aside also.

Put the oil and sugar in a large bowl and beat them for 10 minutes with an electric beater at medium speed, or for 20 minutes if you are beating by hand. Dissolve the baking soda in the orange juice until it fizzes and add them to the oil and sugar mixture; also add the grated orange peel, cinnamon and nutmeg, and with a wooden spoon mix them until the sugar is completely dissolved. Add the baking powder to the flour and add it little by little to the mixture in the bowl until the flour is absorbed and the dough stiffens, then knead the dough until it is smooth. The dough should not be too stiff, otherwise the cookies will be too hard after baking. Preheat the oven to 350°.

Take walnut-size bits of dough and form them into oval-shaped bars by rolling them between your palms. Place them on the bottom of an upside-down cut-glass dish. Then press them lengthwise with the edge of your hand to make a long indentation and at the same time to make a pattern on them, and put ½ teaspoon of walnut filling in the indentation. Fold the edges of the cookie bars together and press them to seal in the filling and then place them on an ungreased cookie sheet, decorated side up. Bake them for approximately 10 to 12 minutes or until they are a light golden color, then remove them from the oven and set them aside until the syrup is ready.

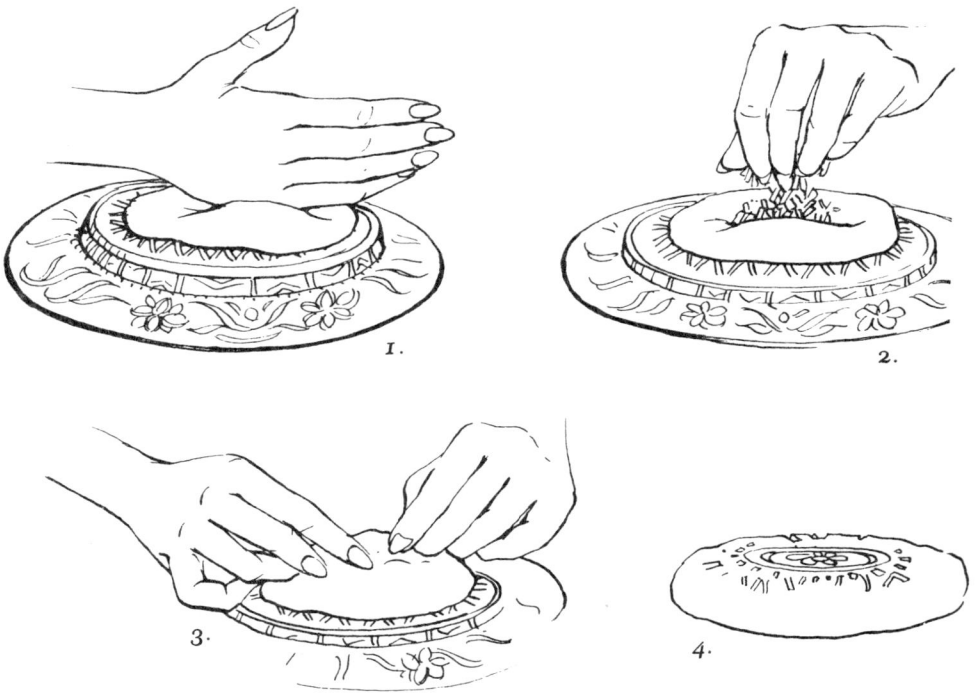

Slowly heat the honey syrup in the saucepan over low heat. When it is hot, drop the baked bars in a few at a time and leave for about 30 seconds, then remove them from the syrup with a slotted spoon and place them on a large deep platter. When all the *phiníkia* have been syruped, pour the remaining syrup over them, sprinkle them with the walnut topping, and let them stand for 24 to 48 hours to absorb the syrup before serving them. Always serve the *phiníkia* from the bottom of the platter first.

THIN-LAYERED PASTRY WITH
WALNUTS AND SYRUP

Baklavás

Baklavás, consisting of layers of paper-thin pastry with sweet spiced nuts in between them, is drenched in orange-scented syrup after it is baked. Known as the "sweet of a thousand layers" and sold in pastry shops, it is eaten by the city islanders mostly after the long afternoon nap to zap them up with energy. The thin dough, which takes skilled hands and hours to prepare, is now available fresh and frozen in Greek and Middle Eastern stores in America in 1-pound packages with 16 to 20 very thin sheets of dough in a package; the frozen variety has to be defrosted in the refrigerator in its own wrapping. Great care should be taken not to expose *phíllo* to the air for long because it dries quickly and crumbles; a damp kitchen towel covering it works well to keep it at the right consistency (page 273). The walnuts used for the filling can be crushed in a mortar and pestle or with a rolling pin, some into small pieces and some powdered. (*Makes 24 to 30 pieces when cut.*)

1 pound unsalted butter
1 pound phíllo

SYRUP
2 cups sugar
1¼ cups water
Juice of ½ lemon
Peel of 1 orange
Peel of 1 lemon

2 cinnamon sticks

FILLING
1¼ pounds crushed walnuts
⅔ cup sugar
1 tablespoon plus 1 teaspoon
  cinnamon
1 teaspoon nutmeg

Clarify the butter (page 269). Combine the syrup ingredients in a saucepan, bring them to a boil, reduce the heat and simmer the syrup gently for 5 minutes. Then set it aside to cool until the *baklavás* is baked. Combine the walnuts, sugar, cinnamon and nutmeg in a bowl, then set that mixture aside.

Preheat the oven to 350°. To assemble *baklavás*, cut the layers of *phíllo* dough with a sharp knife to make them fit a 9″ x 12″ x 2″ baking pan, and set aside 4 of the layers to be used for the very top; use the scraps to make other layers to alternate with the whole ones. Keep covered with a damp dish towel any *phíllo* not in use so that it will not dry out. Brush the baking pan with clarified butter and place it in 4 to 5 layers of *phíllo*, 1 layer at a time, buttering each layer once it is put in the bottom of the pan.

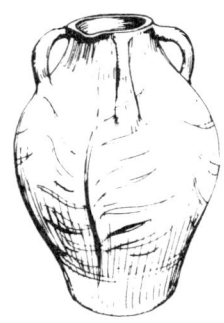

Sprinkle approximately ⅓ cup of filling evenly over these layers and add another 2 to 3 layers of *phíllo*, buttering each and sprinkling with more nut filling. Repeat the process with the remaining layers of *phíllo*, alternating ⅓ cup of filling and buttering each layer, and end with the 4 layers set aside for the top, also buttering each of the layers and the top very generously. Now, using the tip of a very sharp knife, cut through the top 4 layers in diamond-shape pattern as a guide for cutting the *baklavás* after they are baked. Bake the *baklavás* for 45 minutes or until the top is golden, remove the pan from the oven, let it cool slightly, and pour the cool syrup evenly over the top. Cut through all the layers, following the diamond pattern, and let the *baklavás* stand to absorb the syrup overnight before serving them. Sprinkle the tops of the *baklavás* with rosewater if you wish before serving them.

ST. BASIL'S CAKE

Vasilópitta

This New Year's cake has a plain but delicious taste from the sweet spices in it. Instead of inserting a gold coin in the dough before it is baked, you can use a silver one wrapped in foil so that it will not tarnish. (*Serves 15 to 20.*)

3 cups sifted flour
3 teaspoons baking powder
½ pound unsalted butter
2 cups sugar
5 medium-size eggs
1 cup orange juice

1 tablespoon grated fresh
  orange peel
1 teaspoon nutmeg
Blanched almonds (*page
  269*)

Preheat the oven to 350°. Combine the flour and the baking powder and set aside. Cream the butter thoroughly with the sugar in a bowl, and beat the eggs in well 1 at a time, with an electric mixer or by hand. With a wooden spoon stir 1 cup of the flour mixture into the beaten egg and butter mixture, then pour in ⅓ of the orange juice and stir to blend well. Repeat the process with the flour and orange juice until they are all mixed in and the batter is smooth. Mix the orange peel and nutmeg into the batter, drop in the coin, and pour the batter into a well-buttered 9" x 12" x 2" pan. Write the New Year's date on top of the cake with blanched almonds and bake it for 45 minutes to 1 hour until it is golden brown. Let it cool and cut it in squares or diamond shapes.

Fresh Fruits and Spoon Sweets

Golden pyramids of orange and yellow citrus fruits — tangerines, lemons and oranges — fill the marketplaces in winter. As children, my friends and I always looked forward to the citrus season, and when the fruits began turning colors, we climbed the tangerine and orange trees, stretching our arms among the branches to reach the ripest of the barely golden fruits. The oranges we loved the best, and we would first bruise them by rubbing them whole on a hard surface, then we would puncture them with a long, thin wire or stick and suck the juice out, ignoring the still-sour taste that set our teeth on edge. When the oranges are ripe and sweet, the orange flesh is eaten fresh in slices or wedges, and the peel is cooked in small curls and candied in sugar syrup.

SLICED FRESH ORANGES IN SYRUP

Portokália Syropáta

A rather fancy way for an orange to be eaten is in slices like shiny flowers, bathed in a syrup flavored with its peel. They are often served as a dessert with pastries because the tartness of the orange cuts the oversweetness of the pastries; but served alone, they are a delightful finish to a Greek meal. (*Serves 6.*)

4 fresh seedless oranges   *1½ cups water for the syrup*
1 cup sugar

Peel very thinly the outer part of the skins off the oranges, being careful not to get too much white with them, and set the oranges aside. Cut the peeled skins into fine slivers, put them into a saucepan with water to cover them, boil them 1 minute, and drain them. Bring the sugar and the water to a boil and add the slivers, then reduce the heat to moderate and cook the syrup until it coats the spoon, approximately 15 minutes. Set it aside to cool.

Remove the white skin from the peeled oranges and cut the flesh crosswise into slices ¼ to ½ inch thick. Arrange the slices in layers in a shallow dish, pour the cool syrup over them, then chill them and they are ready to serve.

ORANGE-PEEL SPOON SWEET

Portokálli Glykó

Pieces of orange peel are rolled and strung with a needle and thread like garlands, then the ends of the threads are tied together. The peels are cooked in sugar syrup and served one piece at a time on little glass plates to visitors — or to sweeten oneself.

Most of the time *nerántzi* peels are used instead of orange peels in the islands. *Nerantziá* is a tree of the same family with fruits of the same size as the orange tree, but with inedible bitter flesh and stronger aroma. They are not available in most parts of this country.

6 medium-size seedless   *2 cups water for the syrup*
   oranges   *Juice of ½ lemon*
2½ cups sugar

Lightly grate the surface of the oranges to remove the shine, being careful not to grate too deeply. Cut the rind skin-deep into 6 vertical sections and peel them off the orange; then with a knife remove the excess white covering from each section. Tightly roll the sections of peel from end to end and with a needle and heavy thread string the rolls one at a time until you have strung 18 rolls. Then tie the ends of the thread together to make a garland. Repeat the process for a second garland, place them in a pan, cover them with cold water, boil for 1 minute and drain them. Repeat the procedure; it is done to take the bitterness out of the peel.

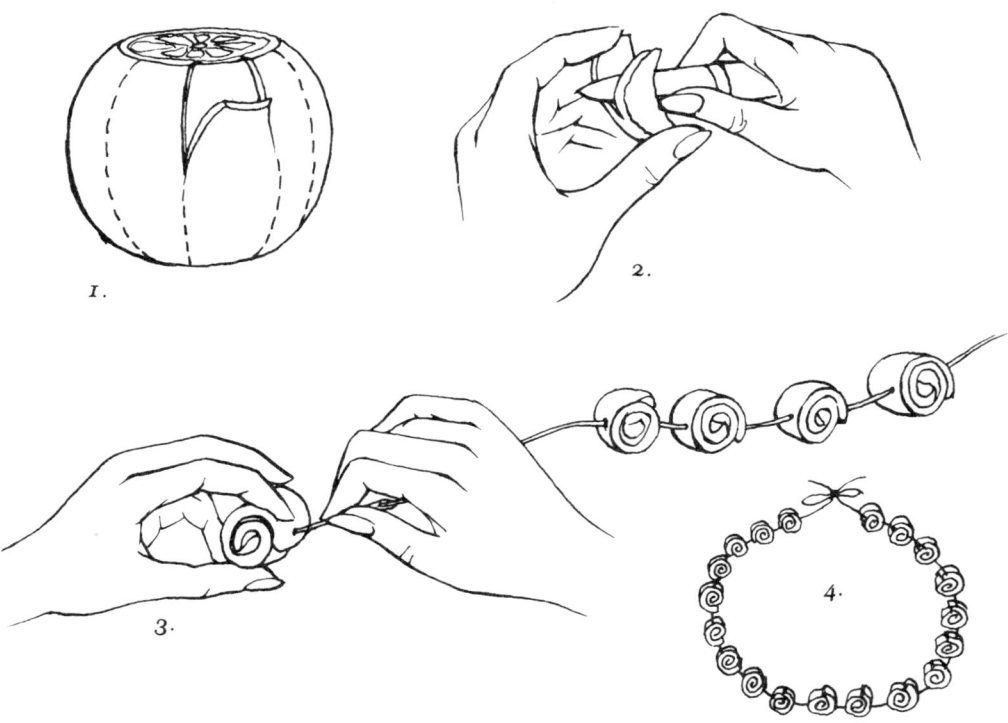

Now put the garlands in a large pot with 3 quarts of fresh cold water, bring the water to a boil over moderate heat, and cook the peels until they are tender, about 30 to 40 minutes. Drain them again, still on the threads, and pat them dry.

Put the water, sugar and lemon juice in a large pot and bring them to a boil, then add the garlands and simmer them uncovered over moderate-low heat for 45 minutes to an hour until the syrup is thick and the peels are glazed. Remove the pan from the heat, let cool, remove the strings. Store the peels in their syrup in a sterilized jar. They need no refrigeration.

Confections

Winter was the time when my mother used to make our favorite confection in her special deep, black frying pan over the wood fire, while my brothers and I watched the bubbling mixture with delight. *Halvah*, which my brothers loved, is the sweet made from cream of semolina or wheat or rice flour with honey mixed in while it is cooking, and it has the consistency of fudge after it is spread out and cooled. But *melekoúni*, made with sesame seeds and honey, is the sweet I remember most of all, a sweet still passed out from house to house in the villages as a wedding invitation, a lovely custom left over from pre-Christian days.

HOMEMADE HALVAH

Halouvás Spitísios

The color and consistency of *halouvás* depends on the ingredients used. Made with different kinds of flours or grains, shortenings and sometimes dried fruits and nuts, this homemade halvah is totally different from that sold in markets, which has ground sesame seeds as the basic ingredient. (*Makes a plateful.*)

SYRUP	HALVAH BASE
1 cup sugar	1/4 pound unsalted butter
1 1/2 cups water	3/4 cup rice flour
1 teaspoon grated lemon	1/2 teaspoon nutmeg

First make the syrup. Combine the ingredients in a saucepan, boil them for 1 minute, and set the syrup aside.

Melt the butter over moderate heat in a saucepan, add the rice flour and nutmeg and mix them vigorously for 2 minutes until the mixture turns a slightly golden color, then remove the saucepan from the heat. Mixing slowly but continuously, add the syrup to the pan, then cook the mixture for 2 minutes more, stirring constantly until it pulls away from the sides of the pan and toward the middle. Pour it into a small 4" x 8" x 2" pan slightly buttered, and with the back of a spoon spread and smooth the mixture. Cut it in squares and serve it hot or cold.

SESAME AND HONEY CANDY

Melekoúni

Roasted sesame seeds and honey saved with the other winter supplies from the fall harvest are prepared and cut into diamond shapes for another kind of a sweet that is still made in homes and also sold in shops as candy bars. When you are roasting the sesame seeds and cooking the honey, you must watch them constantly so they do not burn, and when you pour the mixture out of the pan you must be careful not to let it come in contact with your hands. (*Makes several bars.*)

1 1/2 cups sesame seeds	1 cup Greek or any thick honey

Preheat the oven to 350°. Spread the sesame seeds in a medium-size shallow pan and roast them in the oven for approximately 5 minutes, stirring them at least twice. Put the honey in the saucepan and boil it over moderate heat until it foams; then remove it from the heat and add the sesame seeds. Cook it for 2 to

3 minutes longer, stirring constantly. Lightly oil a marble or Formica surface; pour the hot sesame seed–honey mixture on it, and flatten the mixture with a damp spatula. When the mixture cools slightly, wet your hands with cold water and smooth it. If you are making a very large quantity, roll out the mixture evenly with a rolling pin that has been dampened with water, simultaneously straightening the edges to make an oblong shape ½ inch thick before the *melekoúni* completely cools. Wet the edge of a large knife and cut it in 2″ x 3″ diamond-shaped pieces. When the *melekoúni* is cold, remove it to a plate and store it in a cool, dry place.

Teas

Besides the imported tea that Greeks have adopted as one of their hot breakfast drinks, there are teas made from the aromatic bushes and herbs that grow wild in the mountains. Sage, called *alesfakiá* by the islanders and *faskomiliá* by the rest of the Greeks, is what the villagers make into tea to drink on winter mornings. During my visits to the village, my aunt used to make my favorite tea for me with boiling hot water in a cup and a spray of dry sage dipped in it, which I moved around in the clear water until it became almost a chartreuse color. The sweet marjoram, called *sápsihos*, and mint, *diósmos*, are other herbs made into tea the same way for people with colds; and the beautiful camomile, *hamómilo*, whose yellow and white little daisylike flowers are used for a delicate tea, is always given as a first drink to the newly born baby.

SAGE AND OTHER HERB TEAS

Alesfakiá ke álla Tsáia

Sage, sweet marjoram and mint are picked in small branches in late summer, tied to dry in bunches, and hung with the other herbs in the food storage room for winter use. Camomile is put in cheesecloth bags, also to hang until it is thoroughly dry. (*Serves 4.*)

3 tablespoons sage, marjoram,   5 cups boiling water
*   or mint*

Place the herb in a warmed earthenware teapot (not metal; it changes flavors) and pour the boiling water over it while stirring. Let the tea steep for 5 to 7 minutes, or longer if you want stronger tea. Strain the tea and serve it in regular tea cups with or without sugar.

SPICED TEA

Tsái Mirotháto

Sometimes a cup of tea is the only breakfast a Greek islander has until the ten o'clock food break called *kolatsión*. This tea is spiced with clove and cinnamon and bits of dry orange peel before it is brewed. (*Makes 60 cups of tea.*)

¼ pound orange pekoe or   7 crushed cloves
*   English breakfast tea   2 tablespoons dried orange*
1 tablespoon crushed   peel (page 272) cut in
*   cinnamon sticks   small bits*

Mix together the tea, cinnamon, cloves, and orange peel and store the mixture in a tightly covered tin.

When you are making tea in small amounts, use ½ to 1 teaspoon of the tea mixture per cup of boiling water, according to the strength desired. Place the tea in a warmed earthenware teapot, pour the boiling water over it, and let it steep for 2 to 3 minutes. If the tea is too strong, strain it and dilute it with boiling water. Serve it with or without sugar.

ALL SEASONS

All Seasons

There are foods very basic to Greek cooking that don't belong to any one of the four seasons. Some of these foods are used for main dishes, others as part of the meal, but all of them are used throughout the year. So I thought I would gather all such recipes in one "all seasons" section. Here are the recipes for different kinds of bread used by Greeks at all times of the year in village and city alike — such as the round flat bread, *pítta*, used by peasants for centuries and now also used in the cities, usually eaten stuffed with bits of broiled meat or salad, and sold in small eating places or by food carts on street corners for snacks but also used at home; large brown loaves of whole-wheat bread, *psomí sitarénio*, which village women still bake in the outdoor ovens; and the ordinary city bread, *psomí tis hóras*, with loaves long and crusty baked fresh every day, this bread is never absent from the table.

Greeks adore pastas and rices — especially the favorites, *makarounátha* and *piláfi* — plain or warm with sauces. Included here also are the cold sauces, the ones most frequently used with poached and fried fish, and the dressings that are used over cooked vegetables and salads. Stocks, the basis of delicate chicken-egg-lemon soup and island fish soup, are present in this chapter, together with wine marinades to tenderize meats and give them good flavor. Also, a recipe for batter to dip anything in before frying to become golden and crisp; and of course coffee, which is used throughout the day in any season, at breakfast, in between meals and at the end of eating — the best way to end a Greek meal.

Breads

The freshly baked breads displayed in the windows of city bakeries are irresistible to passersby, and men going home for lunch and siesta usually stop and buy a still-hot crusty loaf to accompany their midday meal. But the bread aromas I remember most are those of the wheat and barley bread baking, which fill the air of small villages on Saturday, baking day.

Bread-making is a weekly village ritual. Flour for bread is ground the previous day in the village windmill, a circular stone structure that looks more like a tower and is large enough to hold the huge wooden works, the miller and one customer at a time. On the outside, the enormous cloth-covered wooden wings of the mill, practically reaching the ground, face the north side, where the summer winds blow most often and make them go around, turning the millstones inside. There the peasant women take their grain in sacks loaded on donkeys, and then stay until the miller grinds it into flour, to make sure they get their own back. For the housewife bread-making begins the night before, with the preparation of the starter, *prozími*, which is made in an earthenware bowl out of some flour and the leavening — a piece of dough saved from the previous batch — then let rise overnight to be used in making the new bread. Every Saturday the flour is sifted into a large boat-shaped wooden basin, *skáfi*, through a mesh made of horsehair stretched over one side of a wooden colander, called *kóskino*, to remove the excess bran. The flour in the *skáfi* is kneaded together with the starter to make dough, then the dough is divided and rolled on a low circular wooden table, *syní*, to make large round loaves of bread. Some small doughnut-shaped breads are also made, one for each child in the family.

Preparing the outdoor beehive oven is also a long process, which involves the man of the house having to find enough dry shrubs and branches on the mountains to load a donkey full — the amount needed to heat the oven and bake the breads. First

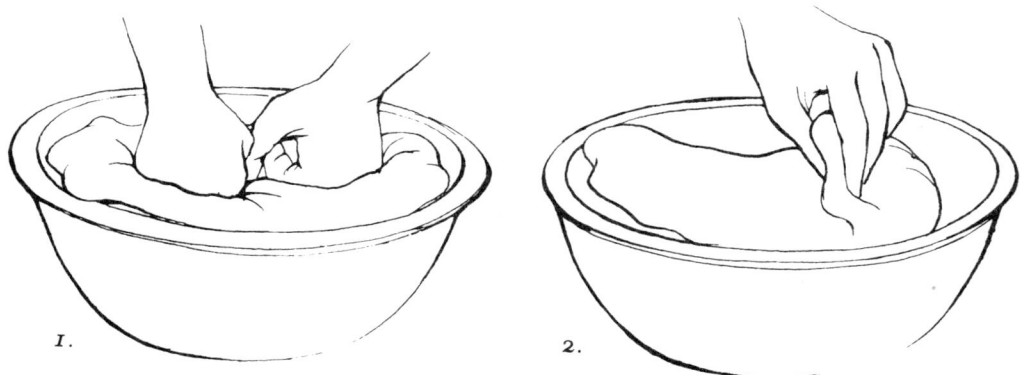

How to knead bread

the floor of the oven is carefully swept clean of coals and ashes with wet sage sprigs. When the sleeping breads rise they are transferred to the all-purpose *syní*, then with a long wooden paddle one by one they are set on the hot oven floor to bake. The children's breads are the first to finish baking and are pierced through as soon as they are out of the oven with a small branch of the very aromatic shrub *askinós*, so that the child can hold his hot bread without burning his fingers, and so that the heat of the bread on the leaves will flavor the bread. When large loaves are baked they are cooled slightly then covered with a thick hand-woven cotton cloth and stored in a basket hanging from the ceiling beams to last until the next bread-making day.

For leavening I use the yeast available in America as cake yeast, which dissolves in warm water at 80° to 85°, and as dry granular yeast, which comes in little envelopes and needs water a bit warmer, 110°, to dissolve. Both types of yeast must always be tested to make sure they are active (page 274) I knead dough in the bowl, pressing hard on it alternatively with my two fists, then pulling and folding the edges of the dough from the sides of the bowl toward the middle with my fingers, continuing until the dough feels elastic and smooth and is no longer sticky. But any other type of kneading you may prefer can be used. Letting the dough rise to double its volume — called in recipes "double in bulk" — is essential to making good bread. Different types of bread will take less or longer time to rise depending on the ingredients and the temperature of the room, usually 1 to 2 hours for the first rising and ½ hour for the second. To test the risen bread, press the top with your finger; if a dent is left, it has risen sufficiently and is ready to be punched down and kneaded again or to be baked. A baked loaf should feel light in weight and have a hollow sound when you tap it on the bottom with the second knuckle of your finger.

WHOLE-WHEAT BREAD

Sitarénio Psomí

Because of climate and sun, wheat flour varies a great deal from country to country. I find that American whole-wheat flour lacks the sweetness of that of the Greek islands, so I add brown sugar and olive oil to make the dough richer. This recipe may be cut in half if you wish. (*Makes 4 9" x 5" loaves and 6 8" x 4" loaves.*)

5 yeast cakes or 5 envelopes
    dry granular yeast
6 tablespoons brown sugar
5½ cups hot tap water
5 pounds whole-wheat flour

(20 cups)
4 tablespoons salt
⅔ cup olive oil or melted
    salt butter

Combine the yeast and sugar in a bowl, add to it 1 cup of the hot water and let it stand for 10 minutes to dissolve the yeast and also proof it (page 274).

Put the flour and salt in a large mixing bowl and pour on the oil or butter, mix them, then take handfuls of the flour mixture and rub it between your palms for about 7 to 10 minutes to incorporate the oil into the flour. Make a well in the middle of the flour, pour in the yeast mixture and 4 cups of the hot water, and work the mixture with your hands until it becomes dough and the yeast is mixed in. Knead the dough about 5 minutes, then add the rest of the water to the bottom of the bowl to moisten any crumbs and flour left loose, and add it to the large ball of dough. Continue the kneading for about 5 minutes longer, until the dough is smooth. Cover with a towel and let the dough rise about 1 hour or until it doubles in bulk. Preheat the oven to 350°. Punch the dough down, knead it for 1 minute, and divide and shape it into loaves. Put them in well-buttered bread pans. Cover the dough in the pans with towels and let the loaves rise in a warm, draft-free place until they double their bulk, brush the tops with the water, and bake them for about 40 to 50 minutes until they are brown and crusty. Remove the bread from the pans to racks to cool slightly, then wrap them immediately in a heavy towel to cool completely. Bread keeps well when wrapped in sealed plastic bags, and also freezes successfully.

HOLIDAY BREAD

Tsouréki

Braided and sweet, *tsouréki* is the bread eaten at Easter and Christmas. Made by the housewives in the city, it is kneaded and let rise many times to produce its fine texture, and it crowns Greek tables at breakfast and coffee hour and sometimes at dinner. I make this bread once a week and use the flavoring of mastic, the sap of the mastic bush, sold in Greek stores. This bread can be frozen successfully after it is baked. (*Makes 4 small loaves or 3 medium-size loaves.*)

*2 yeast cakes or 2 envelopes
    dry granular yeast
½ cup warm water
½ pound unsalted butter
    softened at room tem-
    perature
1¼ cups sugar plus 1
    tablespoon
5 large eggs
2 cups warm milk*

| 10 cups all-purpose un-
   bleached flour | Sesame seeds (optional)
½ teaspoon pulverized mastic |

Dissolve the yeast in the warm water with 1 tablespoon of the sugar added and set it aside for 10 minutes to ferment and proof it.

Beat the butter and sugar in a large bowl with an electric mixer until the mixture is light and creamy. Using a wooden spoon, beat in 4 of the eggs 1 at a time to mix well with butter and sugar, and slowly pour in the warm milk, stirring constantly.

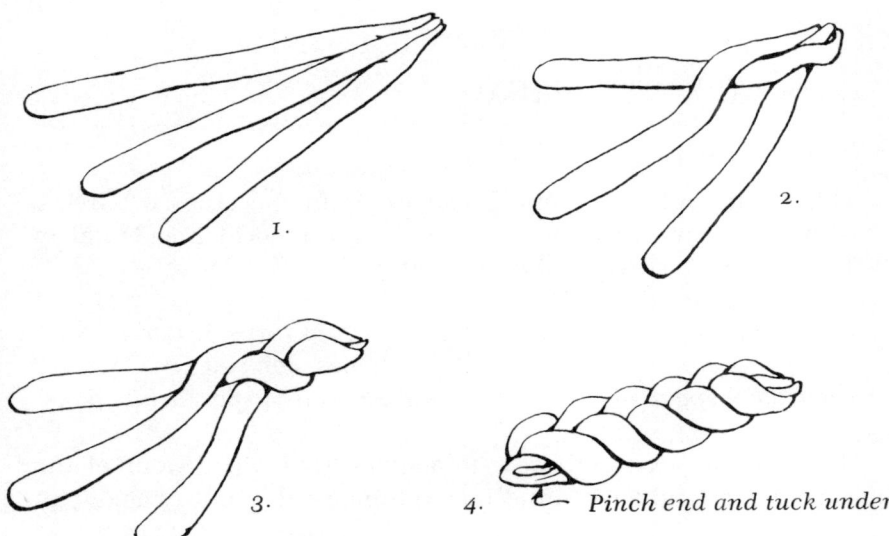

Pinch end and tuck under

Add 1 cup of the flour and stir it to blend with the other ingredients, then add the mastic, then the dissolved yeast and, slowly, the remaining flour, stirring constantly with the wooden spoon until the batter becomes too thick to stir. With both hands dipped in flour to prevent them from sticking, knead the dough, which should be pliable but not stiff, until it is smooth. Cover the dough in the bowl with a towel and let it rise until it doubles in bulk, about 1 hour, then knead it again for 1 minute. Repeat the process once more and divide the dough into 12 orange-size balls for 4 loaves or 9 balls for 3 loaves. Roll each ball on a board into a rope 1½ to 2 inches thick and 15 to 20 inches long, sprinkle each with sesame seeds, and braid three strips together to make a loaf. Press the ends of the loaves tightly, turn them under, and set each of them on a well-buttered baking sheet to rise, covered, in a draft-free place, until they double in bulk. Preheat the oven to 275°. Beat the last egg lightly with a fork until it is well mixed and brush the tops of the braided loaves with it. Bake the loaves for 15 minutes at 275° then lower the heat to 250° and continue to bake until they are light golden. about ½ hour. Remove the cooked loaves from the baking sheets to towels to cool and store them in air-tight bags.

ORDINARY CITY BREAD

Psomí tis Hóras

This is the ordinary white bread made in the cities of Greece with just flour, salt, water and yeast, the kind of bread sold in all bakeries every day. (*Makes 2 loaves.*)

1 cake yeast or 1 envelope	*1½ cups warm water*
dry granular yeast	*1 tablespoon salt*
1 teaspoon sugar	*4 cups all-purpose white flour*

Combine the yeast and sugar in a small bowl with ½ cup of the warm water and let it stand for 10 minutes to proof (page 274)

and ferment it. Dissolve the salt in the remaining warm water. Put the flour in a large mixing bowl, make a well in the middle, pour in the salt water and the yeast mixture and mix it with your hands into dough. You may need slightly more or less water depending on your flour. Knead the dough in the bowl with your fists for 10 to 15 minutes until it is smooth. Cover the dough in the bowl with a clean towel and let it rise in a draft-free place to double in bulk, about 1 to 2 hours. Punch it down and knead it 1 minute, then cover it and let it double in bulk again, about ½ hour.

Preheat the oven to 375° to 400° then punch the dough down for the second time, divide it in half, and roll each half into an oblong, rounded loaf. Set the loaves on a lightly greased baking sheet, cover them, and let them rise to double in bulk again. Then with a sharp razor slash three slits diagonally ⅛ to ¼ inch deep in the top of each loaf, brush them with a little water, and bake them for 40 minutes or until they are golden brown.

ROUND FLAT BREAD

Pítta

This flat bread, *pítta,* was cooked in the village fireplace on an upside-down iron saucer, *víssalon,* heated by wood coals. My village aunt cooked it in an iron skillet on bread-making day with some of the dough made for the large loaves. She flattened the dough with the tips of her fingers, turning it around on a board. When the *pítta* was cooked, she split it and stuffed it, still hot, with cold summer salad for lunch. My mother made *píttas* for us by frying the dough in olive oil in a skillet, then sprinkled them with sugar and sweet spices. (*Makes 6 to 8 medium-size píttas.*)

1 cake yeast or 1 envelope
   dry granular yeast
1 tablespoon sugar
1½ cups warm water

2 teaspoons salt
4 cups white all-purpose flour
1 tablespoon olive oil

Combine the yeast and sugar in a small bowl, add ½ cup of the warm water, and let it stand for 10 minutes to proof (page 274) and ferment it. Dissolve the salt in the remaining warm water. Put the flour in a large mixing bowl, make a well in the middle, and put the dissolved yeast and salt water into it. With your hands blend the yeast, flour and water into dough. You may need a bit more or less water depending on your flour. Then knead the dough in the bowl with your fists for 10 to 15 minutes or until it is smooth. Pour the olive oil over the dough and knead it a few minutes longer until the oil is absorbed. Cover the dough in the bowl with a towel and set it in a draft-free area to rise to double its bulk (1 to 2 hours), then punch it down and knead it for 2 minutes.

Preheat the oven to 350°. Then cut pieces of dough egg-size or larger, depending on the size of the *pítta* desired, shape them into balls with your hands, and roll them out over a lightly floured board or pastry cloth to ¼-inch thickness. Set 2 to 3 *pittas* at a time on a lightly oiled cookie sheet and bake them on the lower rack of the oven 2 to 3 minutes on each side. *Pittas* should be white and soft, but if overcooked become hard. Wrap the baked *pittas* in a clean towel until they are cool, then store them in plastic bags to prevent them from drying out.

Pastas and Rice

There is a name for pasta in every language and there are as many ways to cook it, with a different sauce for every one. The pasta we had when I was growing up was excellent, bought from the two-room shop in the center of town, which had the most fascinating display of different kinds of pasta — ribbons, shells, bows, and stars — in large glass-front drawers in the front part of the store. In the back room, a flour-covered man made pasta, some types forced through a machine and others draped on rods to be cut later into different lengths and let dry. It was this fresh pasta my mother always bought; thin and pliable and needing only minutes to cook, it tasted so much better than the packaged variety I now get in the stores.

The noodles my mother made herself with eggs and flour. She kneaded the dough and rolled it into sheets, then folded them and cut them in narrow strips. She cooked them in a lot of water until they were tender, and while they were still hot she would drench them with melted butter and grated cheese.

Rice is used more frequently than pasta in Greece and is cooked alone as pilaf, or with meats, or stuffed in vegetables and leaves. There are many types of rice but the long- and short-grain are the ones most commonly used, each for certain dishes.

The island villages in the past used cracked wheat, called *pergoúri*, instead of rice, very old and basic and still quite popular now. The housewife prepares it every year by boiling wheat and drying it in the sun, then grinding it between two round flat stones; she turns the top stone by hand. *Pergoúri* makes a delicious pilaf with any meat stock for a base.

LONG THIN PASTA WITH TOMATO-MEAT SAUCE

Makarounátha

(Serves 6.)

Tomato-meat sauce (pages 249–250)	*¼ pound salt butter*
1 pound thin spaghetti	*⅓ cup grated hard cheese,* kephalotíri *or Parmesan*
2 tablespoons salt	

Prepare the tomato-meat sauce and set it aside to simmer until the pasta is cooked.

Bring to a boil 6 quarts of water with 2 tablespoons of salt added, carefully put in the pasta, stirring often to prevent it from sticking together and to the bottom of the pan, and over moderate-high heat, continue to boil it uncovered until it is tender. Drain it in a colander, rinse it with hot water, and transfer it to a large bowl. Melt the butter in a small saucepan over low

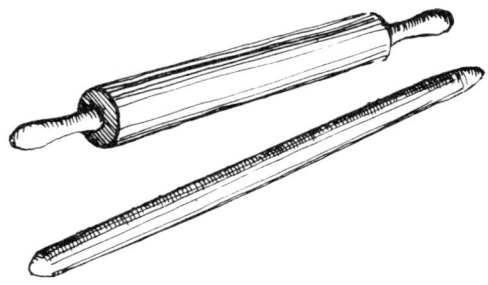

heat, being careful not to burn it, pour it over the pasta, and toss the pasta to coat it. Sprinkle half the grated cheese over the pasta and toss it again, then transfer it to a large platter and pour the hot tomato-meat sauce over it, then sprinkle the rest of the grated cheese over the sauce. Serve with a leafy salad.

HOMEMADE EGG NOODLES

Hilópittes-Mátsi

This recipe explains how to prepare the dough and cut the noodles by hand. (*Serves 4 to 6.*)

2¼ cups (*approximately*) sifted flour plus extra for dusting
3 medium-size eggs plus 2

yolks, lightly beaten with a fork
1 tablespoon olive oil
1 teaspoon salt

Put the flour in a large bowl, make a well in the center of it, and put the eggs, yolks, olive oil and salt into it. With your fingers continually push the flour from the sides of the bowl over the eggs and oil and mix them until they turn into dough. If any dry bits of dough mixture remain in the bottom of the bowl, moisten them with a few drops of water and knead them into the mass of dough, then knead for 5 minutes until it is smooth. The dough will be a bit sticky and elastic.

Divide the dough into 3 parts and place 1 at a time on a flour-dusted board and roll it out, rolling away from you with a rolling pin. Turn the dough around and flour it between rolls to open it into a thin, round sheet. Let each one stand for 15 minutes, then dust it with flour and roll it up like a jelly roll. Cut across the rolls in strips the width you want your noodles to be, then unroll them into noodles and spread them out until you are ready to cook them. Fresh noodles can be cooked immediately or kept for two days wrapped in plastic and refrigerated. They also may be dried in a warm oven then stored in a box.

EGG NOODLES WITH BUTTER AND CHEESE

Hilópittes Tsigharistés

(*Serves 4 to 6.*)

1 tablespoon salt
2 tablespoons olive oil

Homemade egg noodles (*page 239*)

| ⅓ pound salt butter or 1⅓ sticks | ½ pound grated hard cheese, kephalotíri or Parmesan |

Bring 4 quarts of water with the salt and olive oil added to a rapid boil and drop the noodles in. Bring the water to a boil again, reduce the heat to moderate, and cook for 8 to 10 minutes or until they double in size and are tender, stirring occasionally with a wooden spoon. Drain them in a colander, then transfer them to a bowl. Heat the butter over low heat in a small saucepan until the foam subsides, pour it over the cooked noodles, and toss to coat them. Sprinkle the noodles with cheese, toss them again gently, and serve.

How to make noodles

Another variation for serving noodles — noodles made without eggs and used during Lent in the Greek islands — is with a sesame seed and honey topping. But egg noodles can be used for this dish, *hilópittes nistísimes,* which is eaten between meals or at the end of a meal. For 1 serving mix 2 tablespoons crushed sesame seeds with ¼ teaspoon powdered cinnamon. Dribble 1 tablespoon of honey over the hot noodles, sprinkle them with the sesame-cinnamon mixture, and serve.

SAUTÉED RICE PILAF

Rízi Piláfi

There are two basic methods of making pilaf. One is adding the rice to the boiling liquid to simmer, and the other is sautéing the rice in butter before any stock is added. Both methods require exact measurements. Rice used to make pilaf should be long-grain and of good quality so that the grains do not stick together or expand to get soggy. The converted rice available in American markets, which is parboiled while still in the hull then enriched with vitamins, makes pilafs that never fail, although it is not suitable for stuffing or puddings. (*Serves 4.*)

6 tablespoons salt butter
1 cup uncooked long-grain
*   rice*

2 cups chicken stock (page
*   255)*
Salt and pepper to taste

Melt the butter in a 2-quart saucepan over moderate heat until the foam subsides and add the rice, stirring about 2 minutes over the heat to coat the grains evenly with the butter. Add the stock to the rice, season with salt and pepper, and bring the mixture to a boil, stirring constantly. Reduce the heat to low, cover the saucepan, and simmer the rice for 20 to 25 minutes until the stock is absorbed and the rice is tender. Remove the pan from the heat and set a folded towel between the pan and cover for a few minutes to absorb any steam from the rice before serving.

TOMATO-BASE PILAF

Domatopílafo

This pilaf, usually made in summer, is a favorite all over Greece. (*Serves 8.*)

1 cup tomato sauce (pages
*   248–249)*
8 tablespoons salt butter

3 cups beef or chicken stock
*   (pages 255–256)*
Salt and pepper to taste

2 cups uncooked long-grain rice

Combine all the ingredients except the rice in a large saucepan and bring them to a rolling boil over high heat. Add the rice and bring it to a boil again, stirring constantly, then reduce the heat to low, cover the saucepan, and simmer the rice about 25 to 30 minutes until the liquid is absorbed and the rice is tender. Remove the pan from the heat and set a folded towel between the pan and the lid to absorb the steam from the rice for a few minutes before serving.

TWO-TONE PILAF

Thítono Piláfi

Kritharáki, or orzo, a barley-shaped pasta available packaged in American markets, is combined here with rice to make this popular pilaf. (*Serves 4 to 6.*)

8 tablespoons salt butter (¼ pound)	*¾ cup* kritharáki *(orzo)*
	¾ cup rice
6 peeled and finely chopped scallions, some greens included	*3 cups hot chicken or beef stock (pages 255–256)*
	Salt and white pepper to taste

Melt the butter in a heavy saucepan and over moderate-low heat sauté the scallions until they are soft. Add the *kritharáki* (orzo) and cook, constantly stirring until it turns the color of straw, then add the rice and mix it with the orzo and cook for 2 minutes longer. Stir in the hot stock and salt and pepper, raise the heat, and bring the mixture to a boil, then reduce the heat to low, cover, and simmer 30 minutes, stirring occasionally, or until the stock is absorbed and the rice is cooked.

Eggs and Omelets

The modest, inexpensive egg can be prepared on its own, with care to retain its natural flavor, to make the simplest of foods. But when combined with cheese, vegetables and herbs, it makes the elegant *sfongáta* of the islands, which are sometimes served in place of meat or fish. It resembles a semiscrambled, inverted omelet, very delightful to eat. In the city bits of liver or fish are mixed in with the eggs, and then it is called the butcher's and fisherman's *sfongáta*.

Eggs, fried or baked, are common everyday food, but at Easter time the egg is in its glory. Eggs adorn the islander's house in the large *avghoúlas* made of roped dough worked in intricate designs around dozens of them dyed red, a traditional gift from children to their godparents, which they hang on the wall for decoration on Easter Sunday, later to eat.

SCRAMBLED ZUCCHINI SQUASH OMELET

Kolokithákia me Avghá Sfongáto

(*Serves 2.*)

3 tablespoons olive oil
2 cups fresh, unpeeled
   zucchini squash cut in
   ¼-inch cubes
Salt and pepper to taste

1 tablespoon fresh or ½
   teaspoon dry dill weed
4 eggs lightly beaten with a
   fork

Heat the olive oil in a skillet until a haze forms in it and fry the zucchini in it over moderate heat until it is tender, stirring occasionally. Season with salt, pepper and dill weed and stir in the eggs in a circular motion, scrambling them to mix with the squash. Reduce the heat to low and let the omelet cook to set, shaking the pan often. Put a plate larger than the frying pan over the pan, hold it down firmly with one hand, and turn the pan upside down on the plate with the other hand. Gently slide the omelet into the pan again, cooked-side up and cook it for a minute longer. The omelet is turned this way so that it will not fall apart in the process. Invert the omelet onto a plate, using the method described above, and serve.

SCRAMBLED POTATO OMELET

Patátes me Avghá Sfongáto

(*Serves 1.*)

2 tablespoons olive oil
1 *medium-size peeled and*
   diced potato

Salt and pepper to taste
3 eggs lightly beaten with a
   fork

Heat the olive oil until a haze forms in it and fry the potato in it until it is golden. Season with salt and pepper and add the eggs. Reduce the heat to low and scramble the eggs in a circular motion to mix them with the potato. Let the omelet set and cook.

Invert and finish the omelet as described in the recipe for zucchini omelet above and serve it with a green salad.

TOMATO OMELET

Domáta me Avghá Sfongáto

This omelet, more liquid than the others, is not inverted; instead it is cooked slowly until the eggs solidify. (*Serves 1.*)

1 tablespoon olive oil	Pinch oregano
1 cup peeled and diced tomatoes	3 eggs, slightly beaten with a fork
Salt and pepper to taste	

Heat the olive oil in a shallow skillet until it becomes hazy and cook the tomatoes in it uncovered over moderate heat for 10 to 15 minutes or until most of the liquid evaporates from the tomatoes. Season with salt and pepper and add the oregano, then add the eggs and scramble them in a circular motion to mix with the tomatoes. Turn the heat to low and let the omelet cook until the eggs solidify, shaking the pan frequently. Remove the omelet with a spatula to a plate, cooked-side up, and serve.

CODFISH OMELET

Bakaliáros Sfongáto

(*Serves 2.*)

¼ pound dry salt cod	Pepper to taste
1 tablespoon chopped fresh flat-leaf parsley	4 eggs
	3 tablespoons olive oil

Cover the dried cod in cold water and soak it overnight in the refrigerator, changing the water several times, then drain it. Bring 4 cups of fresh water to a boil in a saucepan, remove the pan from the heat, add the soaked cod and let it stand for 5 minutes, remove it from its broth, pat it dry with a towel, and grind it in a food chopper or puree it in a blender, then transfer it to a bowl. Add the parsley and pepper to the cod and stir, then add one egg at a time, mixing each one well with the cod mixture. Heat the olive oil in a skillet until a haze forms in it,

How to invert an omelet

and over moderate heat cook the cod mixture until it sets at the edges. Lower the heat and continue to cook the omelet until it solidifies, shaking the pan often. Invert and finish the omelet as described in the recipe for zucchini omelet above.

EGGS FRIED IN OLIVE OIL

Avghá Tiganitá

(Serves 1.)

2 tablespoons olive oil
2 eggs

Heat the olive oil in a skillet until it becomes hazy and fry the eggs over moderate heat until the white solidifies. Add 1 teaspoon water and quickly cover the skillet tight for a minute or two so that the steam can cook the clear part on top of the yolk. Remove the eggs with a spatula to a dish and serve.

EASTER EGGS

Avghá tis Lambrís

These eggs may be used with the sweet *tsouréki* dough (pages 232–233) before it is cooked to make Easter *avghoúles*. Place the dyed eggs in the braided dough of *tsouréki* before it is set aside to rise, and bake according to the time specified in that recipe.

Medium-size white eggs   *Olive oil*
Commercial egg dye

Place the eggs in a metal egg or deep-fry basket and set them in a pot in enough hot water to cover them, then bring the water to a boil and cook the eggs over moderate heat for 10 to 12 minutes. Immediately remove the basket from the hot water and plunge the eggs into cold water for a few minutes, then drain them, dry them, and proceed with the dyeing according to the instructions of the brand of dye you are using. When the eggs reach the intensity of color you want, drain and dry them, wipe them with a lightly oiled cloth to shine them, then wipe them again with a dry cloth to remove the excess oil.

Sauces and Dressings

There are only a few leading sauces of the Greek islands cuisine but they are used to crown many of the dishes. Tomato, egg-lemon and white are known as the warm sauces, and *mayonéza* and garlic the cold. The dressings, combinations of olive oil and vinegar or lemon, with their piquant flavor, add a finishing touch to leafy raw and cooked vegetable salads.

TOMATO SAUCE

Domatósaltsa

Appearing daily in Greek family meals, tomato sauce flavors meats and vegetables and gives rich color to noodles, pasta and grains. In summer it is made from fresh tomatoes and herbs combined sometimes with thick tomato paste left from the winter supply, which is made from the preserved tomatoes that every housewife prepares from summer's abundance. (*Makes 2 cups.*)

¼ *cup olive oil*
½ *cup finely chopped onion*
3 *cups peeled and diced fresh*
   or 3 cups canned tomatoes

3 *tablespoons tomato paste*
3 *tablespoons finely chopped*
   fresh or 1 tablespoon dried
   parsley

2 tablespoons fresh chopped   *oregano*
   or ½ teaspoon dried   *Salt and pepper to taste*

Heat the olive oil in a saucepan and cook the onion in it over moderate heat until it is soft. Stir in the rest of the ingredients,

partially cover the pan, and simmer the mixture over low heat for 40 to 50 minutes or until it thickens, stirring occasionally. Press the sauce through a sieve to strain it and store it in covered jars in the refrigerator.

TOMATO-MEAT SAUCE

Kimás Sáltsa

This sauce is delicious over rice, noodles, or other pasta. (*Serves 4 to 6.*)

¼ cup olive oil
½ cup finely chopped onion
1 pound ground meat
1½ cups tomato sauce (pages 248–249)
2 tablespoons chopped fresh

flat-leaf parsley
2 tablespoons tomato paste diluted in ½ cup water
2 slit garlic cloves
1 bay leaf
Salt and pepper to taste

Heat the olive oil in a large saucepan until it becomes hazy and cook the onion in it over moderate heat until it is soft. Add the ground meat to the pan and cook, stirring constantly, until the red color disappears and the meat crumbles. Add the remaining ingredients, bring the mixture to a boil, reduce the heat to low, and simmer it partially covered for 45 to 60 minutes, stirring occasionally with a wooden spoon and adding a little water from time to time if it is needed. The finished sauce should be thick. Remove the bay leaf and garlic before serving.

WHITE SAUCE

Áspri Sáltsa

The quantity can be cut down to a half or a third, as your main recipe requires. (*Makes 3 cups.*)

6 tablespoons butter	*3 cups hot milk*
5 tablespoons all-purpose flour	*Salt and white pepper to taste*

Melt the butter in a saucepan over low heat and gradually stir in the flour. When the mixture starts to foam, gradually pour the milk in, stirring constantly and rapidly until it thickens and is smooth. Season the sauce with salt and pepper, simmer it for 3 minutes longer, then remove it from the heat and cover it tightly until you are ready to use it.

EGG-LEMON SAUCE

Sáltsa Avgholémono

There are several ways of making this tangy sauce, which is used in soups or for thickening or over vegetable dishes. I mention here three types of sauces of different consistency to be used for specific dishes. Sauce I, very light and fluffy, is the one islanders use in chicken and fish soups. Sauce II is the one best for thickening pork and other meat dishes, also braised vegetables. Sauce III has more body than I and II and is best used over stuffed vegetables, stuffed cabbage and grape leaves.

SAUCE I

3 eggs, separated
1 tablespoon water
1/3 cup fresh lemon juice

1 cup warm chicken stock
from the soup

Combine the egg whites and water in a bowl and beat them with a fork, whisk, or electric beater until soft peaks form. Add the egg yolks to the whites one at a time, beating constantly until they are well blended. Still beating, but now with a fork, gradually add the lemon juice to the egg foam. In the same way add the stock; this is to avoid shocking the eggs with the heat of the stock and curdling the sauce. Remove the soup pot from the heat and let it stand uncovered a few minutes, then stir the sauce into your soup and serve immediately.

SAUCE II

3 eggs
1 tablespoon water

3 tablespoons lemon juice

Combine the eggs and water in a bowl and beat them with a fork until they are well mixed and fluffy. Gradually add the lemon juice, still beating. Pour the sauce over the meat casserole, gently stirring it in, and heat the casserole until the sauce thickens but does not boil.

SAUCE III

3 eggs
1 tablespoon cornstarch
4 tablespoons fresh lemon

juice
1 cup hot chicken stock (page 255)

Beat the eggs in a bowl with a fork, whisk, or electric beater until they are fluffy. Add the cornstarch and gradually the lemon juice, then gradually the hot stock, stirring gently with a spoon. Transfer the sauce to a saucepan and cook it over low heat stirring constantly, until it thickens. Pour it over a meat or vegetable casserole and serve.

GARLIC SAUCE

Skorthaliá

This is my grandmother's *skorthaliá*, made smooth, white and thin with garlic and moist, crustless bread pounded in a special wooden mortar and pestle and combined with oil and vinegar. She poured it over summer and winter dishes of fried vegetables and fish. Some people substitute boiled potatoes for the bread and make a thick, spreadable sauce served in separate small dishes. Bread *skorthaliá* keeps for a week in sealed jars in the refrigerator. (*Makes approximately 1 cup.*)

7 to 10 slices white bread	*½ teaspoon salt*
½ cup hot water	*⅓ cup white wine vinegar*
3 garlic cloves	*½ cup olive oil*

Remove the crust from the bread and break the white part into small pieces, moisten them with some cold tap water, and set them aside in a bowl. Mash the garlic cloves with the salt in a wooden mortar, a wooden bowl or a blender, and slowly stir in half of the hot water, the vinegar and the bread until they are all well mixed. Gradually add the olive oil, while still mixing, until the sauce is smooth. Mix in the rest of the hot water, adding a little more if it is needed to make the sauce thin, and pour it over fried vegetables or fish.

EGG-GARLIC SAUCE

Aliátha

This sauce is very easy to make in a blender and is delicious with hot or cold poached fish. (*Makes 1 cup.*)

1 egg	*¾ cup olive oil*
¼ teaspoon salt	*1 tablespoon fresh lemon*
3 cut up garlic cloves	*juice*

Put the egg, salt and garlic in a blender and blend at low speed until they are well mixed and frothy. Add gradually, a few drops at a time, the olive oil, then the lemon juice, keeping the blender at low speed until the sauce is thick. Remove the sauce to a bowl, and serve it with any fish.

HERB MAYONNAISE

Mayonéza me Vótana

This blender sauce is much lighter than one made by hand and lasts longer in the refrigerator before it starts to separate. A whole egg is used instead of just yolks and it takes less than a minute to prepare. (*Makes approximately 1⅓ cups.*)

1 egg
½ teaspoon prepared or ¼ teaspoon dry mustard
⅓ teaspoon salt
1½ to 2 tablespoons lemon
juice
⅓ cup firmly packed fresh tarragon or thyme or both
1 cup olive oil

Combine all the ingredients except half the olive oil in the blender, cover it, and blend them at medium speed for 10 seconds or until the mixture is smooth. Uncover the blender without stopping it, add the remaining oil very slowly in a very thin thread. Blend the sauce a few more seconds at high speed until it thickens and becomes smooth. Store the sauce in a covered jar in the refrigerator and use it as directed in recipes.

OLIVE OIL–VINEGAR DRESSING

Lathóxitho

This dressing should stand at room temperature for 1 hour before using it so that the garlic can release its flavor. You can double the ingredients below to make a larger quantity of dressing, which can be stored at least a week in a covered jar or bottle in the refrigerator. (*Makes ⅔ cup.*)

2 tablespoons red wine
   vinegar
½ cup olive oil
1 large slit garlic clove

¼ teaspoon fresh ground
   pepper
½ teaspoon salt

Combine all the ingredients in a bowl and beat them vigorously with a fork or whisk until they are well mixed. Pour over salads and vegetables.

LEMON-OIL DRESSING

Lemonólatho

This dressing is used on salads, boiled greens, or vegetables. It should stand at least 1 hour at room temperature before being used. (*Makes ⅔ cup.*)

½ cup olive oil
3 tablespoons fresh lemon
   juice

1 split garlic clove
¼ teaspoon white pepper

Combine all the ingredients in a bowl and beat them vigorously with a fork or whisk until they are well mixed. Let the dressing stay at room temperature if it is to be used right away. If not, store it in a glass jar in the refrigerator. It will last for a week.

Stocks, Marinades and Batter

CHICKEN STOCK

Zomós Órnithas

The vegetables are added to give flavor and color to the stock and are later discarded. Stock can be frozen in plastic containers to last for months. (*Makes 8 to 10 cups.*)

1 4-pound fowl or 3½ pounds
   chicken parts (backs,
   necks, giblets)
1 unpeeled and quartered
   onion
2 washed and quartered
   carrots

2 washed and quartered
   celery stalks
5 sprigs flat-leaf parsley
1 teaspoon salt
1 teaspoon pepper
4 quarts water

Combine all the ingredients in a large pot, bring the water to a boil, and skim off the froth that has collected on top. Reduce the heat to low, cover the pot, leaving a small opening for the steam to escape, and simmer for 2 to 3 hours. Remove the fat from the top of the stock, discard the chicken bones and the vegetables, and strain the rest through a fine sieve. Correct the seasoning.

BEEF STOCK

Zomós Vothinós

(*Makes 8 cups.*)

4 to 5 pounds beef bones or
   beef and veal bones, and 1
   pound raw beef trimmings
1 large peeled and sliced
   onion

2 stalks cut-up celery
5 sprigs flat-leaf parsley
1 tablespoon salt
10 peppercorns
4 quarts water

Place all ingredients in a stock pot or large pan, add the water, and bring them to a boil over moderate heat. Remove the froth from the top as it accumulates and reduce the heat to simmer, with the pot half covered, for 3½ hours. At the end of the cooking, there should be 2 quarts of liquid left. Remove and discard the bones and the vegetables and strain the stock through a clean cheesecloth. Pour the stock in jars when cool, and before storing in the refrigerator, remove the fat that has collected on top. The stock will keep 5 days in the refrigerator, or may be frozen in plastic-covered containers and stored in the freezer.

FISH STOCK

Zomós Psarioú

(*Makes 3 cups.*)

1 sliced onion
1 sliced carrot
3 sprigs flat-leaf parsley
1 bay leaf
1 sliced celery stalk

1 cup dry white wine
5 cups cold water
1½ pounds fish bones, heads
   and trimmings
Salt and pepper to taste

Combine all the ingredients except the fish, salt and pepper, in a large saucepan. Bring the water to a boil over high heat and add the fish. Bring the liquid to a rolling boil again and simmer uncovered for 25 to 30 minutes. Do not cook longer or the stock will take on a strong, very undesirable fishy flavor. Remove the pan from the heat, and strain the contents through a sieve, then return the stock to the saucepan and boil it to reduce it to about 3 cups, depending on the strength desired. Season the stock to your taste. Use the stock immediately in recipes that call for it or cool then store in a plastic container in the freezer.

COLD WINE MARINADE FOR MEATS

Marináta ghiá Kréata

Always use an earthenware or a glass bowl or pot and a wooden spoon for preparing marinades and for marinating meats. Red wine should be used for game meat, deer, beef and lamb, and white wine for rabbit. (*Makes approximately 4½ to 5 cups.*)

2 cups dry red or white wine
½ cup red or white wine vinegar
⅓ cup olive oil
1 sliced onion
2 sliced carrots
2 chopped celery stalks

2 bay leaves
5 sprigs flat-leaf parsley
½ teaspoon dried rosemary or sage
½ teaspoon salt
¼ teaspoon ground pepper

Put all the ingredients in an earthenware or glass bowl and mix them well. Place the meat in the marinade so that the liquid covers it; cover the bowl with wax paper or plastic wrap, and refrigerate it according to the recipe. Sometimes part of the marinade is used in cooking with the meat. The strained liquid from the marinade will keep for a few days in a glass jar in the refrigerator to be used again.

COLD MARINADE FOR POULTRY AND BIRDS

Marináta ghiá Órnithes ke Pouliá

(*Makes approximately 1⅔ cups.*)

⅓ cup olive oil

⅓ cup fresh lemon juice

1 cup dry white wine

1 3" x 1" strip lemon peel

1 minced garlic clove

5 to 8 peppercorns

2 tablespoons bruised fresh or
1 teaspoon dried thyme

5 chopped scallions

½ teaspoon salt

Combine all the ingredients in an earthenware bowl, beat them vigorously with a fork, and place the chicken or birds in it. Cover the bowl with wax paper or plastic wrap and refrigerate according to the recipe.

FLOUR BATTER

Kourkoúti-Salangoúta

Vegetables, fish and meat become golden crisp fritters when they are dipped in this batter before being fried. Let the batter stand, covered, at room temperature for ½ hour before using it. (*Makes 1½ to 2 cups.*)

1 cup flour

¾ cup warm water

1 tablespoon olive oil

1 teaspoon salt

Dash of pepper

1 egg beaten light and creamy
with a fork

Put the flour in a bowl and make a well in the center of it. Stir in the water a little at a time until the mixture is smooth and like pancake batter. Mix in the olive oil, salt and pepper and fold in the beaten egg. Use as directed in recipes.

Coffee

I recall the roasting of coffee over a charcoal fire in a particular clay pot used only for that, and the beans turning from green to black, scattering an aroma so familiar around the neighborhood

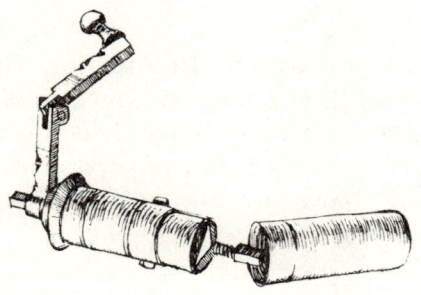

on Friday afternoons. This weekly chore, so faithfully executed by the older women of the family, was the beginning of the centuries-old coffee ceremony. Next, the black beans were set in a wooden bowl to cool and then ground in a tall, cylindrical shiny brass hand mill into powder and brewed with or without sugar in boiling water in different sizes of coffeepots, called *bríki*, according to the number of people to be served. The coffeepot has a wide bottom narrowing to the neck and then widening again on the open rim, and a long handle designed for holding it without burning the hands while the coffee is cooking. The shape of the top allows the coffee to foam on top and make *kaimáki*, which is distributed equally in the small cups before the coffee is poured. Coffee is brewed to the preference of the person who is to drink it, in the choices of *skéttos* (straight without sugar), *métrios* (medium sweetness), *glikós* (sweet), and *varíglikos* (very sweet). Coffee-drinking in Greece is an activity that takes place throughout the day, during business or rest hours with men and during socializing time with women. Part of the ceremony of coffee-drinking among women is that when the coffee is drunk, each cup is turned over for the sediment left in the bottom to drain in the saucer, leaving a pattern that is interpreted by a

woman future-teller. In America, Greek coffee is sold by the pound in little stores in Greek and Middle Eastern neighbor-hoods and stores that sell only coffee and in sealed 1-pound cans on the foreign food shelf of supermarkets.

Bríkia, pots, are also sold in the same Middle Eastern and Greek stores.

COFFEE FOR TWO

Thío Kaféthes

⅔ cup cold water   4 level teaspoons Greek coffee
3 level teaspoons sugar

Bring the water to a boil in the *bríki,* add the sugar, and bring it to a boil again. Remove the pot from the heat, stir in the coffee, return it to the heat immediately, and bring it to a boil again, always holding the handle with one hand and a spoon in the other. Watch it carefully! When it foams, lift the pot up from the heat and stir the foam with the spoon so it will settle; repeat the procedure, not allowing the coffee to spill over. When it rises for the third time, it is ready to serve. Spoon some of the froth into each cup, pour the coffee over it, and serve it immediately.

Wine

To reach the vineyards that grow on the steep, terraced slopes of the mountain sections of the islands, one ascends the narrow, snaking, uphill road, where the sweet smell of growing sage fills the air in the summer afternoons. The grapes, hanging from the vines in dense clusters, look deep purple against the setting sun which, like a giant gold piece, sets behind the mountains of the neighboring islands across the sea. There are other vineyards, with white grapes, growing on the flatlands near the sandy beaches. Day after day, the heavy, early spring rains water these vines and the hot summer sun drenches them, and they yield sweet and juicy grapes, which make the sweet and dry wines of Greece; the same wines ancient Greeks, from Homer to Plato, wrote about. The ancient Greeks drank their wines at rituals and festivals and they even had a god, Dionysios, to protect their vineyards — vineyards that continued to produce good wines throughout the Roman invasion and up through the Byzantine Empire. However, when the Turks occupied Greece (roughly 1400–1900) the quality of the wines declined and most of the vineyards were destroyed because, for one reason, the Turks did not drink wine (Muslim dietary laws forbid it), and for another, the subjugated Greeks were more concerned with gaining their freedom than with keeping up and improving their wines. It was not until the early 1900's, when the Greeks were free again, that once more they concentrated on cultivating their vineyards, producing wines of warm red and pale straw in the same centuries-old tradition. These wines were always drunk by Greeks — most often they had come from family vineyards and were drunk by the family — and were unknown outside Greece; some people say that this was because the Greek people guarded their secret of wine-making very closely.

The islanders have always made their own wine, from family vineyards. My mother's people in the village still do so today, using a different kind of grape for each kind of wine. For red, they use the grapes that grow in large, dense bunches with dark purple berries called *mourianó* (which means "dark berrylike"); for white, the translucent white berry called *ahíri* (which means "like the straw"); and for rosé, other large ones called *rodítis* (which means "Rhodian, named after Rhodes").

The grapes are still hand-picked in bunches in late summer or early autumn, cut off the vine with the *klatheftíri,* the curved knife that peasants always carry in their sash-style belts. They are put in large willow baskets, loaded onto donkeys, and taken to the family wine press — a stone trough attached to the outside of the house — where they are unloaded and stomped by the little girl relatives with scrubbed feet. The must, or juice, flows to the spout of the trough, where it is strained through small bunches of mountain shrubs into a container, and the women of the family rush to transfer it in clay jugs, *vitinári,* to wooden barrels and demijohns with baskets woven around them. The wine is stored in dark walk-in closets, *appatarós,* in the house, with the containers left open for the gasses to escape, and just a bunch of mountain savory stuffed in the opening to keep anything from dropping in. The savory also collects the froth from the fermenting bubbles, simultaneously flavoring the wine lightly with its aroma.

The wine is ready to be drunk at the end of autumn; and it comes out some years sweet, some years semisweet, and some years very dry and robust, which is called *proúsko.* One thing always stays the same year after year, and that is the full-bodied richness of these wines, with the smoothness of velvet that even children like. With Sunday dinners a half-full glass is served to each child if he or she wants it; and I remember, growing up, the deep ruby color of this wine in the clear glass flask on our dinner table in the winter, and the almost amber color of the white wines we drank in the following spring, chilled in carafes set in ice-cold water drawn from the well. Then the barrels were empty again in late summer, and it was time to wash them once more with water scented with mountain herbs and prepare them for the new wine. For those men whose wives received no vineyards in their dowries — because it is through one's wife that one gets these things, handed down from generation to generation, unless there are only sons in the family, in which case the vineyards are divided among them — and for the city people, too, there were always some small commercial wineries to supply them with their choice of wine.

It is the sunny, nonhumid, climate and the good drainage in the soil that makes Greece the good place that it is for growing grapes. Today these commercial wineries have increased their vineyards and expanded their wineries to supply many European countries and the United States. Greek wines can be found throughout America and I am delighted to find them once more in many more varieties that I knew growing up, wines that complement Greek dishes and are available at moderate prices. Contrary to the mistaken opinion that Greek wines come only resinated (flavored with the sap of pine trees), they come in many varieties and most of them are unresinated.

The wines, aperitifs and brandies that follow are produced by the Nicolaou, Metaxa, and Samos wineries in Greece and are well known and widely available throughout the United States. The list was provided graciously by Mr. M. G. Citarella and Mr. E. Kostick of the Austin and Nichols Company, Inc.

APERITIFS

Oúzo: flavored with anise, clear, drunk straight or mixed with water, in which case it turns milky white
Mastíha: flavored with the sap of the aromatic mastic tree, clear, similar to ouzo and drunk the same way.

DINNER WINES

Róbola: dry, white, full-bodied wine, usually served chilled.
Mount Ámbelos White: dry, delicate, served slightly chilled.
Mount Ámbelos Red: dry, deep red, served at room temperature.
Rodítis: dry, rosé, served chilled.

RESINATED WINES

There are only two resinated wines in Greece, which will surprise many Americans:
Retsína: dry, white, served well chilled.
Kokkinélli: dry, brilliant red, slightly resinated, served slightly chilled.

AFTER-DINNER WINES

Mavrodáphni: sweet, red, rich, served at room temperature.
Fokkiós: sweet, dark amber, served at room temperature.
Múscat: sweet, light amber, served at room temperature.

BRANDIES

Metaxa makes the best Greek brandies. They are well known throughout the United States. The brandies come with three, five, and seven stars on the bottles. *Grand Fine* is the exquisite forty-year-old brandy, very smooth and with a light bouquet and unique taste.

The following wines are made by various Greek wineries and are listed under name and vineyard location. Some of these wines are available in the United States through wine distributors.

DRY WHITE WINES

Aphrodíte	Cyprus
St. Panteleímonas	Cyprus
Deméstika	Achaia
Coróna	Thessaloniki
King and Mínos	Crete
Mantína	Peloponnisos
C.A.I.R. White	Rhodes
St. Heléna	Peloponnisos
Theotóki	Corfu
Vissánto	Sandorini

DRY RED WINES

Kamínia	Lemnos
Naméa	Namea
Pendíli	Athens
Naoússa	Macedonia
C.A.I.R. Red	Rhodes
Veratéa	Zande

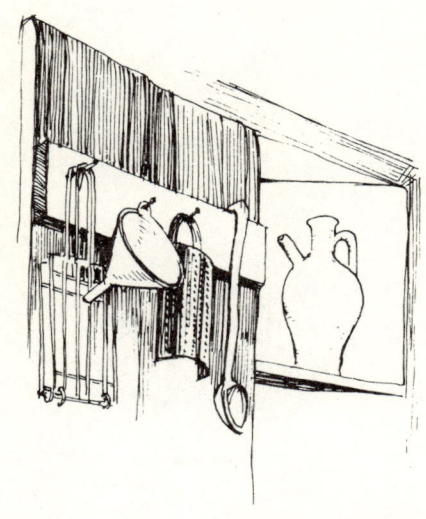

BASIC TECHNIQUES OF
GREEK ISLANDS CUISINE

TRADITIONAL KITCHEN
UTENSILS OF THE
GREEK ISLANDS

TABLE OF MEASURES
AND EQUIVALENTS

INDEX

Basic Techniques of Greek Islands Cuisine

I hope the notes and suggestions in this section are helpful to readers who are not familiar with certain basic procedures used in the preparation of the Greek islands cuisine, and will make cooking more enjoyable.

ALMONDS: *to blanch.* Cover the almonds with boiling water, let them stand in it for a few minutes, then drain off the water. Rub the soaked almonds between your thumb and forefinger to remove the skins, then place the blanched almonds in a shallow baking pan in a very low oven for a few minutes to dry.

BUTTER: *to clarify.* Melt the butter over low heat in an enamel or stainless steel saucepan and let it stand for 15 minutes to settle and separate into layers. With a spoon remove and discard the frothy top layer, the casein, then carefully transfer the middle layer of gold liquid, the butter, to a bowl or jar. Discard the bottom layer, the unusable whey.

CHICKEN AND GAME BIRDS: *to pluck and clean.* Half fill with water a pan larger than the bird to be plucked and bring it to a boil. Remove the pan from the heat, set it beside the sink, and set the whole bird into the hot water for a few minutes to soak the feathers. Lift the bird out of the water into the sink and while it is still hot, begin to pull the wet feathers off with your hands.

Continue to dip and pluck the bird until it is completely plucked. Any very fine feathers left on the bird can be burned off with a lit candle. Cut off the neck, head and feet and cut the bird from the bottom of the breastbone all the way down. Remove the organs, taking care not to puncture the small green sac on the liver, which would bitter the flesh with the bile. Wash inside and out of the bird and pat it dry.

EEL: *to skin, clean and cut.* Place the slippery eel on a flat surface, hold it down firmly with a towel, and with a sharp knife slit the skin around its neck just below the head. Now, holding the eel by the head with the towel, grip the skin with a pair of pliers and pull it slowly downward to peel off inside out to the end of the tail. Slit the stomach lengthwise to remove the intestines, then wash the eel under running cold water. Remove the head and slice the eel into the desired lengths.

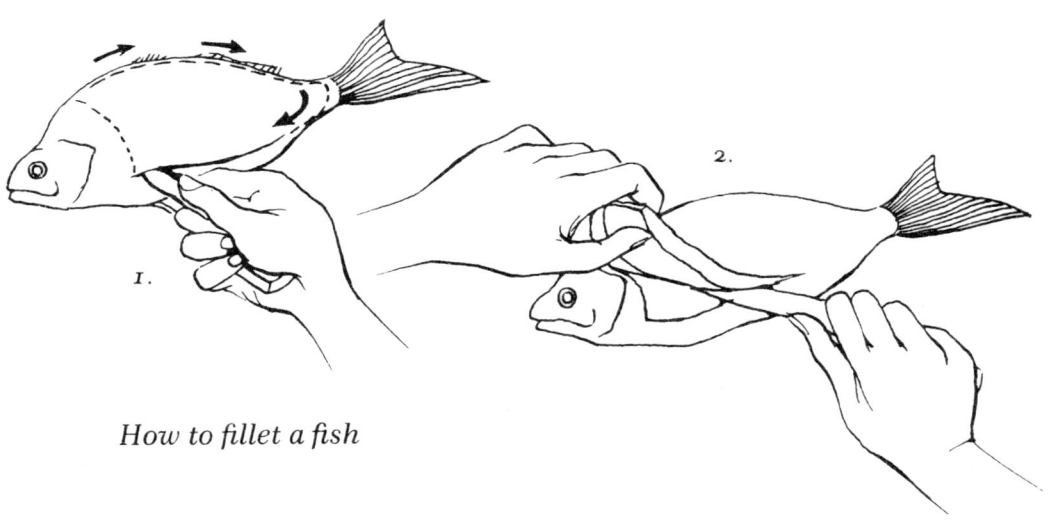

How to fillet a fish

FISH: *to buy.* The skin and scales of fresh fish should be bright, the flesh firm, the eyes clear as a mirror, the gills light red and the fish should smell like the fresh sea. Old fish looks limp and dim, with opaque eyes and dark gills.

to clean. Wear gloves while cleaning fish to avoid being pricked by the fins. With a scissors or knife trim off the fins and tips of the tail, because they have a tendency to burn before the fish is cooked. Hold the fish by its tail and with a knife or a scaler, scrape both sides toward the head to remove the scales. Make a cut below the small stomach fins 1 or 2 inches across depending on the size of the fish, remove the guts, and rinse the fish under running cold water. If the head is to be left on, insert your index finger into the gills one side at a time and pull them out. If you wish to remove the head, just cut it off across below the gills with a knife and rinse the fish well.

to defrost. Do not defrost fish at room temperature; it loses moisture and becomes dry. Defrost overnight in the refrigerator or, if you are in a hurry, under running cold water.

to fillet. With a small all-purpose knife or a fillet knife cut along the back of the scaled and gutted fish from the head all the way to the tail and continue around until you reach the abdominal cavity. Make a flesh-deep cut across the fish just below the head and work your knife between the main bone and the flesh toward the tail while gently pulling the fillet away from the bone all the way down to the tail. Repeat the same procedure on the other side. If you wish the fish skin removed, place the fillet on a flat surface skin-side up and slide your knife in between the fillet and skin, working the knife with one hand while pulling the skin with the other to loosen it.

GAME BIRDS. *See* chicken.

LAMB: *to buy.* In America spring or young lamb is up to 5 months old and yearling up to 1 year; after that it is mutton. A leg of spring lamb weighs no more than 5 pounds and its flesh is pale pink. Yearling lamb, the type of lamb most plentiful in American markets, has a more robust flavor and darker flesh, and a leg of it weighs 7 to 9 pounds. Whether of a spring lamb or a yearling, a short leg of lamb (the lower part around the shank bone), even though more expensive than other cuts of lamb, has more meat and less waste. It can be cooked as a roast, sliced for steaks, or cut in pieces for a casserole.

LEG OF LAMB: *to bone.* Work with a sharp knife or boning knife around the rump knuckle bone at the large end of the leg to loosen it without making an outside incision, then remove it from

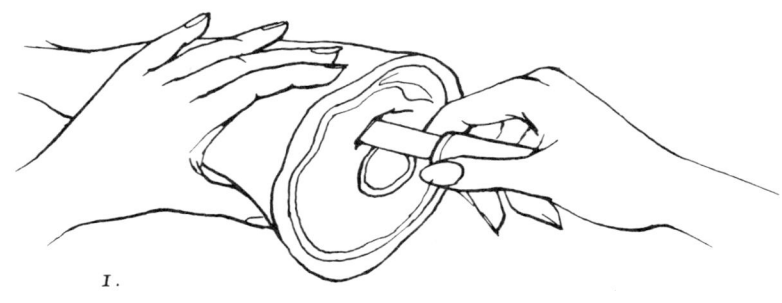

1.

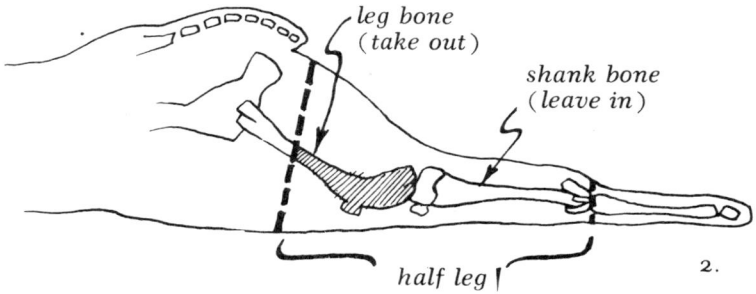

leg bone
(take out)

shank bone
(leave in)

half leg

2.

How to bone a half leg of lamb

the joint of the connecting shank bone, leaving the shank bone in the leg for a more attractive roast.

LEMON: *to get more juice out of.* Roll the lemon on a hard surface with your palm to bruise it before cutting and squeezing it.

NUTS: *to crush.* Use a mortar and pestle and pound a handful at a time or crush them on a flat wooden surface with a rolling pin.

to pulverize. Use an electric blender at high speed, or keep on crushing!

ORANGE PEEL: *to dry.* With a small knife, peel the orange skin off the orange in one piece and hang it in your kitchen to dry. Drying takes only a couple of days. When it is dry, cut it up into small pieces and use it with tea or to flavor stuffings. Keep it in a jar or a box.

PHÍLLO DOUGH: *how to work with*. This paper-thin dough is usually made with just water and flour, and skilled hands and much work are needed to make it. *Phíllo* is sold in America in all Greek and Middle Eastern markets and in many supermarkets in 1-pound boxes or packages that contain approximately 16 to 20 layers (depending on the thickness of the layers) 10" x 15" or 12" x 18" in size. *Phíllo* is better fresh but a lot of stores sell it frozen and then it has to be defrosted overnight in the refrigerator, still sealed in the package. Cut the sheets of dough into the size called for in your recipe. When a recipe specifies the dimensions of *phíllo* strips, as in cheese triangles (3" x 10" or 3" x 12") and the nut-stuffed pastries (5" x 10" or 5" x 12"), cut them as shown in the drawing. A "double strip" means 2 layers of cut strips used together. Take great care not to expose the *phíllo* to

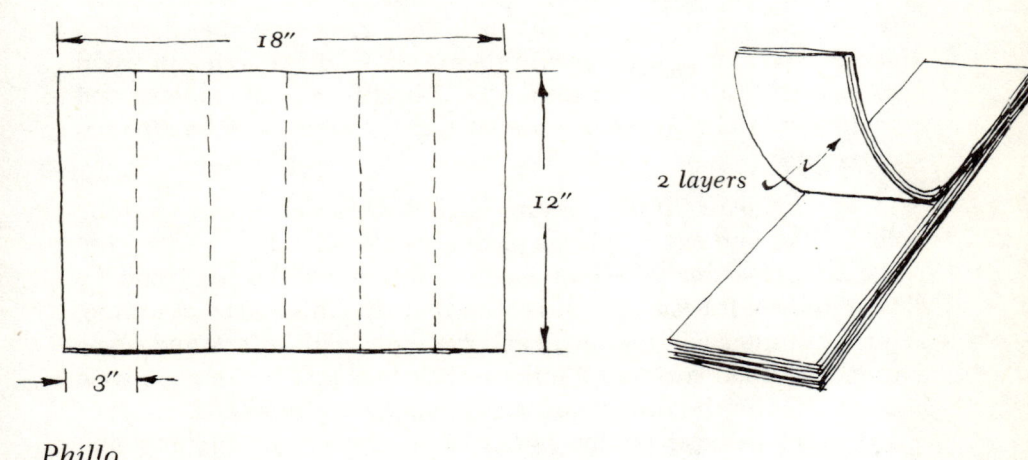

Phíllo

the air for a long time; work with only a few pieces at a time, covering the unused portion with wax paper and a damp towel or placing it in plastic bags to keep it from drying and crumbling.

PAXIMÁTHIS (ZWIEBACK): *to make*. Preheat the oven to 225°. Cut a *tsouréki* loaf (pages 232–233) into slices ¾ to 1 inch thick and place them on an ungreased cookie sheet in the oven to dry for

35 to 40 minutes, turning them once. Let them cool on racks and store them in plastic bags or cookie jars. Use them when called for in recipes or for breakfast with sweet butter and honey.

SHRIMP: *to defrost.* Submerge the shrimp in cold clam juice (2 pounds of shrimp to 3 cups clam juice) in a saucepan, cover the pan, and over low heat bring the liquid almost to a boil. Remove the pan from the heat, stir the shrimps, cover the pan, and let the shrimps cool in the broth. Then drain the shrimps, pat them dry with a towel, and proceed with the recipe. The shrimp looks firm and fresh but not cooked.

TOMATOES: *to freeze.* Tomatoes freeze well to be kept and used only for cooking, but they must be peeled before they are frozen. Quarter peeled tomatoes, put them into plastic containers or bags in groups of 3 or 4, seal them and freeze them. When a recipe calls for tomatoes, simply remove them from the container and put them still frozen into the cooking pot.

to peel. Dip a few tomatoes at a time for a few seconds into water that has been brought to a boil, removing them with a slotted spoon and submerging them into cold water for the skin to loosen. With a small knife slit the skin of each tomato and remove it, and also remove the base of the stem. Use as directed in recipes.

TRIPE: *to clean.* Rinse the unprepared tripe well under running cold water and cut it in large pieces for easy handling. Bring 3 to 4 quarts of water to boil in a pot, then remove the pot from the heat and set it beside the sink. Dip the tripe in, a piece at a time, for 1 minute each, then lift each piece out with a fork and place it on a wooden surface. While each piece is still hot, scrape with a small knife the brown substance off the entire outside surface and from in between the honeycombs, repeatedly dipping and scraping the piece until it is white all over. Rinse the pieces well and cut them in 1½ inch pieces. Use as directed in recipes.

YEAST: *to proof.* Dissolve yeast cake or granular yeast in warm (80° to 105°) water in a small bowl with sugar added (in quantities according to your bread recipe) and set the bowl in a pan of hot water for 10 minutes to determine whether the yeast is active. Active yeast will ferment and rise in a bubbling mixture.

Traditional Kitchen Utensils of the Greek Islands

Akloúmbi: gourd used as a water dipper.
Alaterón: hanging clay salt holder.
Amourghí: clay milking bucket.
Bríkis: brass coffeepots, in varying sizes.
Foufoú: clay charcoal cooker.
Fournístra: wooden shovel for putting bread into the oven.
Ghirístra: wooden spatula.
Ghthin: brass mortar and pestle for crushing spices and nuts.
Ghthin xílino: wooden mortar and pestle for making garlic sauce and other sauces.
Honí: tin funnel.
Kanní: colored glass sprinkler for blossom water.
Kappamás: covered clay oven pot for baking Easter lamb or kid.
Kastaniá: tin-lined copper lunch box.
Kazáni: large copper pot for collecting grape must or for heating water.
Klatheftíri: peasant knife men carry for slicing bread, harvesting fruits and vegetables, and pruning.
Kolokítha: gourd used as a water carrier.
Kopanáki: wooden paddle for shelling dry legumes by paddling them.
Kóskino: round wooden flour sifter with wire or horsehair mesh.
Koutála xílini: large wooden spoon.
Koutalothíki: clay holder for spoons and cutlery.
Mangáli: coal-burning brazier for heating the home and broiling food.

Maskiá: coal tongs.

Matsóxilon: rolling pin.

Mílos kaffé: brass coffee mill.

Petrómilos: stone hand mill for grinding wheat.

Pinakotí: wooden box where bread dough rises.

Pithári: large clay jug for storing oil.

Píthos: clay crock for pickling cheese or olives.

Sfahtári: utensil with flat metal front for moving bread around in the oven.

Shára: wire grill for broiling fish.

Siní: versatile low wooden dining table also used for many other things.

Skáfi: wooden box for mixing and kneading bread dough.

Skálathros: oven utensil used for breaking up hot wood coals.

Skoúpa: wild rush broom.

Sourátha: clay water pitcher.

Soúvles: metal skewers for *souvlákia.*

Stámnos: clay jug for carrying water.

Tapsí: tin-lined copper baking pan.

Tentserí: shallow tin-lined copper cooking pot.

Téntsero: deep tin-lined copper cooking pot.

Tipári: wooden bread pattern stamper.

Tirikón: rush cheese form.

Tripitón: colander.

Triviás: wooden rubbing utensil used in making *mizíthra* cheese.

Tsoúka: clay cooking pot.

Tsoukáli: clay bean pot.

Vitinári: clay jug for transferring wine or olive oil from the press to the wine barrel or oil *pithári.*

Xístros: tin grater.

Table of Measures and Equivalents

The following table of measures and equivalents is compiled for the convenience of those who wish to translate the American measurements into English and metric.

EQUIVALENT LIQUID MEASURES

American Spoons — Cups — Ounces	English Ounces — Pints	Metric Grams	Liquid Liters
1 teaspoon = ⅙ ounce	⅙ ounce	5	5 milliliters
1 tablespoon = 3 teaspoons	½ ounce	14	14 milliliters
2 tablespoons = ⅛ cup	1 ounce	28	28 milliliters
4 tablespoons = ¼ cup	2 ounces	57	57 milliliters
8 tablespoons = ½ cup	⅕ pint	113	113 milliliters
1 cup = 16 tablespoons	⅖ pint	227	
1 cup + 2 tablespoons		250	¼ liter
2 cups = 1 pint		454	½ liter minus ½ deciliter
2½ cups = 20 ounces	1 pint	567	
4 cups = 1 quart		907	1 liter minus 1 deciliter
4⅓ cups	1¾ pints	1 kilo- gram	1 liter

EQUIVALENT DRY AND SOLID MEASURES

American	English	Metric (Grams)
1 pound *fétta* cheese	16 ounces	454
1 cup granulated sugar	½ pound	200
⅔ cup granulated sugar		125
2 tablespoons granulated sugar		25
1 cup all-purpose flour	5 ounces plain flour	120
1 cup uncooked rice	½ pound	200
1 stick (8 tablespoons) butter	4 ounces	125
1 tablespoon butter	½ ounce	15
1 cake or envelope granular yeast	¼ ounce bakers' yeast	7
1 envelope (1 tablespoon) granulated gelatin	3 to 4 sheets (4" by 9") (Enough to jell 2 cups of liquid)	

CONVERSION FORMULAS — AMERICAN, BRITISH, METRIC

To Convert	Multiply	By
Grams to ounces	the grams	0.035
Ounces to grams	the ounces	28.35
Liters to U.S. quarts	the liters	0.95
Liters to British quarts	the liters	0.88
U.S. quarts to liters	the quarts	1.057
British quarts to liters	the quarts	1.14
Centimeters to inches	the centimeters	0.39
Inches to centimeters	the inches	2.54

FAHRENHEIT AND CENTIGRADE TEMPERATURE CONVERSION

Fahrenheit Degrees (American and British)	Centigrade or Celsius Degrees	American Oven Temperature Terms	British "Regulo" Oven Thermostat Settings
225	107	Very slow	
230	110		No. ¼ (241°F)
250	121		
275	135		No. ½ (266°F)
284	140	Slow	No. 1 (291°F)
300	149		
302	150		
320	160		No. 2 (313°F)
325	163		
			No. 3 (336°F)
350	177	Moderate	
356	180		No. 4 (358°F)
375	190		
390	200		No. 5 (379°F)
400	205		No. 6 (403°F)
410	210	Hot	
425	218		No. 7 (424°F)
428	220		
437	225		
450	232		No. 8 (446°F)
475	246	Very hot	No. 9 (469°F)
500	260		
525	274		
550	288		

Index

Skáfi

Foufoú

Tirikón

Alaterón

Koutalothíki

Skoúpa

Tapsí

Kopanáki

Sourátha

Tripitón

Klatheftí

Kóskino

Kastaniá

Tipári

Tsoúka

Matsóxilon

Akloúmbi

Petrómilos

Píthos

* See glossary for English translation